■ 2004 Annual Gift Edition

OUR DAILY BREAD®

For Personal and Family Devotions   *Since 1956*

CONTENTS   PAGE

Copyright © 2003 RBC Ministries, Grand Rapids, Michigan, USA
Internet Address: www.rbcinternational.org • E-mail: rbc@rbc.org
Printed in Colombia.

ACKNOWLEDGMENTS

COVER PHOTO:

Alex Soh, © RBC Ministries
Sheep grazing in Scotland, UK

WRITERS:

Henry G. Bosch • J. David Branon • Dennis J. De Haan
M. R. De Haan, M.D. • Martin R. De Haan II • Richard W. De Haan
David C. Egner • Vernon C. Grounds • Albert Lee
Julie Ackerman Link • David C. McCasland • Haddon W. Robinson
David H. Roper • Herbert Vander Lugt • Joanie E. Yoder

POEMS:

February 11 — Carol Cymbala, © 1989 Word Music
February 26 — Jim Hill, © 1965 Ben L. Speer
May 5 — William Sherbert, © 1978 William F. Sherbert
July 11 — John W. Peterson, © 1958 Singspiration, Inc.
July 23 — Oswald J. Smith, © Renewal 1960 Rodeheaver
August 4 — Rhea F. Miller, © Renewal 1950 Chancel Music
August 31 — John W. Peterson, © 1957 Singspiration, Inc.
September 3 — Thomas O. Chisholm, © Renewal 1951 Hope Pub. Co.

Introduction

It is with great joy that we introduce to you the gift edition of *Our Daily Bread* from RBC Ministries. This is a devotional that you can use to give as a present to family members, friends, and co-workers.

As you may know, RBC Ministries also offers a quarterly edition of *Our Daily Bread.* If you request it, we will send a copy to your home automatically every 3 months. Along with *Our Daily Bread,* you will receive an article written by RBC president Mart De Haan, and you'll have an opportunity to receive a Discovery Series study booklet.

As a quarterly recipient of *Our Daily Bread,* you will receive information about special offers, and you'll hear about our goals and plans as a ministry. All these resources will be available to you.

So, don't delay! Begin to receive your quarterly *Our Daily Bread* by completing the form on the last page of this book and mailing it to the RBC office in your region (listed on page 381).

OUR DAILY BREAD

Delivered right to your home every quarter!

What could be better than getting *Our Daily Bread*? How about having it delivered directly to your home every quarter?

You'll also have an opportunity to receive study booklets written on topics such as learning how to forgive or overcoming life's struggles.

Plus, during the year you'll learn about special offers and hear how *Our Daily Bread* is touching lives around the world.

SIGN UP TODAY!
And begin to receive *Our Daily Bread* at home every quarter.

Just complete the order form on the last page of this book and send it to the RBC Ministries office nearest you (listed on page 381).

NEW YEAR'S CELEBRATIONS

READ:
Psalm 31:14-24

I trust in You, O LORD
. . . . My times are in
Your hand.
—Psalm 31:14-15

THE BIBLE IN ONE YEAR:
■ Genesis 1–2

I don't know what your family does to bring in the new year, but it's celebrated in many different ways around the world.

• In Japan, people dress in new clothes and decorate their houses with bamboo and pine branches — symbols of long life.

• In Scotland, groups of friends or families get together for dinner at a host's house and exchange gifts soon after midnight.

• In Greece, the children leave shoes by the fireplace, hoping St. Basil will fill them with gifts.

For many years, my wife and I have spent New Year's Eve with friends, eating dinner together, playing games, and enjoying good conversation. As midnight approaches, we read from the Bible and pray. We thank God for the year that has passed, and we ask Him to use us to accomplish His will in our troubled, suffering world in the year ahead.

The times and seasons and years, including this new year, are in God's hand (Psalm 31:15). As Christians, we have nothing to fear, for God's goodness is great (v.19). We can walk with Christ each day and join the psalmist in saying, "As for me, I trust in You, O LORD; I say, 'You are my God' " (v.14). — Dave Egner

God will never fail us, He will not forsake;
His eternal covenant He will never break,
Resting on His promise, what have we to fear?
God is all-sufficient for the coming year. — Havergal

THE FUTURE IS AS BRIGHT AS THE PROMISES OF GOD.

WILL WE PASS THE TEST?

READ:
Genesis 3:1-19

When the woman saw that the tree was good for food, that it was pleasant to the eyes, . . . she took of its fruit and ate.
—Genesis 3:6

THE BIBLE IN ONE YEAR:
■ Genesis 3–5

Coyotes can't resist a tasty sheep dinner. That's why a number of years ago researchers experimented with about 500 different chemicals to develop a solution to spray on sheep that would make them "coyote proof." A compound that tasted like spicy hot sauce offered the most promise.

Scientists theorized that if the tests were successful, coyotes might lose their taste for sheep. If that were to happen, the temptation that makes coyotes a public nuisance in sheep country would be gone, and man would become the wild dog's best friend.

Sometimes I wonder why God didn't do something like that in the Garden of Eden. Why didn't He make the tree of the knowledge of good and evil bear ugly fruit? Why didn't He surround it with a chain-link fence with barbed wire at the top? Why did God even create the tree in the first place? Part of the answer, I believe, is that temptation to do evil brought Adam and Eve face to face with the ultimate moral question: Would they show confidence in their Creator and lovingly obey Him with all their heart?

We face a similar test every day. What are we going to do? Will we flunk the test? Or will we trust God completely and obey His commands? — Mart De Haan II

> Along life's road are obstacles —
> Our choice becomes a test;
> Help us, O Lord, to know Your way
> That we may choose what's best. — D. De Haan

EVERY TEMPTATION IS AN OPPORTUNITY TO TRUST GOD.

IN THE SAFE HANDS OF GOD

READ:
Luke 1:26-38

Mary said, "Behold the maidservant of the Lord! Let it be to me according to your word."
—Luke 1:38

THE BIBLE IN ONE YEAR:
■ Genesis 12–15

At age 16, Madame Jeanne Guyon (1648-1717) was forced into an arranged marriage with an invalid 22 years older. She found her marriage to be one of utter humiliation. Her husband was often angry and melancholy. Her mother-in-law was a merciless critic. Even the maid despised her. In spite of her best attempts at devotion to her husband and family, she was subjected to relentless criticism.

Forbidden by her husband to attend church, she sought God in His Word and worshiped Him in secret. She learned that even in the midst of her dreary circumstances she was "perfectly fine — within the safe hands of God." In her book *Experiencing The Depths Of Jesus Christ*, she wrote, "Abandonment [to Christ] is the key to the fathomless depths. Abandonment is the key to the spiritual life."

How can we respond to difficult circumstances with acceptance and abandonment? Mary's response to the angel in Luke 1:38 shows us. The only way to have that same attitude is to believe that God's will is "good and acceptable and perfect" (Romans 12:2), and to lay down our will and patiently submit to Him day by day.

This can be our prayer: Let it be to me according to Your word. — David Roper

When we're abandoned to God's will,
We need not doubt nor fear;
We'll know that He is in control,
That He is always near. — Sper

HE WHO ABANDONS HIMSELF TO GOD WILL NEVER BE ABANDONED BY GOD.

GOD SEES YOU

READ:
Genesis 16:1-13

**She called the name of the LORD who spoke to her, You-Are-the-God-Who-Sees.
—Genesis 16:13**

THE BIBLE IN ONE YEAR:
■ Genesis 16–19

H agar, Sarah's handmaid, was being treated unkindly by Sarah, so she fled into the wilderness. As Hagar stood beside a spring in that desolate and lonely place, the Angel of the Lord visited her. He assured her that God Himself was aware of her situation. Hagar responded, "You-Are-the-God-Who-Sees" (Genesis 16:13). She found great comfort in knowing that the Lord God saw her and knew about her distress.

You and I can have that same confidence in God's watchcare. We can be sure that the Lord God is with us wherever we go, and He knows everything that happens to us. As the all-powerful One, He is able to solve every problem, no matter how overwhelming or perplexing it may be. We are never alone, never forgotten, and never beyond hope.

Whatever your troubling circumstances are, whether you're afflicted by illness or injury, brokenhearted over the loss of a loved one, or disillusioned because your dearest friend has betrayed or rejected you, God knows and cares. You may be deeply depressed, or perhaps you're plagued by loneliness and discouragement. But you can be confident that you are under God's watchful eye. Yes, like Hagar, you can know that God sees you. — Richard De Haan

Beneath His watchful eye
His saints securely dwell;
That hand which bears all nature up
Shall guard His children well. — Doddridge

**WE NEED NOT FEAR THE PERILS AROUND US
BECAUSE THE EYE OF THE LORD IS ALWAYS UPON US.**

PUT ON THE BRAKES

READ:
Romans 13:8-14

Love does no harm to a neighbor.
—Romans 13:10

THE BIBLE IN ONE YEAR:
■ Genesis 20–22

A bumper sticker motto expresses the goal of a campaign to curb gossip: "Put the brakes on *loshon hora*." The movement began with Rabbi Chaim Feld in Cleveland, Ohio, who says the Bible forbids speaking words that hurt people in any way. *Loshon hora* is a Hebrew phrase for negative or cruel speech — an evil that causes untold damage.

Rabbi Feld says, "If you've never met Michael, and someone tells you he is a jerk, then Michael has been murdered for you, before you even meet him."

Someone has said, "When tempted to gossip, breathe through your nose." That's a good way to keep our mouths shut, but we also need a solution that gets to the heart of the issue.

The antidote to the poison of gossip is love, which neutralizes the toxin in our hearts before it escapes through our lips. The Bible tells us, "'You shall love your neighbor as yourself.' Love does no harm to a neighbor; therefore love is the fulfillment of the law" (Romans 13:9-10).

Whenever we're tempted to pass along a negative word about someone, even if it's true, let's seek God's help in putting the brakes on gossip. Instead of *loshon hora,* let's speak a word of kindness and love. —David McCasland

> *Lord, guard our tongues so what we say*
> *Won't hurt and carelessly offend;*
> *Give us the gracious speech of love,*
> *With words that soothe and heal and mend.* —Sper

TO SILENCE GOSSIP, DON'T REPEAT IT.

UNLIKELY PEOPLE

READ:
Mark 1:16-20

___

**They were fishermen. Then Jesus said to them, "Follow Me, and I will make you become fishers of men."
—Mark 1:16-17**

___

THE BIBLE IN ONE YEAR:
■ Genesis 23–26

Not only was the Son of God born in an unlikely location and of unlikely parents, He chose His first followers at an unlikely place. He didn't search the religious schools for the most learned scholars. He didn't look among the ranks of brilliant military leaders. He stayed away from skilled statesmen and famous orators. Rather, Jesus went to the shores of Galilee and called out four common fishermen — Peter and Andrew, James and John.

"Bad choice," some might say. "Uneducated. Tough characters. What would they know about starting a worldwide movement? They couldn't work a crowd if they had to."

Now, on behalf of fishermen everywhere, let me say that they have many positive traits. They must be resourceful, courageous, and patient. They must plan carefully and take care of their equipment. Such qualities are no doubt helpful in carrying out the Great Commission (Matthew 28:19-20), but I don't think that's why Jesus chose those men. I believe He wanted to demonstrate how God can transform ordinary people into "fishers of men" (Mark 1:16-17).

God's work is often done by unlikely people from unlikely places — people like you and me. To be successful, we must follow the One who can make us fishers of men. — David Egner

You may not be a superstar,
Your talents may be few;
But God in His enablement
Works out His will through you. — Branon

___

**GOD USES ORDINARY PEOPLE TO DO
EXTRAORDINARY WORK.**

FINDING THE TRUTH

READ:
Colossians 2:1-12

As you therefore have received Christ . . . , so walk in Him, rooted and built up in Him and established in the faith.
—Colossians 2:6-7

THE BIBLE IN ONE YEAR:
■ Genesis 27–29

How would you answer the following questions:
1. Did Jesus ever sin?
2. Was Jesus resurrected?
3. Do all religions teach the same basic ideas?

According to George Barna and Mark Hatch in their book *Boiling Point,* many people who call themselves Christians have a hard time with questions like these. When Barna and Hatch surveyed professing believers, one-fourth said Jesus committed sins, one-third said He did not rise from the dead, and one-third said all religions are basically the same.

These are troubling statistics, for they reveal a serious lack of biblical understanding. The answers to the questions above are concepts that are clearly defined in Scripture and are foundational to the truth of the gospel.

So, what can we do to make sure that we are "established in the faith"? (Colossians 2:7). First, we must dedicate ourselves to read and study the Bible. Second, we should seek the help of godly teachers and dependable resources. Third, we must ask God to lead us to truth and to keep us from error.

As God's people, we must love the truth, look for the truth, and live by the truth. — Dave Branon

FOR FURTHER STUDY
Jesus didn't sin: 2 Cor. 5:21; Heb. 4:15; 1 Pet. 1:19; 2:22.
Jesus was resurrected: John 20–21; 1 Cor. 15:1-20.
Jesus is the only way to God: John 14:6; Acts 4:12.

**TRUTH IS NOT DETERMINED
BY HOW MANY PEOPLE BELIEVE IT.**

CORRECTING ERROR

READ:
2 Timothy 2:22-26

Be gentle to all, . . . correcting those who are in opposition, . . . so that they may know the truth.
—2 Timothy 2:24-25

THE BIBLE IN ONE YEAR:
■ Genesis 30–32

A trio of well-dressed young men arrived at the door of my home. I knew right away they weren't there to sell me a vacuum cleaner. They wanted to convert me to their religion.

I engaged them in polite conversation, commending them for their dedication on a hot summer day. Then I said, "I know you're going to give me some literature, so please allow me to give something to you." I stepped inside the house and picked up some magazines that contained a clear gospel presentation.

They said they wanted to give me a book that is the basis of their beliefs. I told them that I already had a copy and had read portions of it. When they asked what I thought of it, I told them about the differences between it and the Bible, and why I thought their book contained error. No arguing, just a good conversation about truth and error.

When we're confronted by people who distort or deny biblical doctrines, we need to know what the Bible teaches. The goal, as stated by the apostle Paul, is to gently correct those who are in error "that they may know the truth" and "come to their senses and escape the snare of the devil" (2 Timothy 2:25-26). After all, our goal is to help people find the truth, not to win arguments. — Dave Branon

Lord, give us courage to speak out
Against the errors of our day,
For only when the truth is shown
Will sinners see the better way. — D. De Haan

TO REVEAL ERROR, EXPOSE IT TO THE LIGHT OF GOD'S TRUTH.

Proper Preparation

READ:
Acts 20:7-12

In a window sat a certain young man named Eutychus, who was sinking into a deep sleep.
—Acts 20:9

THE BIBLE IN ONE YEAR:
■ Genesis 33–36

Eutychus was probably not the first person to fall asleep listening to a preacher in a church meeting (Acts 20:9), and he certainly won't be the last. Part of the blame can lie with the humdrum nature of the worship service and the dullness of the sermon. But other factors can also be at work.

For instance, as a boy I noticed that men who worked outdoors in the winter found the warmth of a church building most conducive to sleep. A few years later, after working 17 hours on Saturday in a meat market, I struggled to stay awake in the Sunday morning service. Saturday evening social activities can also make for slumberous Sunday mornings.

One of the keys to having a vital encounter with God on Sunday morning is proper preparation the day before. Yes, those in leadership should give much thought and prayer to every part of the worship service. But those of us who sit in the pews should also keep Sunday morning in mind as we plan our Saturday activities. Then we'll be alert and ready to sing, pray, and take in all that is being said, including the truths given in the sermon.

We can have a fresh vision of God's greatness and love, plus a renewed desire to do His will, if we make proper preparation for worship. — Herb Vander Lugt

THINKING IT OVER
In what ways can you better prepare yourself for worshiping God? Consider these: Prayer, Bible study, confession of sin, adequate sleep.

**WORSHIP ON SUNDAY MORNING
SHOULD BEGIN ON SATURDAY NIGHT.**

CUT DOWN TO SIZE

READ:
James 4:1-12

> I say . . . to everyone who is among you, not to think of himself more highly than he ought to think.
> —Romans 12:3

THE BIBLE IN ONE YEAR:
■ Genesis 37–39

A man who had just been elected to the British Parliament brought his family to London. He felt important as he told them about his new job and gave them a tour of the city. When they entered Westminster Abbey, his 8-year-old daughter was awestruck by the size of that magnificent structure. Her proud father asked, "What, my dear, are you thinking about?" She replied, "Daddy, I was just thinking about how big you are in our house, but how small you look here!"

Without knowing it, that little girl said something her father needed to hear. Pride can creep into our lives so easily, and from time to time it's good to be "cut down to size." We need to be reminded not to think of ourselves more highly than we ought to think (Romans 12:3). It's easy to become proud when we stay in our own little circles of life. But when we are thrust into larger situations, with increased demands, pressures, and competition, we come to the shocking realization that "big fish in small ponds" shrink quickly in a large ocean.

James said, "God resists the proud, but gives grace to the humble" (4:6). So let's ask the Lord to help us see ourselves as we really are. With His help, we'll learn to rid ourselves of foolish pride. — Richard De Haan

> *Help us, O Lord, lest our heart become proud,*
> *For all of our talents by You are endowed;*
> *Nothing we have can we claim as our own—*
> *What mercy and grace in our life You have shown!* —DJD

THOSE WHO KNOW GOD WILL BE HUMBLE;
THOSE WHO KNOW THEMSELVES CANNOT BE PROUD.

WISE COUNSEL

READ:
Luke 2:46-52

Jesus increased in wisdom and stature, and in favor with God and men. —Luke 2:52

THE BIBLE IN ONE YEAR:
■ Genesis 40–42

I'll never forget Jake. His legs seemed too thin and spindly to hold him against the current of the river. His patched and discolored waders looked older than he was. His fishing vest was tattered and held together with safety pins; his ancient hat was battered and sweat-stained; his antiquated fly rod was scarred and taped.

I watched as he worked his way upstream to a patch of quiet water and began to cast. Then I took notice! He was fishing the same water I had fished earlier in the day and catching trout where I had caught none. Here was a man who could teach me a thing or two. All I had to do was ask.

We gain insight when we listen to those who have gone before and who know more than we do—insight we miss when our pride stands in the way. We're able to learn from others when we humble ourselves and acknowledge how little we know. Willingness to learn is a mark of those who are truly wise.

Consider our Lord as a young boy, "sitting in the midst of the teachers, both listening to them and asking them questions" (Luke 2:46). Proverbs 1:5 says that "a wise man will hear and increase learning, and a man of understanding will attain wise counsel." Let's ask questions of those who've spent their lives seeking God's wisdom. — David Roper

There's so much wisdom to be learned,
So many ways for me to grow,
Lord, I would listen like a child,
And learn what You would have me know. — K. De Haan

**IF YOU THINK YOU KNOW EVERYTHING,
YOU HAVE A LOT TO LEARN.**

Legacy

READ:
Psalm 46

God is our refuge and strength, a very present help in trouble. —Psalm 46:1

THE BIBLE IN ONE YEAR:
■ Genesis 43–46

Erma Bombeck wrote a column about the conflicts that sometimes occur as siblings divide family items after a parent has died. Whether it's the mixing bowls, grandma's quilts, or the Christmas ornaments, people are often convinced that they alone should have a certain item. Bombeck said she never wanted a TV set or a tote bag to remember her parents, because their true legacy to her was the way they lived, not what they left behind.

Those comments caused me to ask, "What kind of legacy would I like to leave my children?" I've concluded that I would like my kids to feel that their dad helped them learn where to go during the storms of life.

Three times in Psalm 46, the writer refers to the Lord as "our refuge" — a place of protection during times of danger or distress (vv.1,7,11). And in Proverbs 14:26, we read about the God-fearing man as one whose children "will have a place of refuge."

If I learn to find shelter and strength in the Lord today, then my children have an example to follow and know where to turn. I'd be pleased if someday they would all say of that refuge they've found in the Lord: "Dad wanted me to have this." — David McCasland

O God, our help in ages past,
Our hope for years to come,
Our shelter from the stormy blast,
And our eternal home! — Watts

LIVING FOR THE LORD LEAVES A LASTING LEGACY.

WHO OWNS YOUR HOME?

READ:
1 Chronicles 29:10-15

All that is in heaven and in earth is Yours.
—1 Chronicles 29:11

THE BIBLE IN ONE YEAR:
■ Genesis 47–50

My wife and I bought our first home when we moved to Grand Rapids, Michigan. During my years in the pastorate, a parsonage had always been provided. I remember the feeling when I signed a 30-year mortgage. It seemed that I was committing myself to a lifetime of debt.

Another thought has gripped me recently—I'll never own my home, even when the mortgage is paid off. You see, God is the real title holder. Everything belongs to Him.

These musings raise a vital issue in our highly materialistic culture. We as Christians must recognize that God is the rightful owner of our possessions, or they will be a cause of frustration. Our attitude will be reflected in what happens to them. A dent in the fender of our new car, for instance, can bend us out of shape. A coffee spill on the furniture can stain our attitude. A theft can easily rob us of peace.

We need to give up ownership rights and take our stewardship responsibilities seriously. This does not mean adopting a casual, wasteful attitude about material things. In our hearts we must make a transfer of our goods to God, and then keep reminding ourselves who really owns them (1 Chronicles 29:11). This will help us use things wisely, hold them lightly, and enjoy them fully. — Dennis De Haan

God owns the gold in every mine,
The cattle on the hills,
And in His sovereign grace He gives
According as He wills. — D. De Haan

THE REAL MEASURE OF OUR WEALTH
IS THE TREASURE WE HAVE IN HEAVEN.

THE ADVANTAGE OF WEAKNESS

READ:
2 Corinthians 12:1-10

He said to me, "My grace is sufficient for you, for My strength is made perfect in weakness."
—2 Corinthians 12:9

THE BIBLE IN ONE YEAR:
■ Exodus 1–4

I always enjoy talking with my old college friend Tom and getting caught up on what the Lord has been teaching us since we last met.

One day Tom began with a sheepish grin, "You know, I can't believe how many years it has taken me to learn my latest lesson—and I'm a Bible teacher!" He went on to list some of the trials and testings he and his family had been facing and how unworthy he felt teaching an adult Sunday school class. "Week after week I felt I was a total failure," he confided, "and kept wondering if this might be my last Sunday before announcing my resignation."

Then one Sunday a young woman stayed after class to speak to Tom. She was a friend of his family, so she knew what they had been going through. "Tom," she said, "I hope you won't take this the wrong way, but you're a much better teacher when you're going through tough times."

Tom smiled as he told me, "Only then did I feel that I grasped the Lord's response to Paul's thorn in the flesh: 'My grace is sufficient for you, for My strength is made perfect in weakness'" (2 Corinthians 12:9).

When we recognize how much we need God, He will strengthen us. That's the advantage of weakness. —Joanie Yoder

Inadequate but mighty—
How strange, yet wholly true;
Weak servants filled with power
The Lord's great work can do. —Bosch

IN TOUGH TIMES, GOD TEACHES US TO TRUST.

DISCOVER THE TREASURES

READ:
Proverbs 2:1-9

**The LORD gives wisdom; from His mouth come knowledge and understanding.
—Proverbs 2:6**

THE BIBLE IN ONE YEAR:
■ Exodus 5–7

Profitable Bible study involves more than just opening to a chapter and reading what's there. Here are six guidelines to help you make the most of your study of the Bible.

1. Set aside a regular time. Unless you schedule it, you'll neglect it.
2. Before you start reading, ask God for help and understanding.
3. Carefully think about what you are reading. The treasures of the Bible seldom lie like pebbles on the surface. To mine the gold, you have to dig.
4. Before you decide what a passage means to you, try to understand what the author was saying to the original readers.
5. Write down at least one truth or principle you can put into practice.
6. Don't get discouraged. Some parts of the Bible are difficult to understand, but there's much that you *can* understand. And if you apply what you've learned, it will revolutionize your life.

Now read today's passage from Proverbs 2 again, keeping these principles in mind. Then use this method whenever you study God's Word. If you do, you will begin to discover the treasures of the Bible. — Haddon Robinson

Thy Word is like a deep, deep mine,
And jewels rich and rare
Are hidden in its mighty depths
For every searcher there. — Hodder

**GEMS OF TRUTH ARE FOUND IN THE BIBLE—
BUT YOU MUST DIG FOR THEM.**

GOOD INTENTIONS

READ:
Judges 8:22-27

**[The ephod] became a snare to Gideon and to his house.
—Judges 8:27**

THE BIBLE IN ONE YEAR:
■ Exodus 8–10

Have you ever had one of those "I was just trying to help" moments? Maybe you offered to carry the cake to the table and you dropped it. Or perhaps you offered to dog-sit your neighbor's pooch and the little guy ran away.

In Judges 8, it appears that Gideon tried to do a good thing. But the result was tragic. Impressed by his military exploits, the men of Israel asked Gideon to be their king. To his credit, he refused (Judges 8:22-23). But then he asked them to donate gold earrings, which he made into an "ephod" (v.27). This was either a sacred garment worn by the high priest or some type of image. Why did he do this? We don't know for sure, but Gideon may have been trying to provide spiritual leadership. Whatever his motive was, God hadn't told him to do this.

When Gideon set up the ephod in Ophrah, it drew the people's attention away from worship of the Lord and led them into idolatry (v.27). And as soon as Gideon died, the people found it easy to go back to worshiping the Baals (v.33).

Gideon may have had good intentions, but he made the mistake of acting without consulting the Lord. Let's be careful not to allow anything to take our eyes off our loving, holy God — or it will lead us and others astray. —Dave Branon

The Word of God provides the light
We need to see the way;
If we obey what God has said,
We'll not be led astray. —Sper

**GOOD INTENTIONS ARE NO SUBSTITUTE
FOR OBEDIENCE.**

NEW CLOTHES

READ:
Isaiah 64

**We are all like an unclean thing, and all our righteousnesses are like filthy rags.
—Isaiah 64:6**

THE BIBLE IN ONE YEAR:
■ Exodus 11–13

Two men were talking not long after they had become Christians. One was a poor man from a godless background; the other was from an affluent religious environment. After each man told of his conversion, the man with the religious background asked the other, "Why do you suppose you responded the first time you heard the gospel, while so many years passed before I did?"

The poor man answered, "That's easy. Suppose someone came along and offered to give each of us a brand-new suit. I'd jump at the offer. My clothes are old and worn. But your closet is no doubt filled with the finest of suits. That's the way it is with salvation. You were probably satisfied with all your goodness, so it took you a long time to see the need for God's garment of righteousness offered to you through Christ. But I was deeply aware of my sinful condition, and I was eager to receive forgiveness and cleansing."

All people desperately need to be saved. Isaiah said that "all our righteousnesses are like filthy rags" (64:6). Those who recognize their spiritual poverty and accept the priceless gift of salvation that comes through faith in Christ are given "new clothes" of righteousness.

What are you wearing? — Richard De Haan

No one can say he doesn't need
Forgiveness for his sin;
We all must come to Christ by faith
To have new life within. — Branon

**NO ONE IS GOOD ENOUGH TO SAVE HIMSELF;
NO ONE IS SO BAD THAT GOD CANNOT SAVE HIM.**

A CALL FOR JUSTICE

READ:
Isaiah 59

No one calls for justice, nor does any plead for truth.
—Isaiah 59:4

THE BIBLE IN ONE YEAR:
■ Exodus 14–17

When a particular judge was assigned to a potentially volatile trial involving racial issues, many lawyers praised the choice. "He's fair — very fair — and he's just," said one. "He cares about people — victims and defendants," said another. Many others also spoke highly of his qualifications as a fair judge.

Such praise should be common, not the exception, for we expect justice from a judge. But God, the Judge of the universe, requires fairness from all of us and wants us to plead for justice for the oppressed. Israel's failure to do this accounted in part for the nation's downfall (Isaiah 59:9-15).

Today in many countries, more people are living in cities than ever before. And deep within those densely populated areas are conditions that breed anger, hopelessness, and despair. Landlords charge high rent for rundown apartments. Double standards of justice prevail for different races and nationalities. Unfair hiring and housing practices are common. And many other inequalities lead to new injustices.

As Christians, we must be among the first to work for justice in every area of society, not primarily for ourselves but for others. And we must banish prejudice and unfair attitudes from the inner citadel of our hearts. — Dennis De Haan

POINTS TO PONDER
How does my response to injustice
strengthen or weaken my witness for Christ?
How is prejudice related to injustice?

GOD'S JUSTICE LEAVES NO ROOM FOR PREJUDICE.

IN THE CAR WASH

READ:
Isaiah 43:1-13

When you pass through the waters, I will be with you.
—Isaiah 43:2

THE BIBLE IN ONE YEAR:
■ Exodus 18–20

I'll never forget my first experience using an automatic car wash. Approaching it with the dread of going to the dentist, I pushed the money into the slot, nervously checked and rechecked my windows, eased the car up to the line, and waited. Powers beyond my control began moving my car forward as if on a conveyor belt. There I was, cocooned inside, when a thunderous rush of water, soap, and brushes hit my car from all directions. *What if I get stuck in here or water crashes in?* I thought irrationally. Suddenly the waters ceased. After a blow-dry, my car was propelled into the outside world again, clean and polished.

In the midst of all this, I remembered stormy times in my life when it seemed I was on a conveyor belt, a victim of forces beyond my control. "Car-wash experiences," I now call them. I remembered that whenever I passed through deep waters my Redeemer had been with me, sheltering me against the rising tide (Isaiah 43:2). When I came out on the other side, which I always did, I was able to say with joy and confidence, "He is a faithful God!"

Are you in the middle of a car-wash experience? Trust God to bring you through to the other side. You'll then be a shining testimony of His keeping power. —Joanie Yoder

> *How wonderful to know that He*
> *Who watches from above*
> *Will always keep us sheltered in*
> *His ever-present love!* —King

**A TUNNEL OF TESTING CAN PRODUCE
A SHINING TESTIMONY.**

THE CRITIC

READ:
Proverbs 15:1-12

**The way of a fool is right in his own eyes, but he who heeds counsel is wise.
—Proverbs 12:15**

THE BIBLE IN ONE YEAR:
■ Exodus 21–24

When I was a teenager, a family joined our congregation. The wife was quiet, but the husband was loud, critical, and overbearing. I was standing nearby one Sunday morning when he stormed up to the pastor and verbally attacked him for something he had said in the sermon. The man's voice was loud, his tone disrespectful.

The pastor didn't do what I expected. He spoke softly, thanked the critic for his insights, and promised to think through the issue again.

Later, I asked my pastor why he didn't argue right back. He gave me some valuable advice I still try to follow. He said, "Every piece of criticism can be helpful. God may be in it, and if He is, I need to hear what He's saying. The critic just might be right."

When someone criticizes you, here are some biblical principles to follow: First, don't respond in anger (Proverbs 15:1). It will only accelerate the tension between you. Second, realize that you have been presented with a golden opportunity to model Christlike behavior — love, unselfishness, humility, and concern for others (Philippians 2:1-4). Third, the critic may be right; you may need to change. A wise person welcomes advice (Proverbs 9:8-9).

Treat a critic as a friend, and you both win. — David Egner

If criticism comes your way,
Consider its intent;
It may be that some truth from God
To you is being sent. — D. De Haan

**CRITICISM IS A GOOD TEACHER
IF WE ARE WILLING TO LEARN FROM IT.**

JUST A MESSENGER

READ:
Luke 3:1-18

I indeed baptize you with water; but One mightier than I is coming.
—Luke 3:16

THE BIBLE IN ONE YEAR:
■ Exodus 25–27

Dave Thomas, founder of Wendy's restaurants, appeared in more than 800 television commercials. He offered his homespun humor and "old-fashioned hamburgers" to a world-wide audience. Viewers saw him as friendly, funny, believable, and caring. In spite of his popularity, though, Thomas always said he was "the messenger, not the message."

That's a good word to remember as we speak about Christ to our friends and family. While our behavior should always be consistent with what we say, our goal is to point others to Jesus and not to ourselves. The apostle Paul said, "We do not preach ourselves, but Christ Jesus the Lord, and ourselves your bondservants for Jesus' sake" (2 Corinthians 4:5).

John the Baptist knew that his role was to be a messenger for Christ. When people flocked to hear John preach, and to be baptized as a sign of their repentance, many wondered if he was the promised Messiah. John told them, "I indeed baptize you with water; but One mightier than I is coming, whose sandal strap I am not worthy to loose" (Luke 3:16).

Through our words and actions, we testify of Jesus Christ as Savior and Lord. We are His messengers, but He is the message. — David McCasland

I do not ask that men may sound my praises,
Or headlines spread my name abroad;
I only pray that as I voice my message,
Hearers may find God! — *Cushman*

WE WITNESS BEST FOR CHRIST
WHEN WE SAY THE LEAST ABOUT OURSELVES.

HAPPY WITHOUT

READ:
1 Timothy 6:6-11

Those who desire to be rich fall into temptation and a snare, and into many foolish and harmful lusts. —1 Timothy 6:9

THE BIBLE IN ONE YEAR:
■ Exodus 28–31

The ancient Greek philosopher Socrates (469-399 BC) believed that if you are truly wise you will not be obsessed with possessions. Practicing to an extreme what he preached, he even refused to wear shoes.

Socrates loved to visit the marketplace, though, and gaze with admiration at the great abundance of wares on display. When a friend asked why he was so allured, he replied, "I love to go there and discover how many things I am perfectly happy without."

That type of attitude runs counter to the commercial messages that continually bombard our eyes and ears. Advertisers spend millions to tell us about all the latest products that we can't be happy without.

The apostle Paul advised his spiritual son Timothy, "Godliness with contentment is great gain. For we brought nothing into this world, and it is certain we can carry nothing out. And having food and clothing, with these we shall be content" (1 Timothy 6:6-8). If we become enamored with things, Paul warned, we may wander from the faith and be pierced with the pangs of frustrated desire (vv.9-10).

Let's ask ourselves, "What am I truly happy without?" The answer will reveal much about our relationship with the Lord and our contentment with Him. — Vernon Grounds

Lord, help me not to set my heart
On things that pass away;
Make me content with what I have,
And give You thanks each day. —Sper

**CONTENTMENT COMES NOT FROM GREAT WEALTH
BUT FROM FEW WANTS.**

BLAMING GOD

READ:
Exodus 32:15-29

Let no one say when he is tempted, "I am tempted by God."
—James 1:13

THE BIBLE IN ONE YEAR:
■ Exodus 32–34

It's bad enough to blame our parents, peers, or circumstances for our sins, but it's much worse to blame God. I read about a person on a weight-loss program who bought some donuts. When asked why, he implied that it was God's fault, because He had opened up a parking place right in front of the bakery just as he was driving by.

In Exodus 32, we read how the high priest, Aaron, supervised the making of a golden image for worship. This resulted in the death of 3,000 Israelites and brought a terrible plague on the nation. Instead of repenting immediately and taking responsibility as the leader, Aaron first blamed the people, saying they had put such pressure on him that he had no choice. Then he went even further and lied. He said that all he did was throw the gold into the melting pot, and the image of a calf mysteriously appeared (Exodus 32:24).

Moses rejected Aaron's excuse. He confronted his brother with his sin and then prayed for him (Deuteronomy 9:20). We can be sure that the Israelites who acknowledged their guilt were forgiven. But God judged the sin, and many died.

When you do wrong, take the blame. Don't look for scapegoats. Most important, don't blame God. — Herb Vander Lugt

My sin, O Lord, defies Your Word,
It shames Your holy name;
I will not make excuse for wrong —
Christ's blood is all I claim. — D. De Haan

**A GOOD TEST OF CHARACTER: WHEN YOU DO WRONG,
DO YOU ACCEPT THE BLAME?**

THE VALUE OF A LIFE

READ:
2 Samuel 9

Mephibosheth . . . shall eat at my table like one of the king's sons. —2 Samuel 9:11

THE BIBLE IN ONE YEAR:
■ Exodus 35–37

A British factory worker and his wife were excited when, after many years of marriage, they discovered they were going to have their first child. According to author Jill Briscoe, who told this true story, the man eagerly relayed the good news to his fellow workers. He told them God had answered his prayers. But they made fun of him for asking God for a child.

When the baby was born, he was diagnosed as having Down syndrome. As the father made his way to work for the first time after the birth, he wondered how to face his co-workers. "God, please give me wisdom," he prayed. Just as he feared, some said mockingly, "So, God gave you this child!" The new father stood for a long time, silently asking God for help. At last he said, "I'm glad the Lord gave this child to me and not to you."

As this man accepted his disabled son as God's gift to him, so King David was pleased to show kindness to Saul's grandson who was "lame in his feet" (2 Samuel 9:3). Some may have rejected Mephibosheth because he was lame, but David's action showed that he valued him.

In God's eyes, every person is important. He sent His only Son to die for us. May we remember with gratitude how much He values each human life. — Dave Branon

Lord, we would see in those we meet
The likeness of Your image there,
And may their special dignity
Grow stronger from our love and care. — D. De Haan

EVERYONE IS VALUABLE TO GOD.

THE REASON AND THE RISK

READ:
2 Timothy 2:1-13

I endure all things for the sake of the elect, that they also may obtain the salvation which is in Christ.
—2 Timothy 2:10

THE BIBLE IN ONE YEAR:
■ Exodus 38–40

It was the kind of moment that people have nightmares about. A tanker truck filled with 2,500 gallons of propane gas caught fire while parked at a fuel storage warehouse. The flames shot 30 to 40 feet out of the back of the truck and quickly spread to a loading dock. Several large tanks nearby were in danger of exploding.

At that point, the plant manager, after helping to rescue the badly burned driver, jumped into the cab and drove the blazing truck away from the warehouse. His quick action and courage saved lives.

The apostle Paul also risked his life on behalf of others (2 Timothy 2:10). He was stoned and left for dead (Acts 14:19). On another occasion he was mobbed, whipped, and imprisoned (16:22-23). Three times he was shipwrecked, and he was beaten many times with lashes and rods (2 Corinthians 11:23-28). Why did Paul willingly endure such suffering? He was thinking in terms of eternal fire and eternal life, so he gladly undertook the risk.

Do we see the danger as clearly as Paul did? Do we take advantage of opportunities to go to the rescue of people who need the good news of Christ? Are we filled with the same sense of purpose that caused Paul to endure all things for the sake of the lost? — Mart De Haan II

THINKING IT OVER
What risks do we take if we dare to tell others about Jesus? Physical harm? Verbal abuse? Rejection? Ridicule? Loss of possessions? Other?

**IT'S RISKY TO GO OUT ON A LIMB—
BUT THAT'S WHERE THE FRUIT IS.**

BE CAREFUL!

READ:
1 Corinthians 10:1-13

Let him who thinks
he stands take heed
lest he fall.
—1 Corinthians 10:12

THE BIBLE IN ONE YEAR:
■ Leviticus 1–4

Several years ago my wife Carolyn and I were hiking on Mount Rainier in Washington when we came to a swollen, glacial stream. Someone had flattened one side of a log and dropped it across the river to form a crude bridge, but there was no handrail and the log was slippery.

The prospect of walking on the wet log was frightening, and Carolyn didn't want to cross. But she found the courage, and slowly, carefully she inched her way to the other side.

On the way back we had to walk on the same log, and she did so with the same care. "Are you afraid?" I asked. "Of course," she replied, "that's what keeps me safe." Again, fully aware of the danger, she made her way to safety.

Much of life poses moral danger for us. We should never assume in any situation that we're incapable of falling. "Let him who thinks he stands take heed lest he fall" (1 Corinthians 10:12). Given the opportunity and circumstances, *any* of us are capable of falling into *any* sin. To believe otherwise is sheer folly.

We must watch and pray and arm ourselves for every occasion by putting our total trust in God (Ephesians 6:13). "God is faithful" (1 Corinthians 10:13), and He will give us the strength to keep from falling. — David Roper

The hand of God protects our way
When we would do His will;
And if through danger we must go,
We know He's with us still. — D. De Haan

GOD PROVIDES THE ARMOR, BUT WE MUST PUT IT ON.

WHO IS JABEZ?

READ:
1 Chronicles 4:9-10

Jabez was more honorable than his brothers.
—1 Chronicles 4:9

THE BIBLE IN ONE YEAR:
■ Leviticus 5–7

Chinese New Year celebrations are fun for children. When relatives and friends get together, it's the custom for adults to give children small, red envelopes containing token sums of money. Children often rip open their packets just to get the money, and their parents have to remind them that the giver is more important than the gift.

Similarly, when we study the prayer of Jabez in 1 Chronicles 4:9-10, it is important to remember that the Giver, the Lord, is more important than the gift. If we focus solely on the request of Jabez, it could be easy to make the mistake of turning it into a formula for obtaining what we want from God.

We don't know much about Jabez, except that his mother gave him a name that sounds like the Hebrew word for "distress" or "pain." We're also told that when he grew up, "Jabez was more honorable than his brothers."

What made Jabez "more honorable"? On the basis of his prayer, we can assume that he took his relationship with God seriously. There was no magic in the words of his prayer. Rather, he knew that God is the giver of all things. Jabez was honorable, I believe, because he honored the Lord.

Our prayer today should be to emulate the character of Jabez, who lived to please God. — Albert Lee

> *We can't presume to know what's best*
> *When we begin to pray;*
> *So we must ask, "What honors God?"*
> *And seek His will and way.* — Sper

THE PURPOSE OF PRAYER IS NOT TO GET WHAT WE WANT,
BUT TO BECOME WHAT GOD WANTS.

BUILDING A LIFE

READ:
John 20:11-18

To me, to live is Christ, and to die is gain.
—Philippians 1:21

THE BIBLE IN ONE YEAR:
■ Leviticus 8–10

It was a sunny, sad day in 1982 — the day after my husband's funeral. I had gone alone to Bill's grave, hardly knowing why. As with Mary Magdalene who visited Jesus' tomb, the risen Lord was waiting for me. He impressed the words of Philippians 1:21 on my mind, still numbed by Bill's untimely death from cancer.

I wove my prayer around the words of that verse: "Lord, how often I've heard Bill testify, 'For to me, to live is Christ, and to die is gain.' Well, your servant has now died, an untold loss for us, an unspeakable gain for him. I know, Lord, that I too will die someday and enter that gain. But right now I'm still alive. I know I must not live in the past, precious as it is. For to me, to live is You!'"

As I turned to leave, I knew I had prayed a foundational prayer. Much recovery and rebuilding lay before me, but beneath me was the only firm foundation on which to build — Jesus Christ.

Has a loved one's death or the fear of your own death tested your foundation? Let Paul's words, written in the face of death, and Jesus' words to Mary encourage you to offer a foundational prayer of your own. Then begin to rebuild your life on the risen Christ! — Joanie Yoder

It matters not how dark the way,
How thick the clouds from day to day,
God will direct in all we do
If we take time to pray it through. — Mead

LIFE'S BEST OUTLOOK IS A PRAYERFUL UPLOOK!

THE JUDGE'S COMPASSION

READ:
Romans 5:1-11

Christ also suffered once for sins, the just for the unjust, that He might bring us to God.
—1 Peter 3:18

THE BIBLE IN ONE YEAR:
■ Leviticus 11–13

During his years as mayor of New York City, Fiorello La Guardia sometimes presided as judge in a night court. In one case, a man was found guilty of stealing a loaf of bread. He pleaded that he had committed that theft to feed his starving family. "The law is the law," La Guardia declared. "I must therefore fine you $10." When the man sadly confessed that he had no money, the judge took $10 out of his wallet and paid the fine. He also asked each person in the courtroom to contribute 50 cents to help the man.

At the heart of the gospel stands the cross of Jesus Christ. Its message is so plain that even a child can understand it: Jesus took my place and died instead of me. But its truth is so awesome that the wisest of humans can't fully fathom its meaning. The Bible says, "Christ also suffered once for sins, the just for the unjust, that He might bring us to God" (1 Peter 3:18). It also says, "When we were still without strength, in due time Christ died for the ungodly" (Romans 5:6).

As we look at the judge's compassion, we catch at least a glimpse of God's measureless grace. The demands of the law were satisfied. The judge himself paid the fine. The lawbreaker was set free and even blessed with an undeserved gift. What a profound picture of our Savior! — Vernon Grounds

> *There's a wideness in God's mercy*
> *Like the wideness of the sea;*
> *There's a kindness in His justice,*
> *Which is more than liberty.* — Faber

**THE WAY TO FACE CHRIST AS JUDGE
IS TO KNOW HIM AS YOUR SAVIOR.**

TRUE GREATNESS

READ:
Mark 10:35-45

Whoever desires to become great among you shall be your servant. —Mark 10:43

THE BIBLE IN ONE YEAR:
■ Leviticus 14–16

Some people feel like a small pebble lost in the immensity of the Grand Canyon. But no matter how insignificant we judge ourselves to be, we can be greatly used by God.

In a sermon early in 1968, Martin Luther King Jr. quoted Jesus' words from Mark 10 about servanthood. Then he said, "Everybody can be great, because everybody can serve. You don't have to have a college degree to serve. You don't have to make your subject and your verb agree to serve. You don't have to know about Plato and Aristotle to serve. . . . You only need a heart full of grace, a soul generated by love."

When Jesus' disciples quarreled about who would get the places of honor in heaven, He told them: "Whoever desires to become great among you shall be your servant. And whoever of you desires to be first shall be slave of all. For even the Son of Man did not come to be served, but to serve, and to give His life a ransom for many" (Mark 10:43-45).

I wonder about us. Is that our understanding of greatness? Are we gladly serving, doing tasks that may be unnoticed? Is the purpose of our serving to please our Lord, rather than to gain the applause of people? If we are willing to be a servant, we can achieve true greatness. — Vernon Grounds

No service in itself is small,
None great, though earth it fill;
But that is small that seeks its own,
And great that does God's will. —Anon.

**LITTLE THINGS DONE IN CHRIST'S NAME
ARE GREAT THINGS.**

TOUGH TREES

READ:
Romans 5:1-5

**Tribulation produces
perseverance; and
perseverance,
character; and
character, hope.
—Romans 5:3-4**

THE BIBLE IN ONE YEAR:
■ Leviticus 17–19

Bristlecone pines are the world's oldest living trees. Several are estimated to be 3,000 to 4,000 years old. In 1957, scientist Edmund Schulman found one he named "Methuselah." This ancient, gnarled pine is nearly 5,000 years old! It was an old tree when the Egyptians were building the pyramids.

Bristlecones grow atop the mountains of the western United States at elevations of 10,000 to 11,000 feet. They've been able to survive some of the harshest living conditions on earth: arctic temperatures, fierce winds, thin air, and little rainfall.

Their brutal environment is actually one of the reasons they've survived for millennia. Hardship has produced extraordinary strength and staying power.

Paul taught that "tribulation produces . . . character" (Romans 5:3-4). Adversity is part of the process that God uses to produce good results in our lives. Trouble, if it turns us to the Lord, could actually be the best thing for us. It leaves us wholly dependent on Him.

So we should pray not just for relief from our affliction, but for the grace to turn it into greater openness to God and to His will for us. Then we can be strong in calamity, and at peace in the place where God has planted us. — David Roper

Good timber does not grow in ease;
The stronger wind, the tougher trees;
By sun and cold, by rain and snows,
In tree or man, good timber grows. — Malloch

**GOD USES OUR DIFFICULTIES
TO DEVELOP OUR CHARACTER.**

No Lie

READ:
Colossians 3:9-17

Do not lie to one another, since you have put off the old man with his deeds.
—Colossians 3:9

THE BIBLE IN ONE YEAR:
■ Leviticus 20–23

A college football coach resigns after admitting he falsified his academic and athletic credentials. A career military officer confesses to wearing combat decorations he did not earn. A job applicant acknowledges that her stated experience in "food and beverage oversight" was actually making coffee each morning at the office.

Within each of us is a tendency to embellish the truth in order to impress others. Whether on a job résumé or in casual conversation, exaggeration comes naturally — but we pay a price. Small lies usually grow larger as we try to avoid discovery. Then we wonder how we ever got ourselves into such a predicament.

The Bible says, "Do not lie to one another, since you have put off the old man with his deeds, and have put on the new man who is renewed in knowledge according to the image of Him who created him" (Colossians 3:9-10). In other words, if we've placed our faith in Jesus as our Savior, lying is inconsistent with what God expects us to be. The antidote to the poison of self-promotion is a growing Christlikeness — a spirit of mercy, kindness, humility, patience, forgiveness, and love (vv.12-14).

If we genuinely care about people, we won't need to try to impress them at any cost. — David McCasland

Lord, help me to please You by telling the truth,
Being honest in words and in deeds;
And help me to conquer my selfish desires,
To love others and care for their needs. — Fitzhugh

HONESTY MEANS NEVER HAVING TO LOOK OVER YOUR SHOULDER.

THE WAYS OF GOD

READ:
2 Samuel 24:1-17

The LORD is righteous in all His ways, gracious in all His works.
—Psalm 145:17

THE BIBLE IN ONE YEAR:
■ Leviticus 24—27

Have you ever puzzled over statements in the Bible that seem to contradict each other? For example, 1 Chronicles 21:1 states that the one who "moved David to number Israel" was Satan, but 2 Samuel 24:1 says it was the Lord. How do we explain this? We know that God never tempts anyone to sin (James 1:13).

The answer lies in the way the Old Testament writers expressed the ways of God. They sometimes ascribed to God what He merely allowed, knowing that He permits us to make wrong choices and then uses the tragic results to accomplish His good purposes.

In 2 Samuel 24:1, we read that God "moved David" to take a census of Israel. This is clearly a case when God allowed Satan to influence David, for it was an attempt to assess Israel's military strength. This reflected the same sin of pride and self-reliance that was prevalent in the nation. As a result, God judged the people and their king.

So what was the good purpose God accomplished by allowing Satan to influence David? Although many Israelites died, the nation itself was spared and purified. The Lord punished the guilty but also showed His mercy.

God's ways may be beyond our understanding, but we can always trust Him to do what is right. — Herb Vander Lugt

Your ways, O God, are always right,
Your works are always good;
And when we keep these truths in mind,
Your Word is understood. — D. De Haan

GOD MAY CONCEAL THE PURPOSE OF HIS WAYS, BUT HIS WAYS ARE NOT WITHOUT PURPOSE.

MIDNIGHT ENCOURAGEMENT

READ:
Judges 7:1-23

Your hands shall be strengthened to go down against the camp. —Judges 7:11

THE BIBLE IN ONE YEAR:
■ Numbers 1–3

The Midianites and their allies had invaded Israel. It was the time of the judges, and Gideon could muster only 32,000 men against an army "as numerous as locusts" (Judges 7:12). Then God cut the army down to 300 (vv.2-7). Gideon was afraid, so God sent him into the enemy camp at night. Crouching behind cover, the Israelite captain heard one soldier tell another about a dream (vv.13-14). A loaf of barley bread had tumbled into the Midianite camp, destroying one of its tents. His friend saw it as a sure sign that Gideon would win the battle.

Gideon was greatly encouraged. After worshiping God, he returned to the camp, organized his 300 men with their trumpets and lamps, and routed the superior Midianite forces (vv.15-22).

As Christ's followers we're not battling armies, but we are at war. Spiritual foes attack us (Ephesians 6:10-12). They undermine our confidence and sap our strength. We're also battling ourselves — our weaknesses, fears, doubts (Romans 7:15-25). After a while, we can get discouraged.

But our God is the great Encourager. When our resolve weakens or vision fades, by His power He will give us the strength we need (Ephesians 3:16) — even when the enemy seems more numerous than a swarm of locusts. — Dave Egner

As we meet fierce foes on the pathway of life,
Whether Satan or self or sin,
Let us look to the Lord for encouragement;
If we do, the battle we'll win! — Fitzhugh

**TO TRUST IS TO TRIUMPH,
FOR THE BATTLE IS THE LORD'S.**

ROLL 'EM UP

READ:
James 2:14-26

**Show me your faith
without your works,
and I will show you
my faith by my works.
—James 2:18**

THE BIBLE IN ONE YEAR:
■ Numbers 4–6

When Dave Thomas died in early 2002, he left behind more than just thousands of Wendy's restaurants. He also left a legacy of being a practical, hard-working man who was respected for his down-to-earth values.

Among the pieces of good advice that have outlived the smiling entrepreneur is his view of what Christians should be doing with their lives. Thomas, who as a youngster was influenced for Christ by his grandmother, said that believers should be "roll-up-your-shirtsleeves" Christians.

In his book *Well Done*, Thomas said, "Roll-up-your-shirtsleeves Christians see Christianity as faith and action. They still make the time to talk with God through prayer, study Scripture with devotion, be super-active in their church, and take their ministry to others to spread the Good Word." He went on to say they are "anonymous people who may be doing even more good than all the well-known Christians in the world."

That statement has more meat in it than a Wendy's triple burger. Thomas knew about hard work in the restaurant business, and he knew it is vital in the spiritual world too.

In James 2:17, we read that unless our faith is accompanied by works, our faith is dead. Let's roll up our sleeves and get to work. There's plenty to do. — Dave Branon

> *Let's gladly work in serving Christ,*
> *For faith alone is dead;*
> *Let's labor out of love for Him*
> *Who suffered in our stead.* – D. De Haan

A LIVING FAITH IS A WORKING FAITH.

WHO'S GOT YOUR TONGUE?

READ:
Proverbs 12:17-25

The tongue of the wise promotes health.
—Proverbs 12:18

THE BIBLE IN ONE YEAR:
■ Numbers 7–10

It's been estimated that a talkative person may speak 30,000 words a day! But the important question is, how do our words, whether many or few, affect others?

A Greek philosopher asked his servant to cook the best dish possible. The servant, who was very wise, prepared a dish of tongue, saying, "It's the best of all dishes, for it reminds us that we may use the tongue to bless and express happiness, dispel sorrow, remove despair, and spread cheer."

Later the servant was asked to cook the worst dish possible. Again, he prepared a dish of tongue, saying, "It's the worst dish, for it reminds us that we may use the tongue to curse and break hearts, destroy reputations, create strife, and set families and nations at war."

We don't have to eat tongue to grasp that servant's point. But we may have to "eat our own words" quite often before we learn to avoid saying things we'd like to retract.

Solomon wrote: "The tongue of the wise promotes health" (Proverbs 12:18). It affirms and encourages others. The key word in that verse isn't *tongue* but *wise*. The tongue is not in control, but the person behind it is.

If you want your tongue to build people up and not tear them down, ask God to make you wise. — Joanie Yoder

A wise old bird sat on an oak —
The more he saw the less he spoke,
The less he spoke the more he heard;
Lord, make me like that wise old bird. — Anon.

**WISDOM IS KNOWING WHEN TO SPEAK YOUR MIND
AND WHEN TO MIND YOUR SPEECH.**

THE DEVIL'S BAIT

READ:
1 John 2:15-17

Do not love the world or the things in the world. If anyone loves the world, the love of the Father is not in him. —1 John 2:15

THE BIBLE IN ONE YEAR:
■ Numbers 11–14

I once read about an interesting method used by people in North Africa to catch monkeys. A hunter hollows out a gourd and makes a hole in its side just large enough for a monkey to insert his open hand. The gourd is then filled with nuts and tied to a tree.

The curious monkey is attracted by the smell of the nuts and reaches inside and grasps them. The hole in the gourd is too small, however, for the animal to withdraw his fist as long as it is tightly closed around the nuts. Because he refuses to release his prize, the unsuspecting monkey falls easy prey to his captor. Unwilling to relax his grasp, he actually traps himself!

Satan uses a similar method to ensnare us. He tempts us to grasp after more and more material possessions, which we think will bring us security. As long as we tenaciously hold on to them, we are enslaved. How relevant is the biblical warning, "Do not love the world or the things in the world" (1 John 2:15). The apostle John also said that "the world is passing away, and the lust of it; but he who does the will of God abides forever" (v.17).

Remember what happened to the monkey. Don't be fooled by the devil's bait! — Richard De Haan

Take the world, but give me Jesus —
All its joys are but a name;
But His love abideth ever,
Through eternal years the same. —Crosby

YOU CAN'T STORE UP TREASURES IN HEAVEN IF YOU'RE HOLDING ON TO THE TREASURES OF EARTH.

DESERT OF DIVERSION

READ:
Revelation 2:1-7

**You have left your first love. Remember therefore from where you have fallen.
—Revelation 2:4-5**

THE BIBLE IN ONE YEAR:
■ Numbers 15–17

Muynak was once a thriving fishing port on the Aral Sea. But today Muynak sits on the edge of a bitter, salty desert. Sand dunes are strewn with the rusted, hollow hulls of a fishing fleet that once sailed high above on the surface of Central Asia's fountain of life.

Things began changing around 1960 when Soviet government planners began diverting the Aral's water source to irrigate the world's largest cotton belt. No one, however, envisioned the environmental disaster that would result. Weather has become more extreme, the growing season has been shortened by 2 months, and 80 percent of the region's farmland has been ruined by salt storms that sweep in off the dry seabed.

What happened at Muynak parallels the history of the church of Ephesus. Once a thriving spiritual community, the Ephesian believers diverted their attention from Christ to the works they were doing in His name (Revelation 2:2-4). They had lost sight of what was most important in their relationship with Christ — their love for Him.

Lord, help us to recognize and repent of whatever it is that diverts our attention from loving You. Flood the desert of our souls with Your living water. — Mart De Haan

The works we do in Jesus' name
And battles that are won
Will not be pleasing to the Lord
Unless in love they're done. — Sper

**TO RENEW YOUR LOVE FOR CHRIST,
REVIEW CHRIST'S LOVE FOR YOU.**

Thoughts Of Heaven

READ:
Revelation 21:1-5

Behold, the tabernacle
of God is with men,
and He will dwell with
them, and they shall
be His people.
—Revelation 21:3

THE BIBLE IN ONE YEAR:
■ Numbers 18–20

Cartoonists often depict those who have gone to heaven as white-robed, ghostly forms floating among the clouds or sitting on golden stairs playing harps. What a far cry from the picture we find in the Bible!

In 1 Corinthians 15, we read that our resurrection bodies, although not subject to death, will be real and tangible — not mere apparitions. And Revelation 21:1-5 tells us that God will bring about "a new heaven and a new earth." He will bring down "the city of the living God, the heavenly Jerusalem" (Hebrews 12:22), and set it upon the new earth as the "New Jerusalem." It is described as having streets, walls, gates, and even a river and trees (Revelation 22:1-5).

Life in that city will be wonderful, free from all the debilitating effects of sin. There will be no more death, sorrow, mourning, and pain, for God will make "all things new." But best of all, He Himself will come to live among us, making possible a new level of intimacy with Him.

It's difficult to envision such an existence, but what an exciting prospect! It is all possible because of what Jesus did when He died for us on the cross. This should motivate us to worship Him, live godly lives, and tell others how they too can be assured of a glorious future. — Herb Vander Lugt

When all my labors and trials are o'er
And I am safe on that beautiful shore,
Just to be near the dear Lord I adore
Will through the ages be glory for me. —Gabriel

THE MORE WE LOVE JESUS
THE MORE WE'LL LONG FOR HEAVEN.

HE'S BEEN FAITHFUL

READ:
Psalm 119:89-96

**Your faithfulness endures to all generations.
—Psalm 119:90**

THE BIBLE IN ONE YEAR:
■ Numbers 21–24

Jim and Carol Cymbala prayed and praised and preached their way through a personal 2-year nightmare. Their teenage daughter Chrissy had turned her back on the God they loved and served so faithfully. Although their hearts were breaking, Jim and Carol continued ministering to the people of the Brooklyn Tabernacle in New York City.

Some people think that Carol wrote the song "He's Been Faithful" after her daughter's dramatic return to God, but she didn't. She wrote it before. Carol refers to it as "a song of hope born in the midst of my pain." While hurting deeply, Carol said that her song "became like a balm to my heart, strengthening me once again." The words she wrote during that time helped her to move forward. Although her daughter had not yet come back to the Lord, Carol could praise Him for His loving faithfulness in her own life.

Later, when Chrissy showed up at home and fell to her knees begging forgiveness, the truth of Psalm 119:90 became real to Carol: God is faithful not just to our generation, but to all generations! Carol also experienced in a new way a line of her own song that has blessed so many: "What I thought was impossible, I've seen my God do!" — Julie Link

Looking back, His love and mercy I see,
Though in my heart I have questioned,
Even failed to believe,
Yet He's been faithful, faithful to me. — Cymbala

**WHEN WE HAVE NOTHING LEFT BUT GOD,
WE FIND THAT GOD IS ENOUGH.**

BEING REALISTIC

READ:
Psalm 27

**Whenever I am afraid,
I will trust in You.
—Psalm 56:3**

THE BIBLE IN ONE YEAR:
■ Numbers 25–27

Few of us are traveling to heaven in a state of freedom from all fear. Who can honestly testify that they always practice this verse: "In God I have put my trust; I will not be afraid"? (Psalm 56:11). We do trust, and yet we may be troubled at times by gnawing worries. Our common experience is that our trust in God is mingled with episodes of worry.

Even the apostle Paul, who wrote many of the New Testament letters, had some anxieties. He confessed to the Corinthians, "I was with you in weakness, in fear, and in much trembling" (1 Corinthians 2:3).

So don't worry that you have worries! Don't pretend you never have them. If you are troubled by anxieties, admit them to yourself. Share them with a trusted friend. Above all, talk to the all-compassionate Friend, Jesus Christ, who knows your every thought and emotion (Psalm 139:4). With compassion, He says to you, "Do not fear" (Luke 12:32). Ask Him for the grace to help you overcome your fears and worries. Then, "wait on the LORD; be of good courage, and He shall strengthen your heart" (Psalm 27:14).

On your journey through life, whenever you're afraid, trust in the Lord (Psalm 56:3). — Vernon Grounds

All your anxiety, all your care,
Bring to the Mercy-seat — leave it there;
Never a burden He cannot bear,
Never a Friend like Jesus! — Joy

**TRUSTING GOD'S FAITHFULNESS
DISPELS OUR FEARFULNESS.**

LIVING LIFE TO THE MAXIMUM

READ:
John 10:7-11

**I have come that they may have life, and that they may have it more abundantly.
—John 10:10**

THE BIBLE IN ONE YEAR:
■ Numbers 28–30

A veteran mountain climber was sharing his experiences with a group of novices preparing for their first major climb. He had conquered many of the world's most difficult peaks, so he was qualified to give them some advice. "Remember this," he said, "your goal is to experience the exhilaration of the climb and the joy of reaching . . . the peak. Each step draws you closer to the top. If your purpose for climbing is just to avoid death, your experience will be minimal."

I see an application to the Christian's experience. Jesus did not call us to live the Christian life just to escape hell. It's not to be a life of minimum joy and fulfillment, but a life that is full and overflowing. Our purpose in following Christ should not be merely to avoid eternal punishment. If that's our primary motivation, we are missing the wonders and joys and victories of climbing higher and higher with Jesus.

The Lord promised us "life . . . more abundantly" (John 10:10). We cannot experience a full and abundant life if we are living in fear. When we walk by faith, we will see each day of the Christian life as a challenge to be met, and as one more upward step to glory!

Do not live minimally. Live life to the maximum! Climb that mountain with confidence! — Dave Egner

> *God has given life abundant —*
> *Live it fully every day;*
> *Though our time on earth is fleeting,*
> *He goes with us all the way.* — Hess

**WE GET THE MOST OUT OF LIFE
WHEN WE LIVE FOR CHRIST.**

SPEAKING THE TRUTH IN LOVE

READ:
2 Timothy 2:19-26

A servant of the Lord must not quarrel but be gentle to all.
—2 Timothy 2:24

THE BIBLE IN ONE YEAR:
■ Numbers 31–33

There are times when we must "contend earnestly for the faith" (Jude 3). But in doing so, we must never be ungracious or antagonistic. The 17th-century English Puritans were right when they said that faith can never be foisted on another person. Consent must be gained by gentle persuasion and reason.

Today's Bible reading underscores that principle. Paul told Timothy that "a servant of the Lord must not quarrel but be gentle to all" (2 Timothy 2:24). He wanted Timothy to be thoughtful and relevant in proclaiming the truth, not defensive. When people opposed the truth, he was to gently correct them in the hope that God would "grant them repentance, so that they may know the truth, and that they may come to their senses and escape the snare of the devil" (vv.25-26).

What was true for a young leader like Timothy applies to all believers. Those who oppose us are not the enemy but victims of the enemy. They can be delivered, Paul insisted, but we are to speak the truth in love.

Truth without love is dogma that does not touch the heart. Love without truth is sentimentalism that does not challenge the will. When truth is spoken with love, God's Spirit can use it to change another's mind. — David Roper

To speak of the Savior in glowing terms,
To tell how He died in our place,
Will be unconvincing to those who hear
If we fail to show forth His grace. — D. De Haan

TRUTH SPOKEN IN LOVE IS HARD TO REFUSE.

For Better Or Worse?

READ:
Ephesians 5:22-33

Wives, submit to your own husbands, as to the Lord. . . . Husbands, love your wives, just as Christ also loved the church.
—Ephesians 5:22, 25

THE BIBLE IN ONE YEAR:
■ Numbers 34–36

Within a chip shot of our house is a golf course. When I stand in my backyard, I see ponds waiting hungrily for my next errant shot. At times I can imagine sandtraps and trees joking about my bad days.

I mention the sport with mixed feelings. I like to golf occasionally, but living so close to the course reminds me of my failures in playing the game, which has its disadvantages.

A similar problem can occur in marriage. Sometimes a husband and wife can lose sight of the hopes and dreams they once shared. Then the very presence of the other becomes a source of irritation, a reminder of past failures and disappointments.

When the apostle Paul wrote his letter to the Ephesians, he asked husbands and wives to turn their thoughts to their relationship with the Son of God (5:22-33). In Him we find undying love and forgiveness for our failures. In Him we find Someone who loves to forget the worst and bring out the best. He reminds us not of what we've lost but of what we have yet to find.

Forgive us, Father, for focusing on our flaws and failures rather than on the love of Your Son, Jesus Christ. Help us to rediscover our spouse in the light of our Lord's great love for us. — Mart De Haan

REFLECTING ON MARRIAGE
As a couple, recall the hopes and dreams you had when you were first married. Name some that have come true. Share with each other your hopes for the future.

MARRIAGES MAY BE MADE IN HEAVEN,
BUT THEY HAVE TO BE WORKED OUT ON EARTH.

GRASSHOPPER SENSE

READ:
Hebrews 10:19-25

**Let us consider one another in order to stir up love and good works.
—Hebrews 10:24**

THE BIBLE IN ONE YEAR:
■ Deuteronomy 1–3

One grasshopper seems insignificant as it leaps across a field. But when it joins forces with other grasshoppers, the resulting swarm can soon devour all the vegetation in its path.

Grasshoppers demonstrate the power of working together for a common cause. What they cannot do individually, they are able to accomplish together. In the Old Testament book of Proverbs, the wise man Agur observed, "The locusts have no king, yet they all advance in ranks" (30:27).

We can learn a lesson from these little creatures. Followers of Christ can make far greater advances for Him when they act and pray together than they could ever make alone. When Christians are united in serving the Lord, they can become a mighty force for God in fulfilling His purposes for the church.

Although the New Testament urges us to possess a personal faith in Jesus Christ, it says nothing at all about a private faith. We need other believers, and other believers need us (Hebrews 10:24-25).

Let's enjoy and contribute to the strength and fellowship of the unified body of Christ. An effective church will demonstrate the good sense of the grasshopper by our cooperation and unity in the Holy Spirit. — Haddon Robinson

We Christians have a kinship with
All others who believe,
And from that bond of faith and love
A mutual strength receive. — Hess

**WE CAN ACCOMPLISH MORE TOGETHER
THAN WE CAN ALONE.**

February 17

"JOY STEALERS"

READ:
Philippians 1:1-11

He who has begun
a good work in you
will complete it.
—Philippians 1:6

THE BIBLE IN ONE YEAR:
■ Deuteronomy 4–6

Why do many Christians fail to experience real joy, which is listed as a fruit of the Holy Spirit in Galatians 5:22?

In his book *Laugh Again*, Charles Swindoll suggests three common "joy stealers" — worry, stress, and fear. He defines worry as "an inordinate anxiety about something that may or may not occur." (And it usually doesn't.) Stress, says the author, is "intense strain over a situation we can't change or control." (But God can.) And fear, according to Swindoll, is a "dreadful uneasiness over danger, evil, or pain." (And it magnifies our problems.)

Swindoll says that to resist these "joy stealers" we must embrace the same confidence that Paul expressed in his letter to the Philippians. After giving thanks for the Philippian believers (1:3-5), the apostle assured them "that He who has begun a good work in you will complete it until the day of Jesus Christ" (v.6).

Whatever causes you worry, stress, and fear cannot ultimately keep God from continuing His work in you. With this confidence we can begin each day knowing that He is in control. We can leave everything in His hands.

Resist those "joy stealers" by renewing your confidence in God each morning. Then relax and rejoice. — Joanie Yoder

Although our joy will wane at times
From worry, stress, and fear,
God keeps on working in our heart
And tells us He is near. — D. De Haan

HAPPINESS DEPENDS ON HAPPENINGS;
JOY DEPENDS ON JESUS.

INSEPARABLE TWINS

READ:
Ephesians 4:1-16

. . . speaking the truth in love, [we are to] grow up in all things into Him who is the head—Christ.
—Ephesians 4:15

THE BIBLE IN ONE YEAR:
■ Deuteronomy 7–9

A seminary student got into a heated debate with his landlord. They were discussing the teachings of a theologian whom the landlord thought was a heretic. The student, on the other hand, considered himself a follower of the man and his doctrines.

With an attitude of superiority, the young man showed his landlord a well-marked copy of a theology book written by this man. The landlord, who had little education but was a devout Christian, was overwhelmed by the young fellow's greater knowledge. As a result, he felt frustrated and defeated.

Similarly, it's possible for us to misuse the great spiritual truths of Scripture to hurt others. Maybe we've received instruction from a prominent Bible teacher, gained special insights into the Word, or memorized key Scriptures we can quote with ease. This gives us the leverage either to put someone down or to build him up. If we misuse what we know, we may set Christians against each other and break up churches. Or we can use the truth to enlighten, edify, and enrich others when we accompany it with love.

Speaking the truth must never be separated from love (Ephesians 4:15). They're inseparable twins! — Dennis De Haan

Lord, I must speak the truth in love
If seeking hearts would hear it,
For speaking with self-righteous pride
May wound another's spirit. — Fasick

THE TRUTH MAY HURT,
BUT LOVE HELPS EASE THE PAIN.

IT TAKES JUST ONE

READ:
Ephesians 4:17-32

**A perverse man sows strife, and a whisperer separates the best of friends.
—Proverbs 16:28**

THE BIBLE IN ONE YEAR:
■ Deuteronomy 10–12

In 1520, one person stepped off a Spanish ship in Mexico and caused the deaths of thousands of people. The man was a soldier under the leadership of Pánfilo de Narváez, and he had smallpox. The soldier didn't know it, but wherever he went he exposed the citizens to a new disease. As a result of the ensuing smallpox epidemic, many thousands of Mexican citizens died.

One man. That's all it took. His contact with the unsuspecting Mexican people led to a horrible, painful scourge. The devastating effects of that disease traveled from one person to another, infecting a large segment of the population.

The spread of any deadly disease is similar to the spread of a spiritual sickness that sometimes strikes churches — the disease of gossip and unedifying words (Ephesians 4:29-32).

It's not unusual for a happy and well-adjusted congregation of people to be infected after just one person introduces gossip. Soon dissension is running rampant among people who had been eagerly working together, and the church finds itself spending more time on damage control than on ministry.

Each of us should be careful not to spread the sickness of gossip. Instead, let's use our words to strengthen and encourage one another. — Dave Branon

A careless word may kindle strife,
A cruel word may wreck a life;
A timely word may lessen stress,
A loving word may heal and bless. — Anon.

TO SILENCE GOSSIP, REFUSE TO REPEAT IT.

LIFE AFTER MIRACLES

READ:
Exodus 15:19-27

Moses brought Israel from the Red Sea; then they went out into the Wilderness of Shur. —Exodus 15:22

THE BIBLE IN ONE YEAR:
■ Deuteronomy 13–16

On the other side of every miraculous intervention by God on our behalf, there is a road of faith to travel. Whether God's power has touched our health, finances, or family relationships, we must not only praise and thank the Lord but obey Him as well.

After God opened the Red Sea for His people, then released the waters to overwhelm Pharaoh's pursuing army, there was a great celebration of praise to the Lord (Exodus 15:1-21). But then it was time to move on in the journey toward the land of promise. "So Moses brought Israel from the Red Sea; then they went out into the Wilderness of Shur" (v.22). There they traveled for 3 days without finding water, and they began to complain.

In the divine plan, supernatural intervention is not an end in itself, but it is a means of teaching us that we can always trust and obey the leadership of Almighty God. Will we listen to His voice and obey His Word? If He leads us through the sea, will He not also guide us to a well?

The stunning events recorded in Exodus show that it's possible to experience God's power yet remain spiritually unchanged. To keep that from happening to us, let's use the sweet memory of yesterday's miracle to encourage a bigger step of faith today. — David McCasland

Sometimes we see a miracle,
And faith in God revives;
Yet we should see God's gracious hand
At work throughout our lives. — Hess

**THE GOD WHO DELIVERED US YESTERDAY
IS WORTHY OF OUR OBEDIENCE TODAY.**

IS WORK YOUR GOD?

READ:
Exodus 20:1-6

**You shall have no other gods before Me.
—Exodus 20:3**

THE BIBLE IN ONE YEAR:
■ Deuteronomy 17–19

The ability to work is a wonderful gift, but are we taking it too far? In the past, people left their jobs at the office, but now they come home to e-mail and phone messages.

Dr. Dave Arnott, associate professor of management at Dallas Baptist University, says, "I don't know whether work is taking over family and community, or whether family and community are giving up their place to work. But I know the movement is going on. Everyone's job seems to be who they are." We tend to equate our identity with what we do for a living.

The president of the Families and Work Institute says, "How busy you are has become the red badge of courage. . . . It's become a status symbol," even though people complain about it.

Making a god out of work is not a new problem. In the first commandment, God said, "You shall have no other gods before Me" (Exodus 20:3). That includes our jobs. Through God's gift of work, we can honor Him, care for our families, and help people in need. Work is not to be our main source of fulfillment; that must come from God Himself.

No matter what our occupation, we must keep work in perspective. God and family are more important than dedication to a job. Work is a gift, not a god. — David McCasland

*Work hard, but give the glory to
The Father up above;
For all good gifts come from His hand
As tokens of His love.* — Gustafson

**IT'S NOT THE HOURS YOU PUT IN,
BUT WHAT YOU PUT IN THE HOURS THAT COUNTS.**

WHO'S GOING TO HEAVEN?

READ:
Romans 3:21-28

We conclude that a man is justified by faith apart from the deeds of the law.
—Romans 3:28

THE BIBLE IN ONE YEAR:
■ Deuteronomy 20-22

A poll for *U.S. News & World Report* asked 1,000 adults their opinion about who would likely make it into heaven. At the top of that list, to no one's surprise, was a well-known religious figure. Several celebrities were also listed. But it was surprising to me that of the people being surveyed, 87 percent thought themselves were likely to get into heaven.

I can't help but wonder what qualifications for admission into heaven they had in mind. People have many erroneous ideas about what God requires.

Is it virtuous character? Giving generous contributions to deserving charities? Following an orthodox creed? Attending church and being involved in religious activities? Commendable as these qualities may be, they miss by an eternity the one thing God requires for entrance into heaven — a personal commitment to Jesus Christ as Savior and Lord (John 1:12; 1 Timothy 2:5). Although faith in Jesus will no doubt be seen in a person's actions (James 2:14-20), charitable living or religious activity is not a substitute for trusting in Jesus' sacrificial death for our sin.

Are you confident that you're headed for heaven? You can be — but *only* if you're trusting in Jesus. — Vernon Grounds

There aren't many ways into heaven;
The Bible says there's only one:
Confessing Christ Jesus as Savior,
Believing in God's only Son. — Sper

**JESUS TOOK OUR PLACE ON THE CROSS
TO GIVE US A PLACE IN HEAVEN.**

GOD'S PEOPLE, GOD'S HONOR

READ:
2 Samuel 21:1-14

I had concern for My holy name, which the house of Israel had profaned among the nations wherever they went. —Ezekiel 36:21

THE BIBLE IN ONE YEAR:
■ Deuteronomy 23–25

God's reputation is either enhanced or maligned by the attitudes and actions of His people. Today's Bible reading illustrates this truth.

During the reign of David, God punished Israel with a 3-year famine because David's predecessor King Saul had attempted to exterminate the Gibeonites (2 Samuel 21:1). His action violated a solemn promise Joshua and the rulers of Israel had made with Gibeon in the name of "the LORD God of Israel" (Joshua 9:18). God's honor was at stake.

When David asked the Gibeonites how he could make amends, they demanded that seven men from the descendants of Saul be handed over to them to be hanged. The Bible does not tell us that the Lord demanded this retribution, and the death of Saul's sons and grandsons must have grieved God's heart. Yet He allowed the executions to go forward so that the agreement His people had made in His name would be renewed. The Gibeonites therefore knew that God was a God of honor.

Just as Israel profaned God's holy name by their wickedness (Ezekiel 36:22), so too we can dishonor God today by the way we live. Let's pattern our lives after Jesus. Then we will bring honor to God's name. — Herb Vander Lugt

God's reputation is at stake
In all we say and do;
So let us pray for grace to live
A life that's good and true. —D. De Haan

WE HONOR GOD OUR FATHER
WHEN WE LIVE LIKE HIS SON.

EAGLE FLIGHT

READ:
Isaiah 40:29-31

He gives power to the weak. —Isaiah 40:29

THE BIBLE IN ONE YEAR:
■ Deuteronomy 26–28

I was watching an eagle in flight when for no apparent reason it began spiraling upward. With its powerful wings, the great bird soared ever higher, dissolved into a tiny dot, and then disappeared.

Its flight reminded me of Isaiah's uplifting words: "Even the youths shall faint and be weary, and the young men shall utterly fall, but those who wait on the LORD shall renew their strength; they shall mount up with wings like eagles" (40:30-31).

Life's heartbreaks and tragedies can put an end to our resilience, our endurance, our nerve, and bring us to our knees. But if we put our hope in the Lord and rely on Him, He renews our strength. The key to our endurance lies in the exchange of our limited resources for God's limitless strength. And it is ours for the asking.

With God's strength we can "run and not be weary," even when days become hectic and demanding. With His strength we can "walk and not faint," even though tedious, dull routine makes the way seem dreary and long. The psalmist exclaimed in the midst of his weary, tearful pilgrimage, "Blessed is the man whose strength is in You" (Psalm 84:5).

Oh, what an exchange — God's infinite strength for our finite weakness! —David Roper

If you are helpless in life's fray,
God's mighty power will be your stay;
Your failing strength He will renew,
For He's a God who cares for you. —D. De Haan

GOD GIVES STRENGTH IN PROPORTION TO THE STRAIN.

YES OR NO?

READ:
John 5:24-40

**This is eternal life,
that they may know
You, the only true
God, and Jesus Christ
whom You have sent.
—John 17:3**

THE BIBLE IN ONE YEAR:
■ Deuteronomy 29–31

If God were to give professing believers a quiz on Christianity, many would score well. They would be able to answer "Yes, it's true" to questions such as: Did Christ die for your sins? Did He rise from the dead? Is He coming back to earth?

Pastor and author Bruce Larson says that he grew up saying yes to these types of biblical doctrines. But eventually he sensed that God was asking him some new questions: 1. Will you trust Me with your life, yes or no? 2. Will you entrust yourself to My church family, yes or no? 3. Will you serve Me by getting involved with others, yes or no? Only when Larson said yes to these questions did God become real in his life.

To the religious leaders of His day, Jesus said, "You search the Scriptures, for in them you think you have eternal life; and these are they which testify of Me. But you are not willing to come to Me that you may have life" (John 5:39-40). Jesus was saying, in effect, "You can answer true to many facts of Scripture, but you won't say yes to Me."

Can you say you agree with many facts in the written Word but you haven't said yes to Christ, the Living Word? Then do it now, and Jesus will turn your head knowledge into a life-changing heart knowledge. — Joanie Yoder

*Mere mental assent to the truths of God's Word
Is not the response God requires;
Your total dependence on Christ from the heart
Is what God our Father desires. — Hess*

**IT'S NOT ENOUGH TO KNOW THE FACTS OF SALVATION—
YOU MUST ALSO KNOW THE SAVIOR.**

AT THE CEMETERY

READ:
John 11:25-44

He who believes in Me, though he may die, he shall live.
—John 11:25

THE BIBLE IN ONE YEAR:
■ Deuteronomy 32–34

When a loved one dies and we go to the cemetery, we may join a long processional. We may sit or stand around the gravesite and listen respectfully while the minister commits the body to the earth and reads Bible verses about the resurrection. Then the casket is lowered into the ground. We may return later to leave some flowers and stand with heads bowed in memory and respect. Our loved one is dead, and we know we can never bring him back.

When Jesus went to the cemetery, it was different. His friend Lazarus had died, and when Jesus got to the tomb, He exercised His power and authority. He commanded: "Take away the stone" (John 11:39). "Lazarus, come forth!" (v.43). "Loose him, and let him go" (v.44).

We might wish with all our hearts that we could bring a loved one back, but if we were to give those commands nothing would happen. But Jesus has that ability, for He is "the resurrection and the life" (v.25). His power was demonstrated when Lazarus came out of the tomb — alive!

One day, Jesus will again be "at the cemetery." And when He gives the command, all the dead who believed in Him will "come forth" (John 5:28-29; 1 Thessalonians 4:16). What a day that will be! — Dave Egner

There'll be no sorrow there, no more burdens to bear,
No more sickness, no pain, no more parting over there;
And forever I will be with the One who died for me —
What a day, glorious day that will be! — Hill

FOR THE CHRISTIAN,
DEATH IS THE DOORWAY TO GLORY.

A LONG OBEDIENCE

READ:
Philippians 2:1-13

**Work out your own salvation with fear and trembling.
—Philippians 2:12**

THE BIBLE IN ONE YEAR:
■ Joshua 1–3

Every January, health club memberships dramatically increase and exercise rooms become crowded with what some people call "the New Year's resolution crowd." Fitness regulars know that by March many of the newcomers will be gone. "They don't see results as quickly as they think they will," says one club director. "People don't realize it takes a lot of work and perseverance to get in shape."

It's a phenomenon we experience in the spiritual realm as well. Author Eugene Peterson notes that in a culture that loves speed and efficiency, "it is not difficult . . . to get a person interested in the message of the gospel; it is terrifically difficult to sustain the interest." To follow Christ faithfully, Peterson says, requires "a long obedience in the same direction."

Paul urged the Philippians to adopt the same mindset as Christ, whose obedience to the Father was wholehearted and complete (2:8). He encouraged them to keep on obeying the Lord and to "work out [their] own salvation with fear and trembling" (2:12).

As new believers, we may have good intentions when we take our first steps of faith. Then, as we grow in Christ, God's power enables us to keep walking joyfully with Him along the long road of obedience. — David McCasland

The Lord God is faithful, and always will be,
He'll never give up on you or on me;
So let us continue to serve Him each day,
Faithful to follow His will and His way. — Fitzhugh

**FAITH IN CHRIST IS NOT JUST A SINGLE STEP
BUT A LIFE OF WALKING WITH HIM.**

A PURPOSE THAT SUSTAINS

READ:
2 Corinthians 11:21-29

For to me, to live is Christ, and to die is gain.
—Philippians 1:21

THE BIBLE IN ONE YEAR:
■ Joshua 4–6

Austrian psychiatrist Viktor Frankl was imprisoned by the Nazis during the Holocaust. Once set free, he wrote *Man's Search For Meaning*, which became a perennial bestseller. In it, Frankl shared an all-important lesson he had learned from his suffering: "There is nothing in the world, I venture to say, that would so effectively help one to survive even the worst conditions as the knowledge that there is a meaning in one's life."

The apostle Paul also underwent repeated suffering (2 Corinthians 11:23-27). He certainly had a purpose that sustained him. He told the leaders of the Ephesian church, "Now I go bound in the spirit to Jerusalem, not knowing the things that will happen to me there, except that the Holy Spirit testifies in every city, saying that chains and tribulations await me. But none of these things move me; nor do I count my life dear to myself, so that I may finish my race with joy, and the ministry which I received from the Lord Jesus, to testify to the gospel of the grace of God" (Acts 20:22-24).

We too have a purpose and a task — God has called us to bear witness of the Savior. We may not suffer as Paul did, but we can find in our faith a meaning that helps us walk steadfastly through life's toughest experiences. — Vernon Grounds

I shall not fear the battle
If Thou art by my side,
Nor wander from the pathway
If Thou wilt be my guide. — Bode

KNOWING GOD GIVES MEANING TO LIFE;
OBEYING GOD GIVES PURPOSE TO LIFE.

No Nobodies

READ:
1 Corinthians 12:12-31

Those members of the body which seem to be weaker are necessary.
—1 Corinthians 12:22

THE BIBLE IN ONE YEAR:
■ No extra reading today.

A visitor was being shown around a leper colony in India. At noon a gong sounded for the midday meal. People came from all parts of the compound to the dining hall. All at once peals of laughter filled the air. Two young men, one riding on the other's back, were pretending to be a horse and a rider and were having loads of fun.

As the visitor watched, he saw that the man who carried his friend was blind, and the man being carried was lame. The one who could not see used his feet; the one who could not walk used his eyes. Together they helped each other, and they found great joy in doing it.

Imagine a church like that — each member using his or her strength to make up for another's weakness. That's what should be happening in every congregation of believers. Paul likened spiritual gifts to various parts of the human body. Eyes see. Ears hear. Hands work. Feet move the body forward. All are essential. And when each fulfills its function, the whole body benefits.

All of us have weaknesses, but we also have strengths. God's Spirit has gifted each of us for the good of the church. We need each other. In the church, there are no nobodies. — Dennis De Haan

God can take a lowly vessel,
Shape it with His mighty hand,
Fill it with a matchless treasure,
Make it serve a purpose grand. — Bosch

**THERE IS NO SUCH THING
AS INSIGNIFICANT SERVICE FOR CHRIST.**

SPECIAL BUT NOT SPOILED

READ:
Ephesians 6:1-4

Do not provoke your children to wrath, but bring them up in the training and admonition of the Lord. —Ephesians 6:4

THE BIBLE IN ONE YEAR:
■ Joshua 7–9

Family counselor John Rosemond asks, "Is your child special, . . . the most exceptional person in the world?" He answers, "Of course — to you!"

Rosemond says that letting your child know he's special to you is healthy, but no child should grow up thinking he's more special than others. "That child," he warns, "is likely to think he's also deserving of special things and special privileges." He'll easily "justify outbursts of hurtful anger, selfishness, jealousy." How can we counteract this danger?

Christian parents, if they are grounded in the Scriptures, are equipped to get the right balance. First, they can affirm their children without showing favoritism by telling them that they are unique creations of God (Psalm 139:13-16). Second, they can teach their sons and daughters that sin, the great equalizer, is in every individual, and that they too need Christ's saving grace (Romans 3:23).

Parents who impart these perspectives are well on their way to fulfilling the apostle Paul's instruction for child-rearing: "Bring them up in the training and admonition of the Lord" (Ephesians 6:4). Children with this upbringing are more likely to grow up feeling special without being spoiled. —Joanie Yoder

Speak the truth to these your precious ones,
For guidance tell your daughters and your sons
Of One who loves them even more than you,
And who will be their guide a lifetime through. —Anon.

**SPOILED CHILDREN ARE GIVEN WHAT THEY WANT;
WISE PARENTS GIVE THEM WHAT THEY NEED.**

CREDIT DUE

READ:
Romans 16:1-16

Phoebe our sister . . . has been a helper of many and of myself also.
—Romans 16:1-2

THE BIBLE IN ONE YEAR:
■ Joshua 10–12

In 1946, when the US Army unveiled its 30-ton computer called ENIAC (Electronic Numerical Integrator And Computer), two men named John Mauchly and J. Presper Eckert received all the credit. But it was six women behind the scenes who made the computer work.

Before Mauchly and Eckert took the stage to demonstrate ENIAC, the women had programmed the complex machine. They received no recognition at the time, but historians today want to give them due credit.

Women have often gone unrecognized for their achievements and contributions. And sadly, it's also true in the church. But in Romans 16, we have an example of the importance of honoring women who serve faithfully. Paul praised Phoebe as "a helper of many and of myself also" (vv.1-2). He commended Priscilla and her husband Aquila, who risked their lives for Paul's sake (vv.3-4). Tryphena, Tryphosa, and Persis "labored in the Lord" (v.12). Paul mentioned at least eight women for whom he had great appreciation.

Women of faith deserve honor for their service to God and others. Think of the women who are serving faithfully in your church. Why not give one of them a word of thanks and praise today? — David McCasland

O Lord, help me appreciate
The work that women do,
The service given from their hearts,
Their sacrifice for You. — Sper

**GOD NEVER FAILS TO GIVE CREDIT
WHERE CREDIT IS DUE.**

A LIFE - AND - DEATH MATTER

READ:
Romans 8:12-18

**If by the Spirit you put to death the deeds of the body, you will live.
—Romans 8:13**

THE BIBLE IN ONE YEAR:
■ Joshua 13-15

Nature is violent. Life and death are the law of field, stream, and jungle. A lion stalks a gazelle. A heron stands motionless at the edge of a pond, its sharp beak poised and ready to kill. High overhead a red-tailed hawk holds its deadly talons close to its body, watching for movement in the grass below. A leopard family exists at a zebra's expense. Each survives on another's demise. This sounds natural enough, but it's more graphic than most of us care to watch.

The principle that nothing lives unless something else dies extends beyond nature to our daily walk with God. Interests of the flesh must succumb to the interests of the Spirit, or else the interests of the Spirit will succumb to the interests of the flesh (Romans 8:13). In the jungles and fields and streams of our own heart, something must always die so that something else can live.

We can't be committed to Christ and to the world at the same time. We can't be filled with His Spirit if we are protecting the life of selfish interests. That's why our Lord said so pointedly that we will need to die daily to ourselves if we are going to walk with Him (Luke 9:23-24). We must continually choose what will have to die so that Christ can live freely in us. — Mart De Haan

Is there any life so blessed
As one lived for Christ alone,
When the heart from self is emptied,
And instead becomes His throne? — *Anon.*

TO LIVE FOR CHRIST, WE MUST DIE TO SELF.

So Many Blessings

READ:
Ephesians 1:3-14

**Blessed be the God and Father of our Lord Jesus Christ, who has blessed us with every spiritual blessing.
—Ephesians 1:3**

THE BIBLE IN ONE YEAR:
■ Joshua 16–18

When disaster strikes, people are exceedingly generous in their outpouring of assistance. After the terrorist attacks in September 2001, New York City was flooded with an estimated $75 million worth of towels, blankets, flashlights, water bottles, canned beans, shovels, toothpaste, stuffed animals, radios, rubber boots, and thousands of other items. There was so much stuff that those affected could not use it all.

This reminds me of what happens when we turn in faith to Christ as our Savior. We were facing a personal disaster. Our sins put us in danger of an eternity of separation from God. The future was dark, hopeless.

Then Jesus stepped in and offered rescue. When we trusted Him, our heavenly Father lavished us with spiritual riches. Now we have more blessings than we can possibly use up. We are part of God's family (Ephesians 1:5). We have "redemption" and "the forgiveness of sins" (v.7). We are heirs of the One who owns everything (v.11). Our inheritance is sealed by the Holy Spirit (vv.13-14).

The blessings of being a Christian just keep on coming. They'll never run out. What a generous, thoughtful God we serve! Let's praise Him for the countless blessings that overflow in our lives. — Dave Branon

Give me a spirit of thankfulness, Lord,
For numberless blessings given;
Blessings that daily come to me
Like dewdrops falling from heaven. — Dawe

**GOD'S GENEROUS GIVING
DESERVES THANKFUL LIVING.**

FOLLOW ME

READ:
Mark 8:34-38

**Whoever desires to come after Me, let him deny himself, and take up his cross, and follow Me.
—Mark 8:34**

THE BIBLE IN ONE YEAR:
■ Joshua 19–21

During World War II, B-17 bombers made long flights from the US mainland to the Pacific island of Saipan. When they landed there, the planes were met by a jeep bearing the sign: "Follow Me!" That little vehicle guided the giant planes to their assigned places in the parking area.

One pilot, who by his own admission was not a religious man, made an insightful comment: "That little jeep with its quaint sign always reminds me of Jesus. He was [a lowly] peasant, but the giant men and women of our time would be lost without His direction."

Centuries after our Savior walked the streets and hills of Israel, the world with all its advances still needs His example and instruction. When His ways aren't followed, numerous problems and evils arise in our world — including immorality, crime, and greed.

How do we follow Jesus' ways? First of all, we turn from our sin and entrust our lives to Him as our Savior and Lord. Then, we seek His will in His Word each day and put it into practice by the power of the Holy Spirit within us. We learn to deny our selfish desires and give ourselves completely to following Jesus (Mark 8:34-35).

If you want to get in line with the purposes of God, respond to Jesus' invitation: "Follow Me!" — Vernon Grounds

No darkness have we who in Jesus abide —
The light of the world is Jesus;
We walk in the light when we follow our Guide —
The light of the world is Jesus. — Bliss

TO FIND YOUR WAY THROUGH LIFE, FOLLOW JESUS.

HARD SAYINGS

READ:
Luke 6:27-35

**To him who strikes you on the one cheek, offer the other also.
—Luke 6:29**

THE BIBLE IN ONE YEAR:
■ Joshua 22–24

Russian novelist Leo Tolstoy tells a story of an old cobbler named Martin. After the death of his wife and child, he cried out in despair to a godly old friend, "What now is a man to live for?" His friend replied, "For God, Martin. For God." "And how must one live for God?" Martin asked. "Christ has shown us the way," said the believer. "Buy the Gospels and read. There you'll find out how to live for God. There everything is explained," he said.

So that same day Martin bought a New Testament and began to read. The more he read, the more clearly he understood what God wanted of him and what it meant to live for God. And his heart grew lighter and lighter.

Then one day Martin read Luke 6:27-35, and it suddenly hit him that Jesus' words were hard sayings. He pondered the command in verse 29, "To him who strikes you on the one cheek, offer the other also." As he began to see how his life didn't measure up to Jesus' words, he cried out, "O Lord, help me!"

We also may feel that obedience to Jesus' words is too difficult for us. His hard sayings seem impossible to obey. Like Martin, we must cry out, "O Lord, help me!" Without Him we can do nothing. — David Roper

Obeying Christ can seem too hard,
But we must come to see
That all He asks is for our good
To make life full and free. — D. De Haan

**THE COST OF OBEDIENCE IS NOTHING
COMPARED WITH THE COST OF DISOBEDIENCE.**

PRAYER MALFUNCTION

READ:
1 John 3:21-24

This is His commandment: that we should believe on the name of His Son Jesus Christ and love one another.
—1 John 3:23

THE BIBLE IN ONE YEAR:
■ Judges 1–4

In a box of my father's old tools I found a hand drill that was at least 60 years old. I could barely get the wheel to turn. The gears were clogged with dirt, and the pieces that hold the drill bit in place were missing. But I wanted to see if I could get it to work.

I began by wiping the accumulated dirt and sawdust off the gears. Then I oiled them. At first they turned hard and slow, but I kept working them. Soon the gears were turning smoothly. Then I saw a cap at the top of the handle. Unscrewing it, I discovered the missing parts that would hold the bit in place. I placed them in the drill, inserted a bit, and easily bored a neat hole in a piece of wood.

Working with that old drill taught me something about prayer. Jesus said we will receive from God what we ask of Him (Matthew 7:7-8). But there are conditions. For example, John said we must obey God and do what pleases Him (1 John 3:22). This includes believing in His Son and loving one another (v.23). If we don't meet God's conditions, our prayers will be ineffective — just like that old drill.

If your prayer-life is malfunctioning, make sure you're meeting the conditions. When you do, you can be confident that your prayers will be effective. — Dave Egner

Forgive us, Lord, our selfish asking,
All that's petty in Your sight;
Oh, help us pray with godly motives
And to seek what's good and right! — D. De Haan

FAITH AND LOVE ARE VITAL TO EFFECTIVE PRAYER.

GOOD NEWS OR BAD?

READ:
Luke 12:35-40

**Blessed are those servants whom the master, when he comes, will find watching.
—Luke 12:37**

THE BIBLE IN ONE YEAR:
■ Judges 5–8

A teacher tells her young students, "Class, I'm going down the hall to the school office for a few minutes. I don't expect to be away long. I'm sure there won't be any trouble. I'm trusting you to work on your assignments while I'm gone."

Fifteen minutes pass, then 20, then 40. Suddenly the teacher returns. Dennis has just thrown an eraser at Carol, who is doing her math. Steven is standing on the teacher's desk making faces. The students carrying out the teacher's instructions are delighted at the teacher's return, but Dennis and Steven wish she hadn't come back at all.

Jesus is coming back! That stands as both a warning and a promise throughout the New Testament, as in today's reading from Luke 12. It's good news or bad, depending on who hears it.

In church we sing songs like "Come, Thou Long-Expected Jesus." When we partake of the Lord's Supper, we "proclaim the Lord's death till He comes" (1 Corinthians 11:26). On Sunday morning, the second coming of Christ sounds like great news. But during the rest of the week, are we as ready for His return?

Jesus is coming back! It may be soon. It will be sudden. Is that good news or bad? It's up to you. —Haddon Robinson

When Jesus comes to reward His servants,
Whether it be noon or night,
Faithful to Him will He find us watching,
With our lamps all trimmed and bright? —Crosby

WATCH THEREFORE, FOR YOU DO NOT KNOW WHAT HOUR YOUR LORD IS COMING. —Matthew 24:42

A PASSION FOR THE WORD

READ:
Psalm 119:97-104

How sweet are Your words to my taste, sweeter than honey to my mouth!
—Psalm 119:103

THE BIBLE IN ONE YEAR:
■ Judges 9–12

The Bible — how much of it do you know and understand? Does it seem overwhelming? Do you feel it's too late in life to study it seriously?

Consider Cyrus' story. Although his parents were Christians, he didn't have much use for the Bible. He was more interested in Shakespeare and history. By the time he was 12, he had charted the entire course of human civilization. But the Bible? He was not interested.

Cyrus grew up to be a respected lawyer. When he was 36, a friend came to his office and confronted him about why he was not a Christian. This conversation led him to faith in Jesus Christ.

Realizing that he knew almost nothing about the Bible, Cyrus determined to know God's Word better than anything else. Soon it became to him "sweeter than honey" (Psalm 119:103). Thirty years later, in 1909, *The Scofield Reference Bible* was published. The great work of Cyrus Ingerson Scofield was complete.

Do we all have to give up everything else in life to study the Bible fulltime? Of course not. But we must recognize that a consistent study of God's Word is a vital part of our growth as Christians. It's the way we learn what God expects of us, and the way to know God Himself. — Dave Branon

Gaining knowledge of God's Word
Can be a worthy goal
If it leads us to the Lord
And nourishes our soul. —Sper

**ONE OF THE MARKS OF A WELL-FED SOUL
IS A WELL-READ BIBLE.**

DEALING WITH SELF-DOUBT

READ:
Psalm 26

I will walk in my integrity; redeem me and be merciful to me. My foot stands in an even place.
—Psalm 26:11-12

THE BIBLE IN ONE YEAR:
■ Judges 13–15

Sometimes, when I've been falsely accused, I have found myself questioning my sincerity. When I do, I follow the example of David in Psalm 26 as he responded to his critics.

Appealing directly to the Lord, he expressed his firm conviction that he had walked in "integrity" (the Hebrew word means sincerity, not faultlessness). He asked God to vindicate him, for he had renounced the ways of the wicked, declared his love for God's temple, and pleaded for deliverance from the fate of the ungodly (vv.1-10). Finally, he reaffirmed his resolve to live with sincerity, humbly asked God to redeem him, and acknowledged his need for mercy (v.11).

What happened next? God gave David the assurance that he stood in "an even place" (v.12), a symbolic way of saying he was in a place of safety, accepted and protected by the Lord. As a result, he closed his psalm on a note of confidence and anticipation.

Have the painful barbs of critics or the accusations of your conscience filled you with fear and self-doubt? Talk to the Lord. If you need to confess sin, do it. Then put your hope and trust in God. He will replace your insecurity and doubt with His supernatural peace. He has done that for me. He will do the same for you. — Herb Vander Lugt

When you live every hour by the grace of His power
And you know He will guide you aright,
Then day in and day out faith is stronger than doubt,
And faith puts your worries to flight. — Gilbert

FEEDING YOUR FAITH WILL STARVE YOUR DOUBTS.

CHANGED TO BRING CHANGE

READ:
Acts 22:1-16

You will be His witness to all men of what you have seen and heard.
—Acts 22:15

THE BIBLE IN ONE YEAR:
■ Judges 16–18

One night a woman dreamed that she was having a conversation with God. She was angry about all the suffering and evil she saw around her, so she complained to the Lord, "Why don't You do something about all this?" God gently replied, "I did. I created you."

God could send another flood, as He did in Noah's day, to cleanse away the wickedness of the world. He could, but He won't. He has promised never to do that again (Genesis 9:11). Instead, He chooses to work through human beings like us, changing them, then enabling them to function as His agents of change.

He changed Paul from a persecutor of the church to "His witness to all men" (Acts 22:15). Paul's life and letters taught, inspired, and comforted the church in its early days, and they still do today. It was the power of God that changed Paul, then used him to change the world around him.

What about you? Have you been transformed by the power of Jesus Christ? Are you now obediently serving Him to change the lives of people around you?

Let's ask God to work in our hearts and lives so that through us He will bring about change in our families, our communities, and the world. — Vernon Grounds

Father, thank You for Your Spirit,
Fill us with His love and power;
Change us into Christ's own image
Day by day and hour by hour. —Anon.

ONLY WHEN WE ARE CHANGED
CAN WE HELP OTHERS TO CHANGE.

March 12

INTRODUCTIONS

READ:
Philippians 2:19-30

For the work of Christ he came close to death, not regarding his life, to supply what was lacking in your service toward me.
—Philippians 2:30

THE BIBLE IN ONE YEAR:
■ Judges 19–21

I thought it was a misprint when the schedule at a Christian men's conference noted 2½ hours for introductions. But the time was correct and it turned out to be the most meaningful part of the weekend for me.

Instead of giving our own names, jobs, and family information, each man introduced someone else. Some presented longtime friends, and others told about someone they had met only the night before. Every introduction was an affirmation, with special attention given to the uniqueness and value of each individual.

The apostle Paul was a great "introducer" who spoke highly of his colleagues in the faith and ministry. His letters are dotted with the names of men and women to whom and for whom he was deeply grateful. He affirmed Timothy as a person of proven character, who "as a son with his father" had served him in the gospel (Philippians 2:22). He also praised Epaphroditus, who almost died because of his unselfish devotion to Christ and his service to others (v.30).

In a world dominated by put-downs, let's resolve to master the art of building others up by what we say *to* them and *about* them. Such "introductions" can be one of the most important things we do each day. — David McCasland

Help me, Lord, to reassure and strengthen
Others by what I speak today;
I would always try to be affirming,
As I meet with friends along the way. — Hess

**OUR DAY'S WORK ISN'T DONE
UNTIL WE BUILD UP SOMEONE.**

WHAT WILL HAPPEN?

READ:
2 Timothy 4:1-8

There is laid up for me the crown of righteousness, which the Lord . . . will give to me. —2 Timothy 4:8

THE BIBLE IN ONE YEAR:
■ Ruth 1–4

In his book *Spirit Life,* Stuart Briscoe writes, "When I moved to the United States, I was impressed with the number of total strangers who visited my home to wish me well . . . . They all sold insurance!

"One day my visitor was talking about the necessity to be prudent in the preparation for all possibilities. 'If something should happen to you, Mr. Briscoe —' he started to say, but I interrupted with, 'Please don't say that. It upsets me.' . . . He looked totally bewildered and said, 'I don't understand what I said to upset you.' 'Then I'll tell you,' I replied. 'It upsets me that you talk about [life's] only certainty as if it's a possibility. Death isn't a possibility, it's a certainty. You don't say "if," you say "when," whenever death is the subject.' Then I added, 'By the way, when something happens to you, what will really happen?'"

The apostle Paul was very open about his death (2 Timothy 4:6). He knew that its sting had been removed because Christ paid sin's penalty on the cross (1 Corinthians 15:55-57). Death would give way to victory (v.54); he would fully experience Christ's righteousness; and he would be with Christ (2 Corinthians 5:8). Jesus gives that same confidence to all who trust Him as Savior and Lord. —Dennis De Haan

> In life's eventide, at twilight,
> At His door I'll knock and wait;
> By the precious love of Jesus
> I shall enter heaven's gate. —Blom

**ONLY IF WE ARE READY TO DIE
ARE WE READY TO LIVE.**

TRUE SATISFACTION

READ:
Ecclesiastes 2:1-11

The eye is not satisfied with seeing, nor the ear filled with hearing. —Ecclesiastes 1:8

THE BIBLE IN ONE YEAR:
■ 1 Samuel 1–3

A man stopped at a travel agency and said he wanted to go on a cruise. "Where to?" he was asked. "I don't know," was his reply. So the travel agent suggested that he take a look at a large globe that was in the room. He studied it for some time, then with a look of frustration he exclaimed, "Is this all you have to offer?"

The world in which we live has many things that appeal to us. Apart from what is sinful, we can and should enjoy its pleasures. A delicious meal graced with the good fellowship of friends warms our hearts. The beauties of nature inspire and fill us with wonder. Good music refreshes our souls. And work itself can be fulfilling.

Even in a sin-cursed world we can find great enjoyment. And yet these pursuits do not bring full and lasting satisfaction. In fact, people who live only for self-gratification, no matter how lofty their achievements, will always long for more. It makes no difference how deeply they drink from the wells of this world's pleasures, their thirst is still not satisfied. They must agree with Solomon that "all is vanity and grasping for the wind" (Ecclesiastes 2:17).

Only by living for Jesus Christ do we experience true satisfaction. — Richard W. De Haan

*The world is filled with so much good
That brings us joy and pleasure,
But true fulfillment only comes
When Christ we love and treasure.* — Sper

**PUTTING CHRIST FIRST BRINGS SATISFACTION
THAT LASTS.**

AT THE WELL

READ:
John 4:5-26

With joy you will draw water from the wells of salvation.
—Isaiah 12:3

THE BIBLE IN ONE YEAR:
■ 1 Samuel 4–7

A guide in Israel was preparing to lead a tour into the desert. His instructions to the group were simple and clear: "If you do not have these two items, I will not allow you to accompany us. You must have a broad-brimmed hat and a full bottle of water. These will protect you from the sun, and from the thirst caused by wind and dryness."

Water. It's essential to survival. That's why a woman came to the well in Samaria (John 4:7). She came at noon, when few people were there. She was startled when a young Jewish man asked her for something to drink. Jesus broke huge barriers with His request — she was a woman, had been married many times, and wasn't a Jew.

Jesus offered her water far better than that from the well. He had "living water," which only He could give (vv.10,13-14). I believe she took that water and was spiritually cleansed, for she told everyone what she had experienced: "Come, see a Man who told me all things that I ever did. Could this be the Christ?" (v.29).

Are you at the well? Is your soul thirsting for God? Do you need the cleansing and refreshment He offers? He is waiting there to satisfy you with the "living water" of salvation and the gift of everlasting life. — Dave Egner

Gracious and Almighty Savior,
Source of all that shall endure,
Quench my thirst with living water,
Living water, clear and pure. — Vinal

JESUS IS THE ONLY FOUNTAIN
WHO CAN SATISFY THE THIRSTY SOUL.

SERVANTS OF ALL

READ:
Matthew 20:20-28

**Whoever desires
to be first among you,
let him be your slave.
—Matthew 20:27**

THE BIBLE IN ONE YEAR:
■ 1 Samuel 8–10

Robert K. Greenleaf, founder of the Greenleaf Center for Servant-Leadership in Indianapolis, said, "The great leader is seen as a servant first, and that simple fact is the key to his greatness."

Two thousand years ago, Jesus taught that truth to His disciples and lived it out. As the Son of God, He had been given "all authority . . . in heaven and on earth" (Matthew 28:18). Yet He did not force people to follow and obey Him. His leadership model was radically different from what we see in today's world. It was one of humility and unselfish service to others.

Christlike leadership means considering the needs of our neighbors before our own, seeking their good, encouraging their spiritual growth and intimacy with God. It means treating others the way God has treated us. Servant leaders employ gentle persuasion and reason rather than barking orders and ultimatums. They don't dictate or demand but recognize that before God they themselves are but servants who are only doing their duty (Luke 17:10).

Whatever our position of leadership, we will never lose if we lose ourselves for others. Service that cares for others is the basis of true greatness. — David Roper

*Controlling other people's lives
Is not a leader's trait;
It's serving other people's needs
That God considers great.* — Sper

**ONLY THE ONE WHO HAS LEARNED TO SERVE
IS QUALIFIED TO LEAD.**

MARY & GOD

READ:
Colossians 3:22–4:6

Whatever you do, do it
heartily, as to the Lord
and not to men.
—Colossians 3:23

THE BIBLE IN ONE YEAR:
■ 1 Samuel 11–13

Her bright smile and cheerful voice seemed unusual for someone working at a discount store checkout counter early in the morning. I glanced at her nametag, then looked more closely to make sure I had read it correctly. It said: MARY-N-GOD. So I asked her if she and the Lord were doing this job together. "Oh, yes!" she said, beaming. "He works with me and walks with me and talks with me, and we share the most wonderful life together. I couldn't do it without Him."

Mary was a winsome representative of Christ and a vivid illustration of Colossians 3:23, "Whatever you do, do it heartily, as to the Lord and not to men." Although not in the limelight, Mary, through her attitude and actions, witnessed to hundreds of people every day. Mary's pulpit was a checkout counter, and her smile was the opening sentence in a powerful sermon about the difference Christ makes in a life. If someone asked, she was happy to tell them more.

When I told my wife about Mary, she said, "I think she's one of those who seem to be last here on earth but will be first when they get to heaven." I had to agree.

You and I can also be effective witnesses if we know, love, and walk with Jesus the way Mary does. — David McCasland

THINKING IT OVER

What kind of attitudes are revealed in my daily work?
Does my fellowship with Christ shine through in my
demeanor? For whom do I work? Christ or the boss?

**OFTEN IT'S THE JOY BEHIND OUR WORDS
THAT MAKES OUR TESTIMONY RING TRUE.**

March 18

HE'S NEVER GRUMPY

READ:
Luke 11:5-10

Ask, and it will be given to you.
—Luke 11:9

THE BIBLE IN ONE YEAR:
■ 1 Samuel 14–16

While driving my car the other day, I saw a sign that said, "Sometimes I wake up grumpy — but usually I let him sleep." It reminded me of the night my pregnant wife awakened me saying we had to get to the hospital because the baby was on the way. Half-awake, I replied, "Let's go back to sleep and take care of things in the morning." Then suddenly I realized what she had said, and I was up in a flash.

In Luke 11, a man who needed food for a guest went to a friend's house at midnight and asked for three loaves of bread. The awakened friend may have replied somewhat as I did. After all, it was the middle of the night. Yet he got up and provided the requested food (v.8). I don't think the man gave his friend what he wanted just because he wouldn't go away. Rather, he got up because he realized that this friend would not have had the boldness to wake him if he hadn't been desperate.

The point is this: If an earthly friend will overcome his reluctance to meet your need, will not your heavenly Father, who is never reluctant, do far more than that? He never sleeps, He is never grumpy, and He wants the very best for you. Therefore, do not hesitate to ask, seek, and knock (v.9). He will always be there for you. — Herb Vander Lugt

Pray on, then, child of God, pray on;
This is your duty and your task.
To God the answering belongs;
Yours is the simpler part — to ask. — Chisholm

GOD IS NEVER INCONVENIENCED BY OUR PRAYERS.

Our Children Are Watching

READ:
Deuteronomy 6:1-9

**You shall love the LORD your God with all your heart, with all your soul, and with all your strength.
—Deuteronomy 6:5**

THE BIBLE IN ONE YEAR:
■ 1 Samuel 17–20

It can be disturbing to realize that our children often mirror the way we speak and act. I remember being concerned about the way my son angrily lashed out at his sister when she was annoying him. My wife gently pointed out to me that his behavior was a reflection of mine.

A few weeks later, I caught myself lashing out at my son when I was frustrated. Through my wife's encouragement, I apologized to him for my behavior and told him I would learn to treat him with more respect. In the months that followed, I noticed that my son's attitude toward his sister also improved.

Children do not learn to love and obey God only by what we say. They also learn by watching what we do. We are to teach them constantly about God and His Word as we "sit in [our] house, when [we] walk by the way, when [we] lie down, and when [we] rise up" (Deuteronomy 6:7). Along with what we say to our children, we need to set an example by our love and obedience to the Lord.

We can't be perfect parents, but our children must see our desire to please the Lord. And when we fall short, they need to see our repentance. We teach them by both what we say and what we do. — Albert Lee

You're teaching a lesson each day that you live;
Your actions are blazing a trail
That children will follow for good or for ill;
You can help them or cause them to fail. — Bosch

A GODLY PARENT IS A CHILD'S BEST GUIDE TO GOD.

THINK ABOUT IT

READ:
Philippians 4:1-9

**If there is any virtue and if there is anything praiseworthy— meditate on these things.
—Philippians 4:8**

THE BIBLE IN ONE YEAR:
■ 1 Samuel 21–24

According to one little boy, "Think-ing is when your mouth stays shut and your head keeps talking to itself."

The way our head talks to itself tells a lot about how we are doing morally and spiritually. To guard our mind and to keep out the influences that will hinder our walk with God is to use our mind in the way He desires.

The Bible gives us clear guide-lines — spelling out the kinds of things we should think about. For example, Psalm 1:2 and Psalm 119:97 tell us to meditate on God's Word day and night. That should be our first priority in the thinking department.

But we have a life to live, and we can't spend all of our waking moments meditating on Scripture. Yet even when we are thinking about the mundane aspects of life, we need guidance. Paul told us that we should think about things that are true, noble, just, pure, lovely, of good report, virtuous, and praiseworthy (Philippians 4:8). In our daily activities, those words should govern what is on our mind.

When our head "talks to itself," it needs to say, "Keep the impure and ungodly thoughts out of here!" When we're thinking that way, we'll know what to do, how to behave, where to go, and what to say. — Dave Branon

Let us think about what's good —
What's right and pure and true;
May God's Word control our thoughts
In everything we do. — Fitzhugh

RIGHT THINKING LEADS TO RIGHT LIVING.

FIRST IN OUR LIVES

READ:
Psalm 32:1-5

Search me, O God, and know my heart; try me, and know my anxieties.
—Psalm 139:23

THE BIBLE IN ONE YEAR:
■ 1 Samuel 25-28

Actor Sylvester Stallone is applauded for his strongman movie roles as Rocky and Rambo. But what is he really like in his personal life? During an interview he honestly admitted, "If I were watching a home movie of my life, I would shake my head in despair and wonderment. It's a comedy of errors."

Suppose a movie were made of your life or mine. Would it reveal not only errors and poor choices but also a sinful person who doesn't even act like a follower of Christ? Would we be ashamed of some scenes? Would we be motivated, as Stallone says he was, to shift our values and start paying attention to "relationships . . . and putting someone else first"?

Jesus wants to be the "someone else" in our lives whom we put first (Matthew 6:24,33). But how do we do that? It starts with confession of any sin that is between us and Him, and then experiencing the Lord's cleansing and forgiveness (Psalm 32:5). Then we are gradually changed by Him through the work of the Holy Spirit and by the Word of God (Galatians 5:22-23; Hebrews 4:12). If we make our relationship with the Lord Jesus Christ our first priority, He will make us into the kind of people He wants us to be (Philippians 2:3-8). — Vernon Grounds

Search me, O God, and know my heart today;
Try me, O Savior, know my thoughts, I pray.
See if there be some wicked way in me;
Cleanse me from every sin and set me free. — Orr

**THE SPIRIT OF GOD USES THE WORD OF GOD
TO CHANGE THE PEOPLE OF GOD.**

March 22

JUST TELL THE STORY

READ:
Acts 7:59–8:8

Those who were scattered went everywhere preaching the Word. —Acts 8:4

THE BIBLE IN ONE YEAR:
■ 1 Samuel 29–31

The main character in the movie *Up Close And Personal* is a TV newsman who dies trying to get a story in one of the world's trouble spots. After his death, he is remembered for saying, "I once thought reporting was about glory. But I'm here for only one reason — to tell the story."

In Acts 8, we read that Jerusalem's Christians were scattered abroad to escape persecution. Everywhere they went, they preached the message of Christ (v.4). Saul, their persecutor, was later converted and became an apostle. Toward the end of his life, Saul, also known as Paul, decided to go to Jerusalem, where he knew he would be persecuted. But he remained undeterred, declaring that his purpose was "to testify to the gospel of the grace of God" (Acts 20:24).

God still calls people to tell the good news of Jesus to those who don't know Him. In his book *The Conversion Of The Church*, Samuel Shoemaker states, "The demand is human heart-hunger. The supply is the grace of God. We are only distributors." But we don't work alone or with mere human energy. God is working in us (Philippians 2:13).

When witnessing for Christ, may it be with love and humility — motivated by a desire for His glory, not our own. We're just here to tell the story. — Joanie Yoder

I love to tell the story,
For some have never heard
The message of salvation
From God's own holy Word. — Hankey

**GOD HAS LEFT US IN THE WORLD
TO WITNESS TO THE WORLD.**

ONE GOD – NOT THREE

READ:
John 10:22-33

I and My Father are one. —John 10:30

THE BIBLE IN ONE YEAR:
■ 2 Samuel 1–4

It is said that Augustine (354-430), a leader in the early church, was walking on the ocean shore one day and pondering the mystery of the Trinity. He saw a little boy who was playing with a seashell. The youngster scooped a hole in the sand, then went down to the waves and filled his shell with water and poured it into the hole he had made.

Augustine asked, "What are you doing?" The boy replied, "I am going to pour the sea into the hole." Then Augustine thought, *That is what I have been trying to do. Standing at the ocean of infinity, I have attempted to grasp it with my finite mind.*

The concept of the Trinity does not fit the framework of common logic, nor can it be fully analyzed by our intellect. But this is no reason to say it is the invention of theologians. To declare that the one and only God has made Himself known as Father, Son, and Holy Spirit is simply an attempt to define what the Scriptures teach (John 10:29-30; Acts 5:3-4).

To commit our lives to this triune God is to begin to see with the eye of faith His greatness as our Creator, Redeemer, and Sustainer. Doesn't it make sense that the One we worship, and to whom we entrust our lives, should be vastly greater than our limited understanding? — Dennis De Haan

Father, Son, and Holy Spirit —
O Thou blessed Trinity;
One in essence, yet three persons —
Thou art God, we worship Thee. — D. De Haan

THE IDEA OF A TRIUNE GOD STAGGERS THE MIND,
BUT TO KNOW HIM SATISFIES THE HEART.

RIDING OUT THE WAVES

READ:
Psalm 25:1-10

**Lead me in Your truth and teach me, for You are the God of my salvation; on You I wait all the day.
—Psalm 25:5**

THE BIBLE IN ONE YEAR:
■ 2 Samuel 5–8

What can ride ocean currents for years before finally washing ashore and springing to life? According to National Geographic's *World* magazine, it's a nut that is native to South America and the West Indies. Some people call them "sea hearts."

These 2-inch, chestnut-colored nuts are hardy, heart-shaped seeds that grow on high-climbing vines. They often fall into rivers and float out to sea. There they may ride the currents for years before coming to shore and sprouting into a plant.

This life-bearing, time-enduring, wave-riding seed illustrates a basic spiritual principle. God's plans may include extended times of waiting for Him to act on our behalf. This was true of Noah, who endured ridicule while spending 120 years building a ship; of Abraham, who waited for the fulfillment of God's promise that he would have a son in his old age; and of David, God's anointed, who chose to wait for God's timing rather than take the life of envious King Saul.

Sea hearts can't choose to be patient, but we can. Nothing is harder or better for us than to follow the example of David, who wrote Psalm 25. By waiting on the Lord we can have peace, and our faith will grow — even while we are riding out the waves. — Mart De Haan

THINKING IT OVER
What circumstances make it hard to wait for the Lord?
How do we know we won't be disappointed
when we wait for Him?

**GOD STRETCHES OUR PATIENCE
TO ENLARGE OUR SOUL.**

ALPHA AND OMEGA

READ:
Revelation 22:6-13

**"I am the Alpha and the Omega, the Beginning and the End," says the Lord.
—Revelation 1:8**

THE BIBLE IN ONE YEAR:
■ 2 Samuel 9–12

The meaning of the words *Alpha* and *Omega* — terms that refer to the first and last letters of the Greek alphabet — is fairly easy to understand. Like A and Z, they simply mean "the beginning" and "the end."

In life, we understand these concepts. Things begin . . . things end. Jobs start . . . jobs stop. Decades come . . . decades go. Birth . . . death.

But there is something special and unique about the words *Alpha* and *Omega* as they appear in Revelation (1:8,11; 21:6; 22:13). Jesus Christ used those terms to describe Himself — terms that refer to His deity.

When used in Scripture, the words have an almost unfathomable meaning. Jesus, the *Alpha*, had no beginning. He existed before time, before the creation of the universe (John 1:1). As the first cause of all that exists (vv.2-3), Jesus cannot be limited by the word *Alpha*. And as the *Omega*, He is not the "end" as we know it. He will continue to exist into the everlasting, never-ending future.

It's mind-boggling and awe-inspiring — this view of our Lord. He's the one "who is and who was and who is to come" (Revelation 1:8). He's the Alpha and the Omega, the Almighty God. Not only that, He's our Savior (Titus 2:13). As such, He deserves our praise, our lives, our all! — Dave Branon

Alpha, Omega — our God we proclaim,
Eternal, unchanging, always the same;
He's the beginning and He is the end,
He is our Savior, our Lord, and our Friend. — Fitzhugh

**FOR TIME AND FOR ETERNITY,
JESUS IS ALL WE NEED.**

BE AN ENCOURAGER

READS:
Romans 1:8-15

I long to see you, . . . that I may be encouraged together with you by the mutual faith both of you and me. —Romans 1:11-12

THE BIBLE IN ONE YEAR:
■ 2 Samuel 13–15

Ron, a recent Bible-school graduate, had been a youth pastor for about 3 months. Some of the young people seemed to resent him, certain parents were beginning to criticize him, and he was getting discouraged. Then the chairman of the church board invited him to lunch. "Uh-oh," he said to his wife. "Here it comes."

At lunch the chairman looked him straight in the eye and said, "I hear that you are getting some flak. I want you to know that the board thinks you are doing a good job. True, nothing much is happening yet, but we are convinced that it will. You're doing exactly what we asked you to do. Just keep at it."

Ron walked out of that meeting with his head held high and his heart singing. He worked with renewed confidence, and soon the youth group began to grow numerically and spiritually.

Paul told the Roman believers that he wanted to see them so they could encourage each other (1:11-12). You and I know how helpful that can be. We all appreciate an arm around the shoulder or a kind word.

If you've received some unexpected encouragement today, thank God for it. And when the Holy Spirit leads you to encourage someone, go ahead and do it. Be an encourager. Both of you will be glad you did. —Dave Egner

The power in words can build up or tear down—
Create a big smile or produce a sad frown;
So in all your contacts with people each day,
Be sure to encourage in all that you say. —Fitzhugh

**A SPARK OF ENCOURAGEMENT
CAN REKINDLE WARMTH IN THE HEART.**

THE TREASURE CHEST

READ:
Hebrews 11:32-40

Imitate those who through faith and patience inherit the promises.
—Hebrews 6:12

THE BIBLE IN ONE YEAR:
■ 2 Samuel 16–18

When I was a young girl, my mother often let me rummage through her button box as I recovered from an illness. It always cheered me to come across old, familiar buttons and remember the garments they once adorned. I especially liked it when she picked out an old, overlooked button and used it again.

Similarly, I often leaf through my Bible during distressing times and recall familiar promises that have strengthened me. But I'm always encouraged to find help from promises I've never noticed before.

I remember one dark morning during my husband's terminal illness when I was looking for a word from God to sustain me in our painful circumstances. In Hebrews 11, I noted that God had rescued His suffering people in some very dramatic ways. Yet I couldn't always identify with their particular situations. Then I read about some who "out of weakness were made strong" (v.34). God used that phrase to assure me that I too could be made strong in my weakness. At that very moment I began sensing His strength, and my faith was renewed.

Are you being tested today? Remember, there are many promises in the Bible, God's treasure chest. Generations have proven them true, and so can you. — Joanie Yoder

Standing on the promises that cannot fail,
When the howling storms of doubt and fear assail,
By the living word of God I shall prevail,
Standing on the promises of God. — Carter

**GOD'S PROMISES ARE TREASURES
WAITING TO BE DISCOVERED.**

COME HOME!

READ:
Luke 15:11-32

Your brother was dead and is alive again, and was lost and is found.
—Luke 15:32

THE BIBLE IN ONE YEAR:
■ 2 Samuel 19–21

Several years ago, my wife Carolyn and I camped near the town of Brimley, in Michigan's Upper Peninsula. It was a holiday, and we ambled into town for the annual parade. Believe me, it was something to write home about.

There were marshals on horseback, homecoming queens, forest rangers, even Smokey Bear! There was a float featuring Big Bird from *Sesame Street*, and a flatbed truck carrying a brass band of men and women wearing straw hats and dressed in red-white-and-blue uniforms. There were vehicles of all kinds: tractors, trailers, trucks, and kids on tricycles.

But the last float fully captured our attention. It featured a gray-haired old man kneeling at the foot of a cross. Across the back of the float was written: "COME HOME!" — JESUS

Jesus still calls, "Come home!" You're never too far away or too far gone to come back to your Father's love. He stands waiting, just as the father of the prodigal son did. "When he was still a great way off, his father saw him and had compassion" (Luke 15:20). He rejoiced that his son was no longer lost (v.32).

Come home to God. Don't stay away. No matter what you've done, or left undone, He still loves you. — David Roper

O Lord, it's true, I've wandered far
From what I know is right,
But now I want to come back home
And please You day and night. — K. De Haan

IT'S NEVER TOO SOON
TO COME HOME TO GOD.

A Pair Of Moccasins

READ:
2 Samuel 24:18-25

Nor will I offer burnt offerings to the LORD my God with that which costs me nothing.
—2 Samuel 24:24

THE BIBLE IN ONE YEAR:
■ 2 Samuel 22–24

A doctor was working in a remote area of Minnesota many years ago when a Native American family begged him to come and help their elderly grandmother who was gravely ill. He went, diagnosed her condition, and then gave them detailed instructions for her care.

The woman recovered, and a few weeks later the entire family made the journey to the doctor's office in town. They ceremoniously presented him with a 150-year-old pair of moccasins made by a great-great-grandfather. When the doctor protested, because the gift was cherished and valuable, the head of the clan replied, "You saved my mother's life. We insist that you accept these moccasins. We do not express great appreciation with a cheap gift."

We see this same principle in 2 Samuel 24. David was told to offer a sacrifice to God on land owned by Araunah. As king, he could have taken the piece of land and the animals to make the sacrifice, but instead he purchased them. Araunah offered to give David what he needed, but David said he would not "offer burnt offerings to the LORD . . . with that which costs [him] nothing" (v.24).

By definition, a sacrifice has a cost. So when you give to the Lord, give generously. — Dave Egner

What shall I give You, Master?
You have redeemed my soul;
My gift is small but it is my all—
Surrendered to Your control. — Grimes

SACRIFICE IS THE TRUE MEASURE OF OUR GIVING.

LIVING WATER

READ:
Jeremiah 2:4-13

Jesus stood and cried out, saying, "If anyone thirsts, let him come to Me and drink."
—John 7:37

THE BIBLE IN ONE YEAR
■ 1 Kings 1–4

Lee Atwater was a well-known figure in US politics. He engineered the successful 1988 presidential campaign of George H. W. Bush and was the head of the Republican National Committee (1988-1991). But in the midst of all his activities he developed an inoperable brain tumor and died at the age of 40.

During his illness, Atwater came to realize that wealth, honor, and power are not life's supreme values. Admitting to a deep emptiness within himself, he urged people to work at filling up the "spiritual vacuum in American society." In an insightful comment, he confessed, "My illness helped me to see that what was missing in society is what is missing in me — a little heart, a lot of brotherhood."

In his day, Jeremiah perceived that same kind of vacuum in many of his fellow Israelites. He warned them against the danger of personal and national emptiness. They were digging cisterns, he said, "broken cisterns that can hold no water" (Jeremiah 2:13).

What about your own life? Is it spiritually dried up? Ask Jesus, the fountain of living water (John 7:37), to fill you with His presence. Then joy and peace will begin to bubble up and even overflow. — Vernon Grounds

I heard the voice of Jesus say,
"Behold, I freely give the living water,
Thirsty one, stoop down
And drink and live." — Bonar

**THE ONLY REAL THIRST QUENCHER IS JESUS—
THE LIVING WATER.**

March 31

LEND AN EAR

READ:
1 Corinthians 12:12-27

The members should have the same care for one another.
—1 Corinthians 12:25

THE BIBLE IN ONE YEAR
■ 1 Kings 5–7

Someone needs to talk to you today. Are you willing to listen? It may be a deep confession of failure, an expression of faith, an old joke, or a comment about the weather, but it needs to be said. The person may be a child or a senior citizen. Are you ready to lend an ear?

For 10 years, Mary Ridgway, a busy college administrator and educator, has regularly visited Mary Jacobs in an assisted living center. Ridgway began by receiving 50 hours of training to be a caregiver. She wondered if she could learn to step away from her tendencies to fix problems and to fill silent moments with words. Today, Mary Ridgway considers listening an expression of her service to Christ. Mary Jacobs thanks God every night for her faithful friend who cares enough to hear what she has to say.

The Bible calls us as Christians to "care for one another" (1 Corinthians 12:25) by using the gifts God has given each of us by His grace. One of the ways we can care for and serve each other is to listen.

Listening is not the job of a talented few but the privilege and responsibility of us all. Someone needs to tell you something today. Are you ready and willing, for Jesus' sake, to lend an ear? – David McCasland

A caring heart, a listening ear,
A thoughtful word, a gentle tear
Will help to lift the heavy load
Of weary souls along life's road. – *D. De Haan*

A BIG PART OF LOVING IS LISTENING.

THE RUNAWAY BUNNY

READ:
Psalm 139:7-12

Where can I go from Your Spirit? Or where can I flee from Your presence?
—Psalm 139:7

THE BIBLE IN ONE YEAR:
■ 1 Kings 8–10

Margaret Wise Brown is known for her simple yet profound books for children. One of my favorites is *The Runaway Bunny*. It's about a little bunny who tells his mother he has decided to run away.

"If you run away," says his mother, "I will run after you. For you are my little bunny." She goes on to tell him that if he becomes a fish in a trout stream, she will become a fisherman and fish for him. If he becomes a little boy, she will become a human mother and catch him in her arms and hug him. No matter what the little rabbit does, his doggedly persistent, ever-pursuing mother will not give up or go away.

"Shucks," says the bunny at last, "I might as well stay where I am and be your little bunny." "Have a carrot," his mother then says.

This story reminds me of David's words in Psalm 139:7-10; "Where can I go from Your Spirit? Or where can I flee from Your presence? If I ascend into heaven, You are there; if I make my bed in hell, behold, You are there. If I take the wings of the morning, and dwell in the uttermost parts of the sea, even there Your hand shall lead me, and Your right hand shall hold me."

Let's be thankful that God is relentless in His love for us — ever-pursuing, ever-present, and ever-guiding. — David Roper

THINKING IT THROUGH
How can the truth of God's presence be a comfort
in our trials? How can it help us
to avoid and overcome sin in our lives?

**NO MATTER WHERE YOU GO,
GOD GOES WITH YOU.**

BREAK THE ROUTINE

READ:
Mark 1:32-39

When He had sent the multitudes away, He went up on the mountain by Himself to pray.
—Matthew 14:23

THE BIBLE IN ONE YEAR:
■ 1 Kings 11–13

When was the last time you read the Bible while sitting under an oak tree? Have you ever prayed while the cool water of a creek ran across your feet? Wouldn't it be enjoyable to meditate on God's Word while watching the sun come up over the horizon?

It's not possible, of course, for all of us to do all those things — but it is possible for each of us to break the normal routine of our time alone with God. Sometimes, the habits of our devotional life can get in the way of our growing closer to God. In fact, at times they can grow stale and boring.

But there is nothing boring about a God who created the earth in all its splendor and variety. There is no lack of excitement in worshiping a Savior who was willing to die a horrible death for us and pay the penalty for our sins. There is nothing common about being indwelt by the Holy Spirit, who empowers us to accomplish God's will.

So how do we avoid dry devotional times? By breaking the routine of the usual and adding some variety to our personal time alone with God.

In His worship, Jesus found solitary havens away from the busyness of people and ministry (Mark 1:35). We need to do the same. We need to break the routine. — Dave Branon

THINKING IT THROUGH

Are you spiritually dry? Try changing the routine of your quiet time with the Lord — a different time, place, method, book of the Bible, or topic.

TIME SPENT WITH THE LORD IS TIME WELL SPENT.

How To Fail Successfully

READ:
1 John 1:5 – 2:2

**If anyone sins, we have an Advocate with the Father, Jesus Christ the righteous.
—1 John 2:1**

THE BIBLE IN ONE YEAR:
■ 1 Kings 14 – 16

Inventor Charles Kettering has suggested that we must learn to fail intelligently. He said, "Once you've failed, analyze the problem and find out why, because each failure is one more step leading up to the cathedral of success. The only time you don't want to fail is the last time you try."

Kettering gave these suggestions for turning failure into success: (1) Honestly face defeat; never fake success. (2) Exploit the failure; don't waste it. Learn all you can from it. (3) Never use failure as an excuse for not trying again.

Kettering's practical wisdom holds a deeper meaning for the Christian. The Holy Spirit is constantly working in us to accomplish "His good pleasure" (Philippians 2:13), so we know that failure is never final. We can't reclaim lost time. And we can't always make things right, although we should try. Some consequences of our sins can never be reversed. But we can make a new start, because Jesus died to pay the penalty for all our sins and is our "Advocate with the Father" (1 John 2:1).

Knowing how to benefit from failure is the key to continued growth in grace. According to 1 John 1:9, we need to confess our sins — it's the first step in turning our failure into success. — Dennis De Haan

Onward and upward your course plan today,
Seeking new heights as you walk Jesus' way;
Heed not past failures, but strive for the prize,
Aiming for goals fit for His holy eyes. — Brandt

**FAILURE IS NEVER FINAL FOR THOSE
WHO BEGIN AGAIN WITH GOD.**

THE WAY TO PRAISE HIM

READ:
Luke 19:28-38

Blessed is the King who comes in the name of the LORD!
—Luke 19:38

THE BIBLE IN ONE YEAR:
■ 1 Kings 17–19

The triumphal entry of Jesus into Jerusalem a few days before His death focused attention on Him as Lord. When Jesus sent His disciples to get the colt He was to ride, He instructed them to tell its owners, "The Lord has need of it" (Luke 19:31). And when the crowds shouted their praise, they quoted Psalm 118:26, saying, "Blessed is the King who comes in the name of the LORD!" (Luke 19:38).

Jesus is Lord. His name is "above every name" (Philippians 2:9). As part of His title, the word *Lord* refers to His sovereignty. He is the King, and every believer in Him is a member of His kingdom.

We acknowledge Jesus as Lord of our lives by bowing to His authority as King. This means that we live in obedience to Him. We can't be like the man who claimed to be a Christian and yet chose to use illegal drugs and live in an immoral relationship. When his minister confronted him, he glibly replied, "Don't worry, pastor. It's okay. I'm just a bad Christian."

It's *not* okay. Not at all! Not for a person who claims to be a follower of Christ (Luke 6:43-49).

Today, make sure you are honoring Him with your deeds as well as with your words. Then you can join with others in proclaiming, "Jesus is Lord!" — Dave Egner

Take me as I am, Lord,
And make me all Your own;
Make my heart Your palace
And Your royal throne. — Pope

**IF YOU ADORE CHRIST AS SAVIOR,
YOU CAN'T IGNORE CHRIST AS LORD.**

TRASH DISPOSAL

READ:
James 4:11-17

**Do not speak evil of one another.
—James 4:11**

THE BIBLE IN ONE YEAR:
■ 1 Kings 20—22

While riding in a car, I passed a sign that warned: $100 FINE FOR THROWING LITTER ON HIGHWAY. Soon I saw another sign that stated: LITTER BARREL — 1 MILE! A short time later, I passed a garbage truck on its way to the disposal plant.

There are three things you can do with garbage: You can collect it, scatter it, or dispose of it. Some people are garbage collectors; they are always listening for some choice bit of gossip. If they were only collectors, it would not be so serious. But these collectors are often litterbugs, and insist on scattering it all along life's highway. Thank God, there are also those who know how to dispose of it. They put the refuse where it belongs — in the "litter barrel" of forgetfulness.

James 4:11 tells us, "Do not speak evil of one another." If you can't say something helpful, don't say anything. If you hear a damaging rumor, immediately put it in the "litter bag." Then breathe a prayer for the person being talked about, as well as for the one who told you. Don't spread gossip, but dispose of it by silence. Gossip soon dies if it is not repeated.

Today you will find plenty of garbage. You can collect it, scatter it, or dispose of it. Ask God to help you do what pleases Him and is helpful to others. — M. R. De Haan, M.D.

*Button up your lip securely
'Gainst the words that bring a tear,
But be swift with words of comfort,
Words of praise, and words of cheer.* — Loucks

**DO YOUR PART TO SILENCE GOSSIP—
DON'T REPEAT IT.**

EXAGGERATION

READ:
James 3:1-13

He who covers his
sins will not prosper,
but whoever confesses
and forsakes them
will have mercy.
—Proverbs 28:13

THE BIBLE IN ONE YEAR:
■ 2 Kings 1–3

A woman said to a preacher, "I have a habit that I know is hurting my testimony — the habit of exaggeration. I start to tell something and I go on and on enlarging the story. People suspect that it's not true, and they lose confidence in me. I'm trying to get over it. Could you help me?"

He responded, "Let's talk to the Lord about it."

She prayed, "Lord, You know I have this habit of exaggeration . . ." At this point the preacher interrupted, "Call it lying and you may get over it!" The woman was deeply convicted and confessed her wrong.

We often excuse our pet sins by giving them more acceptable names. Our bad temper we call "nerves"; our untruthfulness, "exaggeration"; our dishonesty we call "good business." In seeking to overcome these sins, we need to bring them out in the open, call them honestly by name, and sincerely repent (Proverbs 28:13).

A man entered a dentist's office and sat down to have his teeth fixed. "I can feel a huge cavity with my tongue," he said. The dentist examined the man's teeth and said, "It'll only be a small filling." "But why does it feel so large?" asked the patient. "Just the natural tendency of the tongue to exaggerate," replied the dentist with a twinkle in his eye. We may smile, but aren't we all prone to blow things out of proportion? Indeed, "the tongue is a little member and boasts great things" (James 3:5).

Lord, forgive us for misusing our tongues. — Henry Bosch

TO STRETCH THE TRUTH IS TO TELL A LIE.

BEARING GRAPES

READ:
John 15:1-8

As the branch cannot bear fruit of itself, unless it abides in the vine, neither can you, unless you abide in Me. —John 15:4

THE BIBLE IN ONE YEAR:
■ 2 Kings 4–6

As I read a modern paraphrase of John 15:1-8, I began to reconsider my concept of what it means to be a fruitful Christian. Jesus said, "I am the Real Vine and my Father is the Farmer. He cuts off every branch of Me that doesn't bear grapes. And every branch that is grape-bearing He prunes back so it will bear even more" (*The Message* by Eugene Peterson).

Grapes—they're the result of the life of the vine flowing through the branches. So often I have viewed fruitfulness in the Christian life as activities such as teaching Sunday school or leading a Bible study. These acts of service are good and worthwhile, but Jesus said that being fruitful is allowing His life to flow through me: "As the branch cannot bear fruit of itself, unless it abides in the vine, neither can you, unless you abide in Me" (v.4). No one can bear "grapes" without being connected to Christ, the Vine. Fruitfulness is not primarily a matter of what I accomplish. It's the result of my being in close fellowship with Him.

Whenever you wonder if you're being a "fruitful" Christian, ask yourself, "Am I like Jesus? Is His life flowing through me in the ordinary activities and relationships of each day? Do the 'grapes' of my life point others to the Vine?" —David McCasland

Closer let me cling, my Savior—
You're the all-sufficient Vine;
You alone can make me fruitful,
Blessed source of strength divine. —Bosch

FRUITFULNESS FOR CHRIST
DEPENDS ON FELLOWSHIP WITH CHRIST.

LIGHTEN THE LOAD

READ:
Philippians 4:10-20

**I can do all things through Christ who strengthens me.
—Philippians 4:13**

THE BIBLE IN ONE YEAR:
■ 2 Kings 7–10

I once read about a distraught Christian woman who was extremely upset because her children had become unruly. She telephoned her husband at work one day and tearfully described the visit of a friend who had pinned this verse above the kitchen sink: "I can do all things through Christ who strengthens me" (Philippians 4:13). The friend had meant well. She was trying to be helpful, but her action just made the mom feel even more like a failure.

Sometimes it's not helpful merely to quote a Scripture verse to someone. Philippians 4:13 was Paul's personal testimony that he had learned to be content in all situations, in plenty and in want (vv.11-12). His secret of contentment was that he could "do all things through Christ" who strengthened him (v.13).

We too can live by Paul's secret. We can be victorious through Christ's strength, but we shouldn't force this truth on people who are feeling overwhelmed. Paul also wrote that we should care for one another and share in one another's distress (Galatians 6:2; Philippians 2:4; 4:14).

We need each other, for we all have burdens to bear. Let's use the strength Christ gives us to minister to the needs of others and find ways to lighten their loads. — Joanie Yoder

PUTTING IT INTO PRACTICE
Who needs your encouragement today?
What are some practical ways you can help?
Write a note? Make a meal? Babysit? Just listen?

TO EASE ANOTHER'S BURDEN, HELP TO CARRY IT.

HE DIED FOR ME!

READ:
Isaiah 53

If He is the King of Israel, let Him now come down from the cross, and we will believe Him.
—Matthew 27:42

THE BIBLE IN ONE YEAR:
■ 2 Kings 11–14

William and Mary Tanner were crossing the railroad tracks when it happened. Mary's foot slipped and wedged itself between the rail and the wooden crosswalk. She tried frantically to pull her foot free as the sound of an approaching train was heard. There were but seconds left as the express came rushing toward her around a curve. Will Tanner pulled on her foot, desperately trying to free her.

As the train came closer and its whistle screamed and brakes shrieked, Will held her in his arms. While people shuddered in horror, the train thundered over them. One witness said that just before the engine hit them, he heard the brave man cry, "I'll stay with you, Mary!" That is great love!

This story reminds me of our Savior, who loved us with a love that *can* save us (John 3:16). Death came hurtling at Him as He hung on a cross and took the full penalty we deserved. He heard people cry out to Him to save Himself and come down from the cross (Matthew 27:40). But to save others He chose not to save Himself (v.42).

With divine, sacrificial love, Jesus refused to spare His own life. He died so that He could provide forgiveness of sins for us. Our Savior stayed on the cross — for you and for me! — M. R. De Haan, M.D.

> *Oh, can it be, upon a tree*
> *The Savior died for me?*
> *My soul is thrilled, my heart is filled,*
> *To think He died for me!* — *Newton*

**NAILS COULD NOT HAVE KEPT JESUS ON THE CROSS
IF HIS LOVE FOR US HAD NOT HELD HIM THERE.**

CROSS AND CROWN

READ:
John 3:13-21

. . . even so must the Son of Man be lifted up, that whoever believes in Him should not perish but have eternal life.
—**John 3:14-15**

THE BIBLE IN ONE YEAR:
■ 2 Kings 15–17

In April 2002, along with thousands of others in London, I filed past the casket of Britain's Queen Mother as her body lay in state. In the muffled silence of Westminster Hall, I was struck by the sight of the magnificent crown resting on top of the coffin, and the cross standing nearby — symbols of her life and faith. We had come to pay our respects to a much-loved member of the royal family. But on that night it was clear to me that the cross of the Lord Jesus Christ matters far more than any crown.

For all who trust in Christ, the cross symbolizes our hope both in life and in death. No matter what positions of power we may inherit or achieve, none will follow us beyond the grave. But Christ is the giver of abundant life now and forever.

Before His death on the cross, Jesus said, "As Moses lifted up the serpent in the wilderness, even so must the Son of Man be lifted up, that whoever believes in Him should not perish but have eternal life" (John 3:14-15).

The cross speaks of forgiveness and of peace with God. It points to the merits of Christ and not our own. As we step through the doorway of death, we must lay aside our "earthly crowns." Our only hope is to cling to our Savior, who died so that we could have everlasting life. — David McCasland

Our Lord took death upon Himself
On that cruel cross of pain,
And those who look in faith to Him
Eternal life shall gain! — *Johnson*

CALVARY'S CROSS IS THE ONLY BRIDGE TO ETERNAL LIFE.

ATTEMPTING THE IMPOSSIBLE

READ:
Matthew 27:62–28:8

**God raised up [Jesus], having loosed the pains of death, because it was not possible that He should be held by it.
—Acts 2:24**

THE BIBLE IN ONE YEAR:
■ 2 Kings 18–20

It was the day after Jesus was crucified. His body lay in a tomb. But the chief priests and Pharisees who had engineered His crucifixion had the uneasy feeling that this might not be the end of the Jesus story. So they went to Pilate and told him that Jesus' disciples might steal His body to try to convince the people that He had fulfilled His prediction to rise from the grave. Pilate responded, "You have a guard; go your way, make [the tomb] as secure as you know how" (Matthew 27:65).

A guard was posted and the tomb was secured with an official Roman seal (v.66). The religious and political leaders did their very best to make sure that the body of Jesus remained in the tomb, but they were attempting the impossible. Death could not hold the sinless Son of God in its grasp, and on the third day He rose just as He said He would (20:19; 27:63; 28:1-8).

After the resurrection, the chief priests bribed the soldiers and told them to spread a ridiculous story about the disciples stealing the body (28:11-14). Still today skeptics offer one fanciful theory after another, attempting to disprove the resurrection of Jesus. In spite of their efforts to cast doubt on the historical record, the truth is that Jesus came out of the tomb.

We serve a living Savior! — Herb Vander Lugt

*I serve a risen Savior,
He's in the world today;
I know that He is living,
Whatever men may say.* — Ackley

JESUS AROSE DESPITE HIS FOES.

IN HIS STRENGTH

READ:
Psalm 71:1-16

**I will go in the strength of the Lord GOD.
—Psalm 71:16**

THE BIBLE IN ONE YEAR:
■ 2 Kings 21–22

In his famous painting titled *A Helping Hand,* Emile Renouf depicted an old fisherman seated in a boat, with a young girl beside him. Both the elderly gentleman and the child have their hands on a huge oar. The fisherman is looking down fondly and admiringly at the girl.

Apparently the man has told the child that she may assist him in rowing the boat, and in her desire to help she feels as though she is doing a great share of the task. However, it's obvious that it's his strong, muscular arms that are moving the heavy oar through the water.

I see a parable in this painting. Christ has granted to us the privilege of sharing in His work here on earth. We must never forget, however, that we cannot perform our tasks through our abilities alone, but only as God works in and through us. While He directs us to put our hand on the oar, we must ever be aware of the ultimate source of our power. He is the strength of our life! There can be no true progress spiritually without the power of the Holy Spirit to undergird our life and all that we do.

Let's recognize our own weakness and echo the cry of the psalmist: "I will go in the strength of the Lord GOD" (71:16). Then we will not faint nor fail. — Henry Bosch

God, grant to me the strength of heart,
Of motive, and of will,
To do my part and falter not
Your purpose to fulfill. — Anon.

**OUR GREATEST WEAKNESS MAY BE OUR FAILURE
TO RELY ON GOD'S STRENGTH.**

THE KING'S OFFER

READ:
Matthew 21:1-11

The multitudes . . .
cried out, saying:
"Hosanna to the Son
of David! 'Blessed is
He who comes in the
name of the LORD!'"
—Matthew 21:9

THE BIBLE IN ONE YEAR:
■ 2 Kings 23–25

I have often wondered how many of those people who enthusiastically cried, "Hosanna!" on Palm Sunday shouted, "Crucify Him! Crucify Him!" a few days later. Some may have been keenly disappointed, even angry, that Christ didn't use His miraculous power to establish an earthly kingdom. Hadn't He created a golden opportunity to rally popular support by parading into Jerusalem and offering Himself as King?

Many Jews failed to recognize that before Jesus would openly assert His sovereignty He had to rule in their hearts. Their greatest need was not to be freed from Caesar's rule but to be released from the chains of pride, self-righteousness, and rebellion against God. They wanted the visible kingdom prophesied in the Old Testament with all its material benefits. But the Messiah first had to die for the sins of mankind and rise again to establish the basis for a spiritual rule.

The issue is the same today. Christ does not offer immunity from life's hardships, a cure for every disease, or the promise of financial success. What the King offered then is what He offers today — Himself as the sacrifice for our sins, and a challenge to serve Him. If we accept His offer, we will not be disappointed. —Dennis De Haan

There's no disappointment in Jesus,
He's all that He promised to be;
His love and His care comfort me everywhere;
He is no disappointment to me. —Hallett

**PUTTING CHRIST FIRST BRINGS
SATISFACTION THAT LASTS.**

GIVING AWAY HAPPINESS

READ:
Proverbs 11:16-26

**The generous soul will be made rich, and he who waters will also be watered himself.
—Proverbs 11:25**

THE BIBLE IN ONE YEAR:
■ 1 Chronicles 1–3

A *U.S. News & World Report* cover story explored the subject of happiness. According to the article, scientists have found that "strong marriages, family ties, and friendships predict happiness, as do spirituality and self-esteem. Hope is crucial, as is the feeling that life has meaning." But what if some of these elements are missing in our lives? Researchers say that "helping people be a little happier can jump-start a process that will lead to stronger relationships, renewed hope, and general upward spiraling of happiness."

What we give, more than what we get, produces joy in our lives. The Bible says, "There is one who scatters, yet increases more . . . . The generous soul will be made rich, and he who waters will also be watered himself" (Proverbs 11:24-25).

Is there some small way you can help someone else be happier today? Perhaps it's sending a card, making a phone call, or giving yourself in friendship. Hoarding never produces happiness. It comes as we seek the good of others and give away what God has given us.

The source of such an attitude is found in our relationship with Christ and His Spirit (Galatians 5:22-23). From Him grows the fruit of generosity, happiness, and love.

What will you give away today? — David McCasland

Not what we have, but what we give,
Not what we see, but how we live —
These are the things that build and bless,
That lead to human happiness. — Anon.

IT IS MORE BLESSED TO GIVE THAN TO RECEIVE. — Jesus

GOD CAN SAVE ANYONE!

READ:
1 Timothy 2:1-8

Therefore I exhort . . . that supplications, prayers, intercessions, and giving of thanks be made for all men.
—1 Timothy 2:1

THE BIBLE IN ONE YEAR:
■ 1 Chronicles 4–6

Today, as always, there is an urgent need for us to pray for "all who are in authority" (1 Timothy 2:2). But does the word *all* include the most wicked of leaders? Are there ever people in positions of power and influence who are beyond the help of prayer?

The answer to this question can be found by noting the word *therefore* in verse 1, which calls our attention to the immediate context. In 1 Timothy 1:12-17, Paul admitted that he was once a blasphemer, a persecutor, and a violent man (v.13). He vigorously affirmed that Christ Jesus came into the world to save sinners. Then he added this significant phrase: "of whom I am chief" (v.15).

Paul explained that he received God's mercy so that Christ would display His limitless grace in him as a pattern for those who are going to believe on Him in the future (v.16). In effect, Paul was saying, "If I, the worst of sinners, can be saved, anyone can." Paul *therefore* exhorted us to pray for all in authority, because God our Savior desires all to be saved and to embrace His truth (2:4).

So let's not only pray that honorable leaders will act wisely, but also that ungodly leaders will be saved. Yes, God can save anyone. — Joanie Yoder

No leader is beyond God's grace
When righteous people pray;
For when God's children intercede,
The Lord will have His way. — D. De Haan

TO INFLUENCE LEADERS FOR GOD,
INTERCEDE WITH GOD FOR LEADERS.

YOU MATTER TO GOD

READ:
Luke 15:3-7

Rejoice with me, for I have found my sheep which was lost!
—Luke 15:6

THE BIBLE IN ONE YEAR:
■ 1 Chronicles 7—9

American author Julia Ward Howe is remembered chiefly for her poem "Battle Hymn Of The Republic." According to her daughter, Howe once invited her friend US Senator Charles Sumner to meet a rising young actor. But he declined her invitation, saying, "I don't know that I should care to meet him. I have outlived my interest in individuals." Julia later wrote in her diary, "Fortunately, God Almighty had not, by last accounts, gotten so far."

Aren't you glad the Lord hasn't gotten beyond caring about people? In fact, our heavenly Father is interested in every individual member of the human family.

According to Jesus, the Father is like a devoted shepherd who leaves his flock of 99 sheep in the safety and shelter of the fold and sacrificially goes out to find that one lost lamb (Luke 15:4-6). Indeed, to help us understand the intensely individual nature of God's love, Jesus declared that the very hairs of our head are numbered (Matthew 10:30). It's amazing that this divine Shepherd even laid down His life for us, His sheep (John 10:11).

Are you a lost sheep, needing Jesus the Shepherd to find you? Call out to Him today and let Him rescue you. Remember, *you* matter to God. — Vernon Grounds

I've found a Friend, O such a Friend!
He loved me ere I knew Him;
He drew me with the cords of love;
And thus He bound me to Him. —Small

**WHEN WE FIND CHRIST, WE DISCOVER
WE WERE THE ONES WHO WERE LOST.**

SCAMMED BY SPAM

READ:
Galatians 1:1-10

I marvel that you are turning away so soon from Him who called you in the grace of Christ. —Galatians 1:6

THE BIBLE IN ONE YEAR:
■ 1 Chronicles 10–13

Have you ever been scammed by spam? *Spam* is a computer term that refers to junk mail on the Internet. It's a common problem for people who use personal computers. Sometimes it's harmless, but sometimes it's not.

You open your e-mail, and you get a note saying someone wants to help you. Your credit card is invalid, the message says, and your number has to be reentered to reactivate your account. So, you type it in and hit "send" — thinking you're doing the right thing. Later you get a bill for a bunch of items you didn't buy. You've just been scammed by spam!

What appeared to be helpful is no help at all. You trust the message, do what it says, and you end up losing.

We can also be scammed spiritually. It happens when supposed teachers of the Bible distort the gospel and proclaim a false message that they call the truth (salvation by works, for example). But often it's "a different gospel" (Galatians 1:6).

How can you avoid such a scam? By knowing from the Bible what the true gospel is. Eternal salvation is available only by grace, through trusting in Jesus Christ and His death on the cross for our sins (Galatians 2:16; Ephesians 2:8-9). Don't be fooled. Any other message is a scam! —Dave Branon

WHAT DOES THE BIBLE SAY?
Look up these passages on the gospel:
John 3:16; Acts 4:12; Romans 1:16; 10:8-13;
1 Corinthians 15:1-4; 1 John 5:11-13.

**THERE'S NO BETTER NEWS THAN THE GOSPEL—
SPREAD THE WORD!**

THREE CROSSES

READ:
Luke 23:32-49

**He said to Jesus, "Lord, remember me when You come into Your kingdom."
—Luke 23:42**

THE BIBLE IN ONE YEAR:
■ 1 Chronicles 14–16

There were three crosses on Calvary's hill. On one was a man dying *in* sin — he did not accept Jesus. On another was a man dying *to* sin — he trusted Jesus as Savior and Lord (Luke 23:40-43). And on the middle cross was One dying *for* sin. He could die for others because He was God's Son and had no sin of His own. The center cross made all the difference for those two men hanging beside Jesus — the difference between an eternal hell and an eternal heaven.

The whole world is represented by those two thieves and their response to the Lord Jesus. I see in the three crucified individuals a picture of the sinner, the saint, and the Savior.

A man was asked to receive Christ but put it off by saying, "Oh, don't bother me now. There is always the eleventh hour. Remember the dying thief." He was shocked when the persistent Christian said pointedly, "Which thief? Remember, there were two!" The man responded, "That's right. I had forgotten that. I meant the saved one!" That very night he decided to trust Jesus for his salvation.

Look in faith now to that One in heaven who once hung on the middle cross. You too will hear His word of forgiveness and hope. — Henry Bosch

When Jesus Christ my Savior suffered loss,
He gave Himself because He saw my need;
It was my sin that nailed Him to the cross —
I cannot blame another for the deed. — Hess

GOD'S JUSTICE AND MERCY MET AT THE CROSS.

NEW LIFE ON DEATH ROW

READ:
John 19:16-18

Jesus said to him, "Assuredly, I say to you, today you will be with Me in Paradise." —Luke 23:43

THE BIBLE IN ONE YEAR:
■ 1 Chronicles 17–19

We see two opposite responses to Jesus from the two thieves who were crucified next to Him: One blasphemed, the other believed (Luke 23:39-42). We rejoice over the conversion of the one and Christ's words to him: "Today you will be with Me in Paradise" (v.43). Now, as then, Jesus saves those who truly repent — even at "the eleventh hour."

One such person was Lester Ezzell, who was on death row in Florida. When his former Sunday school teacher Curtis Oakes traveled 750 miles to visit him in prison, Lester said, "You don't give up, do you?" Though Lester still wouldn't listen to the gospel, Curtis gave him a New Testament and urged him to read it.

Later, Lester wrote several letters to Curtis. The first one brought news of his conversion. His final letter in early 1957 read: "By the time you receive this, my life will have been taken. I will have paid for the wrong I have done. But I want you to know this — with that little Testament, and by the grace of God, I have led 47 people to the saving knowledge of Jesus Christ. I just thank you for not giving up on me."

When we witness to others about Jesus Christ, some may not repent until late in life. So, let's never give up on anyone. — Joanie Yoder

> Lord, lay some soul upon my heart,
> And love that soul through me;
> And may I nobly do my part
> To win that soul for Thee. —Tucker

**WHEN YOU KNOW CHRIST,
YOU WANT OTHERS TO KNOW HIM TOO.**

RESURRECTION REALITY

READ:
Luke 24:1-12

I am He who lives, and was dead, and behold, I am alive forevermore.
—Revelation 1:18

THE BIBLE IN ONE YEAR:
■ 1 Chronicles 20–23

The disciples and early followers of our Lord asserted with a zeal born of heartfelt conviction that Jesus of Nazareth was a living Savior, not a martyred teacher and philosopher. They held this truth so dear that they were willing to suffer torture and death rather than renounce it.

This startling message so electrified their ministry that their testimony "turned the world upside down" (Acts 17:6). It is still true today: The Holy Spirit honors the witness of those who proclaim the resurrected Jesus. They do not point primarily to moral codes, religious rituals, or theological creeds (good as these may be in themselves), but to the living God-man who alone can save. It is to Him who is "alive forevermore" (Revelation 1:18) that we should look in these days of dead orthodoxy and spiritual apostasy.

A proud and ungodly professor said to a young child who believed in the Lord Jesus, "My dear little girl, you don't know whom you believe in. There have been many christs. In which of them do you believe?" "I know which one I believe in," replied the child. "I believe in the Christ who rose from the dead!"

Jesus is alive (Luke 24:1-12). Your eternal life depends on it. — Henry Bosch

> *Although our Lord was crucified,*
> *He rose up from the grave;*
> *He paid our penalty for sin,*
> *Then showed His power to save.* —Sper

**CHRIST'S RESURRECTION ASSURES
WHAT CALVARY SECURES.**

You Can Believe It

READ:
Acts 1:1-11

**He also presented Himself alive after His suffering by many infallible proofs.
—Acts 1:3**

THE BIBLE IN ONE YEAR:
■ 1 Chronicles 24–26

In 1957, Lieutenant David Steeves walked out of California's Sierra Nevada Mountains 54 days after his Air Force trainer jet had disappeared. He told an unbelievable tale of how he had lived in a snowy wilderness after parachuting from his disabled plane. By the time he showed up alive, he had already been declared officially dead. When further search failed to turn up the wreckage, a hoax was suspected and Steeves was forced to resign under a cloud of doubt. More than 20 years later, however, his story was confirmed when a troop of Boy Scouts discovered the wreckage of his plane.

Another "survival story" from centuries ago is still controversial. A man by the name of Jesus Christ walked out of the Judean wilderness making claims a lot of people found difficult to believe. He was later executed and pronounced dead. But 3 days later He showed up alive. And there have been skeptics ever since.

But consider the facts of Christ's life, death, and resurrection. His integrity is well-founded. Prophets foretold His coming. Miracles supported His deity. Eyewitnesses verified His resurrection. And today the Holy Spirit confirms to anyone who is seeking to know the truth that Jesus is alive.

Yes, you can believe it! Do you? — Mart De Haan

I know that Jesus lives today,
No matter what the skeptics say;
The evidence that we must weigh
Says, "Jesus is alive!" — Sper

**THE RESURRECTION OF JESUS IS A FACT OF HISTORY
THAT DEMANDS A RESPONSE OF FAITH.**

THE ANSWERS CAN WAIT

READ:
Luke 4:14-22

**This is a faithful saying and worthy of all acceptance, that Christ Jesus came into the world to save sinners, of whom I am chief.
—1 Timothy 1:15**

THE BIBLE IN ONE YEAR:
■ 1 Chronicles 27–29

David Herwaldt, a thoughtful, reflective pastor friend of mine, was slowly dying after 50 years of faithful ministry. He often talked with me about the nature of God and the eternity he would soon enter. We realized that we had only a superficial grasp of these mysteries, but we were not distressed. We knew that God had rescued us from our sin and guilt, and we rejoiced in our salvation. We had all we needed to obey the Lord gladly, live confidently, and serve Him gratefully.

When we are distressed by our inability to answer life's most vexing questions, we must remember that Christ did not come to satisfy our curiosity. Rather, He saw us as fallen and hurt, and He came to lift and heal.

When Jesus read Isaiah 61:1-2 to the people in the synagogue (Luke 4:16-21), He presented Himself as the promised Messiah, whose primary purpose for coming was spiritual. He came to deliver us from the helplessness of our spiritual poverty, to release us from the shackles of our guilt, to heal our sin-caused blindness, and to set us free from sin's enslaving power.

Let us therefore trust Him and make obeying Him our highest goal. This is the path to a grateful, joyous, and hope-filled life. The answers can wait. — Herb Vander Lugt

When trouble seeks to rob your very breath,
When tragedy hits hard and steals your days,
Recall that Christ endured the sting of death;
He gives us hope, and merits all our praise. — *Gustafson*

**CHRIST CAME NOT TO SATISFY OUR CURIOSITY
BUT TO SAVE OUR SOULS.**

ALWAYS ON CALL

READ:
Psalm 34:1-18

**This poor man cried out, and the LORD heard him, and saved him out of all his troubles.
—Psalm 34:6**

THE BIBLE IN ONE YEAR:
■ 2 Chronicles 1–3

If you're frustrated with the health-care system and would like a personal physician who is always on call, you can have one — for a price. Two Seattle doctors are charging wealthy patients $20,000 a year for primary healthcare. They make house calls, give personal, unhurried treatment, and say the service they provide is like other perks available to people with money. Whatever we think of the medical ethics involved, it's a level of care most of us would like to have if we could afford it.

There's another type of "on-call" relationship that cannot be purchased. In fact, it's available only to those who consider themselves poor and needy. I'm speaking of God's never-failing response to His children who cry out to Him for help.

David said, "I sought the LORD, and He heard me, and delivered me from all my fears" (Psalm 34:4). He also said, "This poor man cried out, and the LORD heard him, and saved him out of all his troubles" (v.6).

Jesus has been called "the Great Physician." He is not "on demand" to do as we ask, but He is always "on call" to hear our prayers and provide the deliverance we need. What an encouragement! "The eyes of the LORD are on the righteous, and His ears are open to their cry" (v.15). — David McCasland

Whenever you need Him, whenever you call,
The Lord is close by — He's the One who hears all;
When you are in trouble, when you need His aid,
Just cry out to Jesus, and your fears will fade. — Fitzhugh

THE GREAT PHYSICIAN IS ALWAYS ON CALL.

LIVE ACCORDINGLY

READ:
Colossians 1:15-18

By Him all things were created that are in heaven and that are on earth, visible and invisible.
—Colossians 1:16

THE BIBLE IN ONE YEAR:
■ 2 Chronicles 4–6

I heard about an ethics professor who serves as a consultant in major ethical dilemmas and legal cases all over the world. Again and again he provides deep insights into complex moral questions, and his opinions have influenced corporate decisions of global significance. But the professor himself is not ethical. He cheats on his wife, and he embarrasses the university by his public behavior.

Now, this man knows the law. He has deep insights into right and wrong. But his knowledge doesn't affect the way he lives. He's like a pianist who has all the notes in front of him but doesn't play the music. He's like the builder who has all the plans and materials but doesn't build the building properly. He's like so many who live without Christ — the One who created them and has a design for their lives. Everything that exists has been created "through Him and for Him" (Colossians 1:16), and we would be wise to follow His plan.

Like good musicians and expert builders, when we live according to God's design, we will be successful in carrying out His plan for our lives. As the apostle Paul prayed, may we be "filled with the knowledge of His will in all wisdom and spiritual understanding" (v.9). And then, may we live accordingly. — Dave Egner

Master, speak, and make me ready,
When Thy voice is truly heard,
With obedience glad and steady,
Still to follow every word. — Havergal

TO KNOW LIFE'S PURPOSE,
YOU MUST KNOW LIFE'S CREATOR.

JUST A GLIMPSE

READ:
Ephesians 2:14-18

God forbid that I should boast except in the cross of our Lord Jesus Christ.
—Galatians 6:14

THE BIBLE IN ONE YEAR:
■ 2 Chronicles 7–9

Travelers who drive across the flat landscape of Groom, Texas, are surprised by an unexpected sight. Looming up against the sky is a cross 190 feet high. That giant symbol of the Christian faith was erected by Steve Thomas in the prayerful hope that the thoughts of anyone who sees it might be turned to Jesus. When his handiwork was finished and dedicated, he said, "We want some converts out of this."

All Christians are grateful when a nonbeliever's attention is drawn to Jesus Christ and the cross. The awareness may be fleeting, but who can predict what even a split-second reaction may mean to an immortal soul? Suddenly a sinful person may begin to wonder why Jesus died on the cross. This may prompt him to seek answers from the Bible or from Christians he may know.

What about us as Christians? As we hurry along through life's often dreary landscape, are we grateful for any reminder of our Father's love that sent His Son to die? Through the cross, Jesus has reconciled us to God and given us His peace (Ephesians 2:14,16). Take some time today to reflect on the meaning of the cross, and let it flood your heart with praise to the Savior. — Vernon Grounds

Once from the realms of infinite glory,
Down to the depths of our ruin and loss,
Jesus came, seeking — O Love's sweet story —
Came to the manger, the shame, and the cross. — Strickland

TO KNOW THE MEANING OF THE CROSS,
YOU MUST KNOW THE ONE WHO DIED THERE.

BRIEF AS A FLOWER

READ:
Psalm 103:8-18

**As for man, his days are like grass; as a flower of the field, so he flourishes. For the wind passes over it, and it is gone.
—Psalm 103:15-16**

THE BIBLE IN ONE YEAR:
■ 2 Chronicles 10–13

Years ago, a young boy wandered from case to case in a candy store, trying to decide what to buy. His mother, tired of waiting, called, "Hurry up and spend your money! We must be going." To this he replied, "But Mom, I only have one penny, so I've got to spend it carefully."

So too, we have only one life to live, so we must "spend it carefully!" If we had ten lives, we might be able to afford to spend one of them merely on pleasure or in making money.

In underscoring the brevity of life, the Bible uses many illustrations, among them that of a flower (Psalm 103:15-16). A flower is a thing of loveliness. As a receptacle of nectar, it usually gives forth a pleasing aroma and performs a necessary function in the production of new seed. But what strikes me most about a flower is that its beauty is so brief!

Because our days on earth are few, we should make the most of our "flowering time." The nectar of the love of God in our heart should attract people to the Savior. Our life should be colorful with spiritual service, remembering that we are allowed to bloom for the express purpose of bringing forth new seed (leading others to Christ).

Your life is brief — make it lovely! — Henry Bosch

Living for Jesus a life that is true,
Striving to please Him in all that I do;
Yielding allegiance, glad-hearted and free,
This is the pathway of blessing for me. — Chisholm

**USING YOUR FEW DAYS WISELY
CAN MAKE AN ETERNAL DIFFERENCE.**

HE IS HERE

READ:
Luke 24:36-45

Jesus Himself stood in the midst of them, and said to them, "Peace to you."
—Luke 24:36

THE BIBLE IN ONE YEAR:
■ 2 Chronicles 14–16

Surprise! Surprise! The eleven apostles had gathered together on the day of Jesus' resurrection. They were discussing the strange happenings of the past few days, and had just listened to a report from two men who said they had seen Jesus. Suddenly He was there! Then the Savior said, "Peace to you" (Luke 24:36).

I wonder if we realize when we meet together — at church, in our home, in our prayer meetings, in our gatherings with friends — that Jesus is also there. He said, "Lo, I am with you always, even to the end of the age" (Matthew 28:20). Do we really believe He is with us and listens to every word we say, and that He sees all we do?

Some scholars were discussing the great authors of the past. One asked, "What if Milton should suddenly enter the room?" "Ah!" replied another. "We would honor him and compensate him for the little recognition he received in his day." A third man commented, "What if Shakespeare entered? Would we not all stand and proclaim him King of the Poets?" Then someone ventured, "And if Jesus Christ should enter?" There was a long silence, until finally one said: "But gentlemen, He is here!"

Yes, remember that Jesus is here! He sees, He hears, and He knows! — M. R. De Haan, M.D.

> *Although we cannot see our Lord,*
> *We know that He is here;*
> *His promise is dependable:*
> *He always will be near.* — Hess

**OUR GREATEST PRIVILEGE
IS TO ENJOY CHRIST'S PRESENCE.**

ADDING LUSTER TO LIFE

READ:
Psalm 119:1-16

**I will delight myself in Your statutes; I will not forget Your Word.
—Psalm 119:16**

THE BIBLE IN ONE YEAR:
■ 2 Chronicles 17–19

While traveling on the ocean liner *Vistafjord,* Eleanor Sass and several other passengers were invited by the captain to visit the ship's bridge. There the engineer explained the workings of the intricate equipment, such as the compass and radar.

But what impressed many of the passengers most was all the brass, which gleamed like gold. "How often do you polish all this?" one man asked an officer. "Every day," was the reply. "For the minute you stop polishing it, the brass starts to tarnish."

That reply made Eleanor think about something she had stopped doing—reading God's Word every night. She recognized that her neglect of the Word of God was causing her life to be "tarnished." So, at bedtime that night she took out the Bible she had seen earlier in the dresser drawer. She began again to turn to God in His Word.

Have you been reading the Bible, or have you been neglecting that discipline? Psalm 119 encourages us to seek the Lord with our whole heart, to delight in His statutes, and not to forget His Word (vv.10,16).

If your relationship with God has lost its spiritual luster, it needs to be polished by the faithful habit of daily Scripture reading. — Vernon Grounds

> *The Bible is the Word of God,*
> *Still fresh through all the ages;*
> *But we must read if we're to find*
> *The wisdom in its pages.* —Sper

**TO KNOW THE AUTHOR OF THE BIBLE,
READ HIS BOOK.**

KEEP RUNNING!

READ:
Hebrews 12:1-3

**Let us run with endurance the race that is set before us.
—Hebrews 12:1**

THE BIBLE IN ONE YEAR:
■ 2 Chronicles 20–22

You may have heard the story of John Stephen Akhwari, the marathon runner from Tanzania who finished last at the 1968 Olympics in Mexico City. No last-place finisher in a marathon ever finished quite so last.

Injured along the way, he hobbled into the stadium with his leg bloodied and bandaged. It was more than an hour after the rest of the runners had completed the race. Only a few spectators were left in the stands when Akhwari finally crossed the finish line.

When asked why he continued to run despite the pain, Akhwari replied, "My country did not send me to Mexico City to start the race. They sent me here to finish."

The attitude of that athlete ought to be our attitude as we grow older. There is a "race that is set before us" (Hebrews 12:1), and we are to keep running until we reach the finish line.

No one is too old to serve God. We must keep growing, maturing, and serving to the end of our days. To idle away our last years is to rob the church of the choicest gifts God has given us to share. There is service to be rendered. There is still much to be done.

So let's keep running "with endurance." Let's finish the course — and finish strong. — David Roper

*It will be worth it all when we see Jesus,
Life's trials will seem so small when we see Christ;
One glimpse of His dear face all sorrow will erase,
So bravely run the race till we see Christ.* — Rusthoi

IT'S ALWAYS TOO SOON TO QUIT.

PRAYING WITH BOLDNESS

READ:
Psalm 6

Let us therefore come boldly to the throne of grace.
—Hebrews 4:16

THE BIBLE IN ONE YEAR:
■ 2 Chronicles 23–25

Have you ever found it tough to pray? That can happen when we're reluctant to tell God how we're really feeling. We might abruptly stop in mid-sentence, fearful of being disrespectful of our heavenly Father.

A trip through the book of Psalms can help us pray more openly. There we can overhear David's conversations with God and realize that he was not afraid to be completely open and honest with the Lord. David cried out: "O LORD, do not rebuke me in Your anger" (Psalm 6:1). "Have mercy on me, O LORD, for I am weak" (6:2). "Why do You stand afar off, O LORD?" (10:1). "Do not be silent to me" (28:1). "Plead my cause, O LORD" (35:1). "Hear my prayer, O God" (54:2). "I am restless in my complaint, and moan noisily" (55:2).

Think about David's approach. He was saying to God: "Help me!" "Listen to me!" "Don't be mad at me!" "Where are You?" David boldly went to God and told Him what was on his mind. Yes, God expects us to come to Him with a clean heart, and we need to approach Him with reverence — but we don't have to be afraid to tell God what we're thinking and feeling.

Next time you talk with your heavenly Father — tell it straight. He'll listen, and He'll understand.   — Dave Branon

When you approach the Lord with boldness,
When you pray in Jesus' name,
Just tell Him all the pain you're feeling —
There's no need for fear or shame.   — Fitzhugh

PRAYER IS AN OPEN LINE TO HEAVEN.

WORRIER OR WARRIOR?

READ:
Ephesians 3:14-21

[God] is able to do exceedingly abundantly above all that we ask or think.
—Ephesians 3:20

THE BIBLE IN ONE YEAR:
■ 2 Chronicles 26–29

A missionary wrote a newsletter to thank his supporters for being "prayer warriors." Because of a typing error, though, he called them "prayer *worriers*." For some of us, that might be a good description.

In his book *Growing Your Soul*, Neil Wiseman writes, "Prayer must be more than a kind of restatement of fretting worries or a mulling over of problems. Our petitions must move beyond gloomy desperation, which deals mostly with calamity and despair."

During an anxious time in my life, I became a "prayer worrier." I would beg, "Lord, please keep my neighbor from causing me problems tomorrow." Or, "Father, don't let that ornery person spread gossip about me."

But then the Lord taught me to pray *for* people, rather than *against* them. I began to say, "Lord, bless and encourage my neighbor, and help him to sense Your love." Then I watched to see what God would do. The Lord's amazing answers not only helped others but also helped to cure my own anxiety!

Paul was no "prayer worrier." He prayed for God's people that they might know the strength, love, and fullness of God, who is able to do far more than we can ask or even think (Ephesians 3:14-21). Such confidence made Paul a true "prayer warrior." Are your prayers like that? — Joanie Yoder

As we resolve to live for Christ
In actions, words, and deeds,
We'll yield our anxious hearts to Him
And pray for others' needs. — Branon

FERVENT PRAYER DISPELS ANXIOUS CARE.

JESUS UNDERSTANDS

READ:
Hebrews 2:9-18

[Jesus] was in all points tempted as we are, yet without sin.
—Hebrews 4:15

THE BIBLE IN ONE YEAR:
■ 2 Chronicles 30–32

Seven-year-old Andy had to have his left arm amputated, and it wasn't easy to adjust to the loss. When he returned to school, his teacher wanted his classmates to understand how difficult the normal activities of life were for Andy. So one morning she told the other students to keep their left arm behind their back. That meant they all had to do everything with their right hand.

Little things like turning the pages of a book, writing neatly, and keeping the paper from slipping became difficult. Buttoning clothing took extra effort, and tying one's shoes became impossible. Andy's classmates discovered that the only way they could really understand his problem was to experience for themselves the difficulties he faced.

Because the Lord Jesus, God's Son, became a man, He can identify with our trials and temptations. He understands the heartaches, pain, and difficulties we face. Since "He Himself has suffered, being tempted, He is able to aid those who are tempted" (Hebrews 2:18). And because He was without sin (4:15), He was able to die in our place as the perfect sacrifice for our sins (2:14-17).

How thankful we can be that we have a Savior who understands and cares! — Richard De Haan

God understands your heartache,
He knows the bitter pain;
O trust Him in the darkness,
You cannot trust in vain. — Smith

NO ONE UNDERSTANDS LIKE JESUS.

HAPPILY EVER AFTER?

READ:
1 Peter 3:1-12

**Do not let your adornment be merely outward, . . . rather let it be the hidden person of the heart.
—1 Peter 3:3-4**

THE BIBLE IN ONE YEAR:
■ 2 Chronicles 33–36

Despite what we've heard in countless fairy tales, there's no guarantee that people who get married will live happily ever after. Things go wrong — sometimes terribly wrong. Even with the best of intentions, we may find ourselves in a house full of resentment, hostility, unrest, and misery. There is no heartache quite like the heartache of an unhappy marriage.

Yet, a difficult marriage can be the setting in which God can deal with "the hidden person of the heart" (1 Peter 3:4). Instead of focusing only on what is wrong with our partner, we need to open our heart to the Lord and ask Him to confront the evil in us. He will begin to do so — gently, gradually, graciously. We will begin to see ourselves as we are — and not as the thoughtful, patient, polite, gracious, giving, and self-controlled person we had imagined ourselves to be. We will come to see how much we ourselves need the Savior's forgiveness and the Spirit's help to do what is right and loving (vv.1-12), even when we have been wronged.

Our growth in grace may change our spouse, or it may not. There are no guarantees in life except God's love. But with His help, *we* can change. Although all our marriage ills may not be cured, God's grace can make *us* well. — David Roper

"For better or for worse," we pledge,
Through sickness and through strife;
And by the help and grace of God
We'll keep these vows for life. — D. De Haan

**SUCCESS IN MARRIAGE IS NOT FINDING
THE RIGHT PERSON BUT BECOMING THE RIGHT PERSON.**

PROFITABLE READING

READ:
2 Timothy 3:10-17

**You have known the Holy Scriptures, which are able to make you wise for salvation through faith which is in Christ Jesus.
—2 Timothy 3:15**

THE BIBLE IN ONE YEAR:
■ Ezra 1–4

Bible scholar William Barclay recalls the experience of a group of British soldiers during World War I. For a long time the men were in a relatively quiet standoff with the enemy. Among them was an atheist who, trying to fill up the empty days, went to the chaplain to ask if any books were available. The only book the chaplain had was the Bible.

The atheist refused the Bible at first, but then he took it and began to read the Old Testament at random. He came across the story of Esther and was so engrossed by it that he decided to read the whole Bible. As he did, he realized that what he was reading was true, and he received Jesus Christ as his Lord and Savior.

The apostle Paul stated in 2 Timothy 3:16 that "all Scripture . . . is profitable." It gives people the wisdom that leads to "salvation through faith which is in Christ Jesus" (v.15). Even passages that may seem boring and lacking in spiritual value have the power to transform people's lives.

If in our own reading we come across passages that we find uninspiring at first, let's trust the Holy Spirit to speak to our hearts and change our lives. Remember, when it comes to the Bible, all of it — from Genesis to Revelation — is inspired and profitable (v.16). — Vernon Grounds

The Bible has power to arrest and convict,
To reveal God's truth to our soul;
For in it we find the good news of the One
Who alone can cleanse and make whole. — Fitzhugh

**MANY BOOKS CAN INFORM YOU;
ONLY THE BIBLE CAN TRANSFORM YOU.**

YIELDING CONTROL

READ:
Romans 8:1-11

**To be carnally minded is death, but to be spiritually minded is life and peace.
—Romans 8:6**

THE BIBLE IN ONE YEAR:
■ Ezra 5–7

During a visit with a friend suffering from Lou Gehrig's disease, I asked what lessons God was teaching her as she traveled down this difficult road. Her immediate response was, "Loss of control."

She had always been a highly organized, independent person whose corporate job involved long hours and frequent travel. Now she had to depend on others for everything from getting dressed to brushing her teeth. Unable to move her arms or legs, she had control over only what she thought and what she said. She knew that soon she would even lose her power of speech. "I used to stress over my job," she said, "and never really gave it to the Lord. Now, with almost all control gone, I can stress about [my physical limitation] or surrender it to Christ."

The question facing each of us is, "Will I retain control of my life or yield it to the Lord today?" To live only for what I want is to be controlled by the sinful nature. Paul said that this leads to death, "but to be spiritually minded is life and peace" (Romans 8:6).

To one degree or another, we will all lose control of our lives as we grow older. Yielding control to God is a choice we can make every day — starting today. — David McCasland

> *Although I may not understand*
> *The path You've laid for me,*
> *Complete surrender to Your will —*
> *Lord, this my prayer shall be.* — *Sherbert*

**TRUE FREEDOM COMES NOT FROM CHOOSING OUR WAY,
BUT FROM YIELDING TO GOD'S WAY.**

ON OUR SIDE

READ:
Romans 8:31-39

**If God is for us, who can be against us?
—Romans 8:31**

THE BIBLE IN ONE YEAR:
■ Ezra 8–10

A young Christian was working at his first job, the night shift at a refrigerator assembly plant, trying to earn money for Bible college. The people he worked with were pretty rough, and he was laughed at for being a Christian. The harassment occurred at every break and gradually became more and more vulgar.

One night was worse than the others. They were laughing at him, swearing, and mocking Jesus. He was about ready to quit. Then an older man sitting at the back of the room said, "That's enough! Find someone else to pick on." They immediately backed off. Later the older fellow said to the young man, "I saw that you were having a difficult time, and I wanted to let you know I'm on your side."

Maybe you're a Christian and are standing alone against others who do not know God. It seems as if Satan is winning. The Lord may send a fellow believer to stand with you. But even if He doesn't, you can be confident that He is on your side. He demonstrated that by sending His Son Jesus to die in your place on the cross. You can never be separated from His love and care (Romans 8:38-39).

With assurance you can now say, "If God is for us, who can be against us?" (v.31). — Dave Egner

I stand alone, dear Lord — stay by my side,
In all my daily needs please be my guide;
O grant to me Your grace, for this I pray,
To carry on my work from day to day. — Anon.

WITH GOD ON OUR SIDE WE ARE NEVER OUTNUMBERED.

THE MAN NOBODY MISSED

READ:
2 Chronicles 21:4-20

**He reigned in Jerusalem eight years and, to no one's sorrow, departed.
—2 Chronicles 21:20**

THE BIBLE IN ONE YEAR:
■ Nehemiah 1–3

A man told me that his oldest brother had died. When I expressed surprise that I had not heard the news already, he said, "We never had it announced in any way. He cared about nobody and nobody cared about him."

At first I was shocked by what I heard, and then I remembered a sermon I had read many years ago, titled, "The Man Nobody Missed." In 2 Chronicles 21 we read about that man, King Jehoram. Early in his reign he killed all his brothers and other potential rivals. He led the nation in the worship of false gods, had a troubled 8-year reign, and died from a terrible, painful disease "to no one's sorrow" (v.20).

It's a sad story. Jehoram wasn't missed when he died, because he had been a self-centered and godless person. The Bible gives Jehoram this short and tragic epitaph: "He did evil in the sight of the LORD" (v.6).

Let's remember that the extent to which we care about our relationships — both with God and the people He has put in our lives — will determine how much we will be missed when we pass on. If we keep this in mind and live to please God and show love to others, we'll be missed when we depart this earthly scene. — Herb Vander Lugt

One life for Christ is all I have,
One life for Him so dear,
One life for doing all I can
With every passing year. — Brandt

**MAKE OTHERS HAPPY WHEREVER YOU GO,
NOT WHENEVER YOU GO.**

DYING TO LIVE

READ:
Luke 9:18-26

If anyone desires to come after Me, let him deny himself, and take up his cross daily, and follow Me.
—Luke 9:23

THE BIBLE IN ONE YEAR:
■ Nehemiah 4–6

The cross in Roman times was designed for death. It had no other use. So what did Jesus mean when He said that anyone who wants to follow Him must "take up his cross daily"? (Luke 9:23). He wasn't saying that we must all be crucified. The "cross" to which He was referring is the act of putting to death our own heart's desires and quietly submitting to God's will.

Such dying is denying our need for larger homes, more compliant children, more accommodating mates. It's putting up with misunderstanding, embarrassment, and loss of esteem. It's accepting our unchangeable circumstances. Missionary and poet Amy Carmichael, who knew much about pain and suffering, wrote, "In acceptance lieth peace."

Jesus said we must take up our cross *daily*. We are to rise each morning and cheerfully, bravely shoulder our load, because there is something else that is "daily." It is the continuous, sufficient grace of the One whose strength is made perfect in our weakness (2 Corinthians 12:9), and who will never leave us nor forsake us (Hebrews 13:5). He promises that through our dying He will make us more alive than ever before (1 Corinthians 15:53-57).

Are you dying to live? — David Roper

> *Day by day, to fight the battle,*
> *Day by day, Thy will to do,*
> *Day by day, the cross to carry,*
> *Seeking only to be true.* — Fisher

IN ACCEPTANCE WE FIND PEACE.

SEASONS OF MOTHERHOOD

READ:
Luke 2:1-7,25-35

To everything there is a season, a time for every purpose under heaven.
—Ecclesiastes 3:1

THE BIBLE IN ONE YEAR:
■ Esther 1–3

As a pastor, I've ministered to many women during their seasons of motherhood. I have called on mothers in the hospital and rejoiced with them for their precious baby who had come into the world. I've counseled with anxious mothers and tried to assure them that God was watching over their rebellious teenager. I've stood with mothers at the bedside of an injured or ill child and felt their pain. And I've cried with them in their grief when their son or daughter died.

Mary, the mother of Jesus, also experienced these times of joy and sorrow. What joy when the Christ-child was born! (Luke 2:7). What excitement when the shepherds and later the wise men came to worship Him! (vv.8-20; Matthew 2:1-12). What uneasiness when Simeon prophesied that a sword would pierce her soul! (Luke 2:35). And what heart-wrenching grief as Mary watched her Son dying on the cross! (John 19:25-30). But her seasons of motherhood didn't end with that terrible scene. She rejoiced that He rose from the grave. And because she trusted Him as her Savior, she is now in heaven with Him.

A mother experiences great joys and intense sorrows. But if she submits her life to God, every season of her motherhood serves His eternal purposes. — Herb Vander Lugt

Thank You, Lord, for motherhood
With all its vale of tears,
For happy moments never dimmed
Through all the many years. — Strecker

MOTHERHOOD IS A SACRED PARTNERSHIP WITH GOD.

AWESOME!

READ:
Exodus 33:12-23

Woe is me, for I am undone! . . . for my eyes have seen the King, the LORD of hosts. —Isaiah 6:5

THE BIBLE IN ONE YEAR:
■ Nehemiah 10–13

Just a few miles from New Mexico's Carlsbad Caverns is Lechuguilla Cave. Explorers who have descended into its interior describe a wonderland whose beauty is beyond almost anything they have ever seen.

One geologist noted, "Everything is alien. . . . I've been in caves that are so beautiful that you just have to leave. You just can't take it." That's an interesting dilemma for explorers, isn't it? To be surrounded by beauty that is overwhelming to the eyes.

Their experience gives us a clue to the problem we have with understanding a holy God. He is so arrayed in splendor, so pure in His goodness, and so beautiful in His character that our sin-darkened eyes cannot bear to look on Him. We cannot endure His glory.

This was the experience of two people in the Old Testament. When Moses asked to see God's glory, the Almighty had to shield him from seeing His face (Exodus 33:18-23). And when Isaiah caught a glimpse of God's majesty, he cried out, "Woe is me, for I am undone!" (Isaiah 6:5).

Lord, Your awesome splendor, goodness, and beauty reveal the defects in us. Thank You for being so loving and merciful. And thank You for making us holy and acceptable to You through Christ. —Mart De Haan

Holy, Holy, Holy! Though the darkness hide Thee,
Though the eye of sinful man Thy glory may not see;
Only Thou art holy—there is none beside Thee,
Perfect in power, in love, and purity. —Heber

**GOD'S AWESOME PRESENCE IS BOTH
CONVICTING AND COMFORTING.**

LIGHT UP YOUR WORLD

READ:
Ephesians 5:8-14

**You are the light
of the world.
—Matthew 5:14**

THE BIBLE IN ONE YEAR:
■ Nehemiah 7–9

My daughter Julie and her friend Jenni were driving one evening from their college to a nearby town. Along the way, they passed through a community that had an eerie darkness to it because of a power outage. It was strange — almost frightening — to drive through that blacked-out community.

As they left the town behind, they noticed a light up ahead. It shone like a beacon. And when they reached it, they were pleasantly surprised to find that the only light in the darkness was a church. A house of worship was lighting up their world.

This is exactly how people should see us as Christians — a bright and inviting light in this world darkened by sin. Jesus brought us out of the darkness, and He said that we as His followers are "the light of the world" (Matthew 5:14). And now we are to "walk as children of light" (Ephesians 5:8).

It's a huge challenge that should make us think seriously about how we live. Ask yourself, "Am I a light in anyone's life? Are my life and words guiding people out of the darkness and into the light of Jesus?"

It's dark in the world — and we have the light. Are we lighting the way? — Dave Branon

*Lord, let me be a shining light
In all I say and do,
May Your great love be seen in me
And lead someone to You.* — Sper

**YOUR LIFE WILL EITHER SHED LIGHT
OR CAST A SHADOW.**

AN END TO REVENGE

READ:
Romans 12:9-21

Do not avenge yourselves, but rather give place to wrath; for it is written, "Vengeance is Mine, I will repay," says the Lord.
—Romans 12:19

THE BIBLE IN ONE YEAR:
■ Esther 4–7

The newspaper headline read: NO END TO CYCLE OF REVENGE IN MIDEAST. In the wake of suicide bombings and military retaliation, the article told of a 28-year-old man consumed with avenging his uncle's death. "When someone dear to you is killed," he said, "you can't sleep; you have to do something." But even after killing two men he considered enemies, he still had no sense of satisfaction. No one can ever win by trying to even the score.

Is there a cycle of revenge in your life today? Perhaps it's an ongoing verbal battle with a co-worker, a spouse, or a child. It may be a simmering feud with a neighbor or even someone at church. Whatever it is, our Lord wants it to end.

Revenge is a weapon of such devastating power that God alone can handle it. He said, "Vengeance is Mine, I will repay" (Romans 12:19). The weapon He has entrusted to us is kindness: "If your enemy is hungry, feed him; if he is thirsty, give him a drink . . . . Do not be overcome by evil, but overcome evil with good" (vv.20-21).

This doesn't mean that we shouldn't appeal to courts for justice in some cases. But because God is just, we don't have to personally repay those who wrong us. With kindness and love, we can bring an end to revenge. — David McCasland

> *Now evil prospers, falsehood reigns,*
> *And darkness dims the light;*
> *But we rejoice to know that Christ*
> *Will one day set things right.* — *Sper*

**REVENGE GETS YOU EVEN WITH YOUR ENEMY;
FORGIVENESS PUTS YOU ABOVE HIM.**

PLANTING GOOD SEEDS

READ:
Hosea 10:12-15

Break up your fallow ground, for it is time to seek the LORD.
—Hosea 10:12

THE BIBLE IN ONE YEAR:
■ Esther 8–10

As a new gardener, I soon learned that uncultivated soil was resistant to seed planting and growth. But when I planted good seeds in well-prepared soil, heaven's sun and rain did their part until the harvest came. Well-prepared soil, the right seeds, and God's blessing are essential for fruitfulness, not only in gardening but also in Christian living.

God's prophet Hosea preached this principle to the people of Israel. They had sown seeds of wickedness and trusted in their own way instead of God's. Now they were eating the bitter fruit of lies, especially the lie that their safety and success came from their own military strength (Hosea 10:13).

Hosea pleaded with Israel to go God's way — to break up the sin-hardened soil of their hearts and to "seek the LORD" (v.12). If they would sow seeds of righteousness, they would reap the Lord's mercy and He would rain blessings on them.

Is the soil of your heart resistant to God and His Word, rather than receptive? Do you trust in your own way rather than in God's? Then it's time to seek the Lord in honest repentance, to sow right actions and attitudes in your life, and to grow His way. Above all, depend on His power rather than your own to make you fruitful. —Joanie Yoder

If you sow the seeds of wickedness,
Its lies will cloud your mind;
If you scatter seeds of righteousness,
God's blessing you will find. —Sper

THE FLOWERS OR WEEDS THAT SPRING UP TOMORROW
ARE IN THE SEEDS WE SOW TODAY.

HOW DESERVING ARE WE?

READ:
Deuteronomy 9:1-6

The LORD your God is not giving you this good land to possess because of your righteousness.
—Deuteronomy 9:6

THE BIBLE IN ONE YEAR:
■ Job 1–4

I remember the day our secondhand refrigerator finally broke down. As a young newlywed employed by a Christian ministry, I didn't have much money to spend on repairs. Not knowing where to turn for reliable help, I called a friend in the electrical business. He assured me that he would handle the problem. Later that evening, I found a brand-new refrigerator in our kitchen. I asked myself, "What did I do to deserve such help?"

It's easy to think we deserve the help that others graciously give us. When we're successful, we tend to assume that we deserve our possessions. Success goes to our head. It makes us proud and can even turn us away from God.

In Deuteronomy 9, we read of God's reminder to Israel about the reason they would be successful. God wanted His people to remember that He was leading them into the land to fulfill His purpose and promises. They would succeed because of Him, not because of their own righteousness (vv.4-5). He knew they would be tempted to become ungrateful after they were prospering in the Promised Land.

Ungratefulness is a temptation for us today as well. If our endeavors are successful, let's make sure we are thankful to God for His goodness, help, and protection. — Albert Lee

Help me, O Lord, lest my heart become proud,
For all of my talents by You are endowed;
Nothing I have can I claim as my own —
What mercy and grace in my life You have shown! — DJD

**WE DON'T NEED MORE TO BE THANKFUL FOR,
WE JUST NEED TO BE MORE THANKFUL.**

I Was Deceived

Read:
John 8:34-47

[The devil] is a liar
and the father of it.
—John 8:44

The Bible In One Year:
■ Job 5–7

It was dusk. My wife and I had just strolled across the famous Charles Bridge in Prague when a man approached us with a wad of money in his hand. "Forty-two Czech korunas for one dollar," he said. The official rate was about 35Ks for one US dollar. So I exchanged 50 dollars for 2,100 Czech korunas.

That evening I told my son about my good fortune. "Dad, I should have told you," he apologized. "Never exchange money on the street." We looked at the bills. The 100K note was a good Czech bill, but the two 1,000K bills were worthless. They looked like Czech money but were Bulgarian notes no longer in circulation. I had been deceived — and robbed!

Satan employs similar tactics (John 8:44). He capitalizes on the deceitfulness of sin, using its "passing pleasures" (Hebrews 11:25) to hide the pain that always follows. Sin may be attractive, even offering something that in and of itself is good — but behind it is deception.

Our best defense against that deception is to have a growing knowledge of God's Word. As we follow the psalmist's example, we'll keep from being deceived by sin: "Your Word I have hidden in my heart, that I might not sin against You" (Psalm 119:11). — Dennis De Haan

Give me, O Lord, a strong desire
To look within Your Word each day;
Help me to hide it in my heart,
Lest from its truth my feet would stray. — Branon

GOD'S TRUTH UNCOVERS SATAN'S LIES.

LET'S KEEP DIGGING

READ:
Hebrews 10:32-39

You have need of endurance, so that after you have done the will of God, you may receive the promise. —Hebrews 10:36

THE BIBLE IN ONE YEAR:
■ Job 8–10

Scottish physician A. J. Cronin (1896-1981) was forced by illness to take a leave of absence from his medical practice. He then decided to write a novel. But when half done, he became disheartened and threw his manuscript into a garbage can.

Totally discouraged, Cronin was walking the Scottish Highlands and saw a man digging in a bog, trying to drain it for use as a pasture. As Cronin talked with him, the man said, "My father dug at this bog and never made a pasture. But my father knew and I know that it's only by digging you can make a pasture. So I keep on digging."

Rebuked and remotivated, Cronin went home, picked his manuscript out of the garbage can, and finished it. That novel, *Hatter's Castle,* sold three million copies. Cronin left his medical practice and became a world-famous writer.

At times, you and I may feel trapped by circumstances that demand patience and persistence. Are we willing to keep digging away at whatever "bog" God has assigned to us?

The book of Hebrews tells us that we have "need of endurance" (10:36), and that we must "run with endurance the race that is set before us" (12:1). How? By "looking unto Jesus, the author and finisher of our faith" (v.2). With Christ as our example, let's keep on digging! — Vernon Grounds

Whatever you're doing for Jesus today,
Be sure to keep at it — don't stop or delay;
If you are discouraged, don't give up your place,
For God will sustain you by His matchless grace. —Hess

**IN SERVING THE LORD,
IT'S ALWAYS TOO SOON TO QUIT.**

BETTER THAN GOLD

READ:
Psalm 119:121-128

I love Your command-
ments more than gold.
—Psalm 119:127

THE BIBLE IN ONE YEAR:
■ Job 11–13

The Gideons, a worldwide network of people who distribute Bibles, had been operating in the former Soviet Union less than a year. It didn't take them long to find opportunities to pass out copies of the Scriptures in Russian. Wherever they went, they were welcomed by people who were hungry for the Word of God.

In one town they were given permission to pass out New Testaments at an elementary school. The police chief accompanied them, so when they were driven past the assigned school they wondered if they were being taken in for questioning. After driving 6 or 7 kilometers, they pulled up in front of a different school and were told to hand out the Bibles. They distributed copies to every student and staff member.

Later, the leader of their group asked the chief of police, "Why did we switch schools?" He calmly replied, "Because my two children attend school here. I wanted to make sure they have Bibles."

God's Word is precious and valuable (Psalm 19:10), especially to those who have either limited or no access to it. This Russian official used his power to get copies of the Scriptures for his children — and maybe so he could read it too.

How precious is God's Word to you? — Dave Egner

More precious than gold is God's Word to me,
Much better than pearls from deep in the sea;
For in the Lord's words I take great delight,
And it is my joy each day and each night. — Fitzhugh

**COMPARED TO GOD'S WORD,
THE WORLD'S RICHES ARE FOOL'S GOLD.**

No Partiality

READ:
James 2:1-9

**Do not hold the faith of our Lord Jesus Christ, the Lord of glory, with partiality.
—James 2:1**

THE BIBLE IN ONE YEAR:
■ Job 14–17

A man attended a church regularly for several months, but he was always ignored. Because no one knew who he was, and he looked out-of-place with his old and worn-out clothes, no one ever took the time to speak to him.

One Sunday as he took a seat in church, he intentionally left his hat on. As the pastor stood on the platform and looked out over the audience, he noticed the man with the hat right away. So he summoned one of the deacons and asked him to tell the man that he forgot to remove his hat. When the deacon spoke to the man, he responded with a big smile and said, "I thought that would do it. I have attended this church for 6 months, and you are the first person who has ever talked to me."

There is no place for prejudice or favoritism in the family of God. We who have been born again through faith in Jesus are equals in God's sight. And that equality should be evident in the way we treat other believers.

We must be hospitable and courteous to all, regardless of their race, social status, or appearance. When we show favoritism, we sin against people whom God loves and for whom Christ died. Let's be gracious to everyone and be careful to avoid showing partiality. — Richard De Haan

All those who know and love the Lord
Must show by word and deed
That they will not discriminate
But welcome those in need. — D. De Haan

**PREJUDICE BUILDS WALLS;
LOVE BREAKS THEM DOWN.**

FEEDING JESUS' SHEEP

READ:
John 21:15-19

**Simon, son of Jonah, do you love Me? . . . Feed My sheep.
—John 21:17**

THE BIBLE IN ONE YEAR:
■ Job 18–20

What will keep us serving the Lord in our church and community when the going gets tough? Although we may be sensitive to the needs of others, that alone isn't enough. Nor should we be driven by a need that *we* have—a desire to be appreciated or loved by others. Our needs are deep, and only God can satisfy them. The more we try to satisfy them with anything else—even God's work—the more dissatisfied we will become.

Even love for God's people, His sheep, won't keep us going. People can be unlovable and insufferable. We may come to resent them.

No, the only sufficient incentive for service is our love for the Lord, and it's the love of Christ that compels us (2 Corinthians 5:14). No other motivation will do. In *My Utmost For His Highest*, Oswald Chambers wrote, "If we are devoted to the cause of humanity, we shall soon be crushed and brokenhearted, . . . but if our motive is to love God, no ingratitude can hinder us from serving our fellowmen."

In one of His last conversations with Peter, Jesus asked him, "Simon, son of Jonah, do you love Me?" Peter answered, "Lord, You know all things; You know that I love You." Jesus *then* said, "Feed My sheep" (John 21:17).

Are you motivated by love for Christ? —David Roper

More love to Thee, O Christ, more love to Thee!
Hear Thou the prayer I make on bended on knee;
This is my earnest plea: More love, O Christ, to Thee,
More love to Thee, more love to Thee! —Prentiss

TO LOVE CHRIST IS TO SERVE CHRIST.

A Departing Blessing

READ:
Luke 24:44-53

**While He blessed them, . . . He was parted from them and carried up into heaven.
—Luke 24:51**

THE BIBLE IN ONE YEAR:
■ Psalms 13-15

A cancer-stricken believer was dying. I was in his room as his family gathered around him. One by one he spoke to his children, to their spouses, and to his young grandchildren. He gave each a loving, tender blessing. Even his warnings were spoken with gentleness. He reminded them to keep the Lord in the center of their lives. We wept together, knowing that soon he would no longer be with us. A few days later he was gone.

Our Savior was doing much the same thing just before He ascended to heaven. Rather than weep as they saw Him leave, His disciples were filled with great joy, even though they understood only dimly how they would experience His blessings. But Jesus would soon send the Holy Spirit to indwell them (Acts 1-2). He would carry on a ministry of intercession for them "at the right hand of God" (Romans 8:34). And the promise of His return would comfort them (1 Thessalonians 4:13-18).

As we think about our Savior ascending to heaven, let's rejoice in the blessings He left us. And as we have occasion, let's encourage our loved ones to keep Jesus at the center of their lives. Someday we will depart from this earth, and our example and words may be the most precious blessing we can leave behind. —Dave Egner

Your parting words, O Lord, give hope,
They're filled with promise, joy, and love;
Help us to share what You have done
With grace and power from above. —D. De Haan

**CHRIST DEPARTED SO THAT THE HOLY SPIRIT
COULD BE IMPARTED.**

MISQUOTE

READ:
Deuteronomy 4:1-14

Do not add to His words, lest He rebuke you, and you be found a liar.
—Proverbs 30:6

THE BIBLE IN ONE YEAR:
■ Job 25–27

Imagine the frustration of a mother as she tries to gather her family for supper. Her 8-year-old son comes through the door smuggling a dead bird behind his back. "Call Ann for dinner," says his mother. "Then wash your hands and come to the table."

A minute later the 4-year-old daughter comes running into the kitchen, sobbing uncontrollably. Her brother had just waved the stiff bird under her nose and told her that if she wasn't at the table in 17 seconds, Mom wouldn't let her go out and play for a whole week.

This story about a misquoted mother doesn't begin to capture the confusion that follows when we misquote the heavenly Father. Often we become preoccupied with our own ideas of how things should be, like Job's friends, who didn't speak rightly about the Lord (Job 42:7). The result is that we say more, or less, than God actually said in His Word (Deuteronomy 4:2). We need to make sure we know exactly where His words stop and our opinions begin. If we don't, we may misrepresent Him, and Proverbs 30:6 warns that we are then in danger of being found liars before God.

Let's take care that we don't express our opinions as if they were God's words. — Mart De Haan

Lord, grant us wisdom to discern
The truth that You've made known,
And may we never teach one word
Beyond what You have shown. — D. De Haan

**WE MUST ADJUST OUR LIVES TO THE BIBLE—
NEVER THE BIBLE TO OUR LIVES.**

SHINE!

READ:
Matthew 5:14-16

**I am the light of the world. He who follows Me shall not walk in darkness, but have the light of life.
—John 8:12**

THE BIBLE IN ONE YEAR:
■ Job 28–31

Author Anne Lamott once wrote that the people she admires have "purpose, heart, balance, gratitude, joy . . . . They follow a brighter light than the glimmer of their own candle; they are part of something beautiful."

In my experience, such people are not simply religious. They are committed disciples of Christ. Jesus explained why His followers have a sort of luminous quality. "I am the light of the world. He who follows Me shall not walk in darkness, but have the light of life" (John 8:12). Believing in Jesus as our Savior, we now can light up the world. We are told, "Let your light so shine before men, that they may see your good works and glorify your Father in heaven" (Matthew 5:16).

This doesn't mean we must always display an artificial cheerfulness. Many of us don't possess a sunny disposition. But in the Holy Spirit's power, we can be like the Christians to whom Paul wrote, "You shine as lights in the world" (Philippians 2:15). As Francis of Assisi put it: "Lord, make me an instrument of Your peace! Where there is hatred, let me sow love; . . . where there is darkness, light."

Just as the moon reflects the radiance of the sun, so we who believe and follow the Savior can reflect Him who is the light of the world. — Vernon Grounds

There is sunshine in my soul today,
More glorious and bright
Than glows in any earthly sky,
For Jesus is my light. —Hewitt

**A WORLD IN DARKNESS
NEEDS THE LIGHT OF THE GOSPEL.**

CONFESSION & CONSEQUENCES

READ:
Joshua 7:1-6,19-26

I said, "I will confess my transgressions to the LORD," and You forgave the iniquity of my sin. —Psalm 32:5

THE BIBLE IN ONE YEAR:
■ Job 32–34

She brutally murdered two people in 1983, but in prison Karla Tucker confessed her sins to God and became a vibrant Christian. Many people hoped her transformation would persuade legal authorities to change her punishment to life imprisonment. But the courts rejected all appeals, and her execution was carried out in 1998.

I thought about Karla as I was reading the tragic story of Achan. I was impressed by his confession: "Indeed I have sinned against the LORD God of Israel, and this is what I have done" (Joshua 7:20). Those words make me think it possible that he, like King David many years later (Psalm 32:5), was forgiven by God. But Achan's sin had caused the death of 36 Israelites (Joshua 7:5), and he had to pay the penalty for his actions.

Even after we have received God's forgiveness, we may still have to face the consequences of our sin. If we have lied, mistreated someone, behaved irresponsibly, damaged someone's property, or broken a law of the land, we still must do our best to make right any wrongs we have committed.

Yes, it's wonderful to know we're forgiven when we confess our sins to God. But that doesn't mean we're exempt from all of sin's consequences. That's why confessing sin is good, but saying no to sin is even better. — Herb Vander Lugt

We love You, Lord, and want to do
What's pleasing in Your sight;
Help us to fear sin's consequence,
So we will do what's right. — Sper

SIN BRINGS FEAR, BUT CONFESSION BRINGS FREEDOM.

THE WINNING COMBINATION

READ:
1 Timothy 6:3-19

Godliness with contentment is great gain. —1 Timothy 6:6

THE BIBLE IN ONE YEAR:
■ Job 35-37

I have often been encouraged by people without their realizing it. I remember walking through the main lounge of a Christian retirement community late one evening. The residents had gone to their rooms for the night, except for one elderly woman. Unaware of my presence, she patiently worked on a jigsaw puzzle and joyfully hummed to herself. She seemed to be quite content.

I began to wonder, "How can people find true contentment, no matter what their circumstances?" The apostle Paul addressed this issue in 1 Timothy 6. He warned against corrupt people who see godliness as a means for financial profit (v.5). A more subtle error among Christians is the belief that godliness-plus-money is life's winning combination. Paul corrected both errors by stating the *real* winning combination: "Godliness with contentment is great gain" (v.6). He urged believers to be satisfied with food and clothing (vv.7-8). "The love of money is a root of all kinds of evil" (v.10), but loving and trusting God is the root of all contentment.

How about you? Are you experiencing the joy that comes when godliness is combined with contentment? If so, you've got the winning combination. —Joanie Yoder

O Lord, give me the grace to be
Content with what You give to me.
No, more than that, let me rejoice
In all You send, for it's Your choice! —Anon.

**TRUE CONTENTMENT IS NOT IN HAVING EVERYTHING,
BUT IN BEING SATISFIED WITH EVERYTHING YOU HAVE.**

Our God Is Marching On

READ:
Habakkuk 2:6-20

**The LORD is in His holy temple. Let all the earth keep silence before Him.
—Habakkuk 2:20**

THE BIBLE IN ONE YEAR:
■ Job 38–42

In 1861, during the US Civil War, author and lecturer Julia Ward Howe visited Washington, DC. One day she went outside the city and saw a large number of soldiers marching. Early the next morning she awoke with words for a song in her mind.

She was aware of all the ugliness of the war, but her faith led her to write: "Mine eyes have seen the glory of the coming of the Lord." She saw, I believe, that in spite of and through all the ugliness, God was "marching on" toward the day when He will right the wrongs of the ages.

The prophet Habakkuk came to a similar conclusion. Chapter 1 of his book tells us how troubled he was when he learned that God was going to punish the people of Judah by letting them be conquered by the wicked Babylonians. In chapter 2, God assured His servant that — in spite of and through all the ugliness and wrongs of history — He is "marching on" toward the day when "the earth will be filled with the knowledge of the glory of the LORD" (v.14).

If we believe that God is "marching on," in spite of all the brutal conflicts that mark our day, we will not despair. We can quietly await the final verdict from our Lord, who rules the universe from "His holy temple" (v.20). — Herb Vander Lugt

God rules as Sovereign on His throne,
He judges great and small;
And those who would His earth destroy
Beneath His rod shall fall. — D. De Haan

**SOMEDAY THE SCALES OF JUSTICE
WILL BE PERFECTLY BALANCED.**

A GOOD NAME

READ:
Proverbs 10:1-7

**The memory of the righteous is blessed, but the name of the wicked will rot.
—Proverbs 10:7**

THE BIBLE IN ONE YEAR:
■ Psalms 1–4

On Memorial Day in the United States, thousands of people visit cemeteries and monuments to remember and honor their loved ones. They ponder a name carved in stone and recall the person for whom it stands.

This kind of reflection on the lives of those who have gone before us can encourage us to evaluate the way we are living today. When people hear our name, do they think of someone who is faithfully living for Christ?

King Solomon observed: "The memory of the righteous is blessed" (Proverbs 10:7). "A good name is to be chosen rather than great riches" (22:1). "A good name is better than precious ointment" (Ecclesiastes 7:1).

A solid reputation and loving relationships are high achievements. Honesty, integrity, and generosity in life are more valuable than the most expensive funeral. Perfume fades, but the aroma of our lives lingers on.

By our attitudes and actions, we are creating the memories that will be associated with our names in life and in death. Today we have an opportunity to renew our commitment to Christ and to the making of a good name — a name that honors Him and encourages those we love for years to come.

Do you have a good name? — David McCasland

This is the wish I always make,
The prayer I always pray:
Lord, may my life help other lives
It touches by the way. — Anon.

**THE MEMORY OF A FAITHFUL LIFE
SPEAKS MORE ELOQUENTLY THAN WORDS.**

THE UPSIDE OF SORROW

READ:
Ecclesiastes 7:1-14

**Sorrow is better than laughter, for by a sad countenance the heart is made better.
—Ecclesiastes 7:3**

THE BIBLE IN ONE YEAR:
■ Psalms 5–8

Sorrow can be good for the soul. It can uncover hidden depths in ourselves and in God.

Sorrow causes us to think earnestly about ourselves. It makes us ponder our motives, our intentions, our interests. We get to know ourselves as never before.

Sorrow also helps us to see God as we've never seen Him. Job said, out of his terrible grief, "I have heard of You by the hearing of the ear, but now my eye sees You" (Job 42:5).

Jesus, the perfect man, is described as "a man of sorrows," intimately acquainted with grief (Isaiah 53:3). It is hard to fathom, but even the incarnate Son of God learned and grew through the heartaches He suffered (Hebrews 5:8). As we think about His sorrow and His concern for our sorrow, we gain a better appreciation for what God is trying to accomplish in us through the grief we bear.

The author of Ecclesiastes wrote, "Sorrow is better than laughter, for by a sad countenance the heart is made better" (7:3). Those who don't let sorrow do its work, who deny it, trivialize it, or try to explain it away, remain shallow and indifferent. They never understand themselves or others very well. In fact, I think that before God can use us very much, we must first learn to mourn. — David Roper

When God leads through valleys of trouble,
His omnipotent hand we can trace;
For the trials and sorrows He sends us
Are valuable lessons of grace. — Anon.

**WE CAN LEARN MORE FROM SORROW
THAN FROM LAUGHTER.**

PLENTY OF PENCILS

READ:
2 Corinthians 12:7-10

When I am weak,
then I am strong.
—2 Corinthians 12:10

THE BIBLE IN ONE YEAR:
■ Psalms 9–12

My mother lives alone now. It's been 8 years since my dad died. She can't get out by herself except to take brief walks. She's having a terrible time with her short-term memory. Conversations are limited to a few repeated comments.

Yet she told me something profound. She said, "I was thinking the other day about my troubles, and I decided that I don't have anything to complain about. God's taking care of me and I've got people who are helping. My only trouble is that I can't remember anything, and I've got plenty of pencils and paper to write everything down."

The apostle Paul struggled with what he called "a thorn in the flesh" (2 Corinthians 12:7). But he found that in his weakness he experienced "the power of Christ" (v.9). He said, "I take pleasure in infirmities, in reproaches, in needs, in persecutions, in distresses, for Christ's sake" (v.10).

All of us have struggles. They may be related to age, finances, relationships, or a myriad of other difficulties. But if we truly set our heart to trusting God, and if we stay thankful even in the midst of our troubles, we'll be more likely to acknowledge that we "don't have anything to complain about." — Dave Branon

Even in my darkest hour
The Lord will bless me with His power;
His loving grace will sure abound,
In His sweet care I shall be found. — Brandt

**AS YOU GO THROUGH LIFE, CONCENTRATE ON
THE ROSES INSTEAD OF THE THORNS.**

BATTLE PRAISE

READ:
2 Chronicles 20:1-22

When they began to sing and to praise, the LORD set ambushes against the people ... who had come against Judah.
—2 Chronicles 20:22

THE BIBLE IN ONE YEAR:
■ Job 21 – 24

Visitors to the Military Museum in Istanbul, Turkey, can hear stirring music that dates back to the early years of the Ottoman Empire. Whenever their troops marched off to war, bands accompanied them.

Centuries earlier, worship singers led the people of Judah into battle, but there was a big difference. Whereas the Ottomans used music to instill self-confidence in their soldiers, the Jews used it to express their confidence in God.

Threatened by huge armies, King Jehoshaphat of Judah knew that his people were powerless to defend themselves. So he cried out to God for help (2 Chronicles 20:12). The Lord's answer came through Jahaziel, who said, "Do not be afraid nor dismayed . . . , for the battle is not yours, but God's" (v.15).

Jehoshaphat responded by worshiping and then by appointing singers to lead the army (vv.18,21). As the people sang, "Praise the LORD, for His mercy endures forever," God confused the invaders and they killed one another (vv.22-24).

No matter what battles we may face today, the Lord will help us when we cry out to Him. Instead of retreating in fear, we can march ahead with confidence in God's power and sing praise to Him. — Julie Link

> *Does all the world seem against you*
> *And you're in the battle alone?*
> *It's often when you are most helpless*
> *That God's mighty power is known.* — Anon.

PRAISE IS THE VOICE OF FAITH.

FINDING REST

READ:
Psalm 23

He restores my soul;
He leads me in the
paths of righteous-
ness for His name's
sake. —Psalm 23:3

THE BIBLE IN ONE YEAR:
■ Psalms 16–18

According to a survey conducted by an insurance company, one of every six workers in the US feels too busy to take all the vacation days he or she has earned. Even though studies show that a week's holiday each year can dramatically reduce stress and the risk of heart attack, many people just keep working.

A vacation can be good for body and soul. But many people don't have the luxury of time away from work and daily responsibilities. What can we do when we must remain in demanding circumstances?

Psalm 23 paints a beautiful word picture of a caring shepherd, secure sheep, and a tranquil scene of quiet meadows and still waters. But it is the Lord, our shepherd, who gives rest, not the green grass or the flowing stream. "He restores my soul; He leads me in the paths of righteousness for His name's sake" (v.3).

Rest is a place of peace that our spirits find in God. Neither the presence of those who oppose us nor the dark valley of death can keep us from what hymnwriter Cleland McAfee called "a place of quiet rest, near to the heart of God." Through prayer and meditation on His Word, we can commune with Him. In the Lord's presence we can experience the rest and renewal we so desperately need. — David McCasland

There is a place of comfort sweet,
Near to the heart of God,
A place where we our Savior meet,
Near to the heart of God. —McAfee

**SPENDING QUIET TIME WITH GOD
WILL BRING QUIET REST FROM GOD.**

IT'S TOO EASY

READ:
Romans 4:1-8

To him who does not work but believes on Him who justifies the ungodly, his faith is accounted for righteousness.
—Romans 4:5

THE BIBLE IN ONE YEAR:
■ Psalms 19—21

I read about an instant cake mix that was a big flop. The instructions said all you had to do was add water and bake. The company couldn't understand why it didn't sell — until their research discovered that the buying public felt uneasy about a mix that required only water. People thought it was too easy. So the company altered the formula and changed the directions to call for adding an egg to the mix in addition to the water. The idea worked, and sales jumped dramatically.

That story reminds me of how some people react to the plan of salvation. To them it sounds too easy and simple to be true, even though the Bible says, "By grace you have been saved through faith, . . . it is the gift of God, not of works" (Ephesians 2:8-9). They feel that there is something more they must do, something they must add to God's "recipe" for salvation. They think they must perform good works to gain God's favor and earn eternal life. But the Bible is clear — we are saved "not by works of righteousness which we have done, but according to His mercy" (Titus 3:5).

Unlike the cake-mix manufacturer, God has not changed His "formula" to make salvation more marketable. The gospel we proclaim must be free of works, even though it may sound too easy. — Richard De Haan

Salvation is a gift of God,
Not something earned or won;
He freely gives eternal life
To all who trust His Son. —Sper

**WE ARE SAVED BY GOD'S MERCY, NOT BY OUR MERIT—
BY CHRIST'S DYING, NOT BY OUR DOING.**

DRY SPELLS

READ:
Psalm 119:105-112

**Your Word is a lamp to my feet and a light to my path.
—Psalm 119:105**

THE BIBLE IN ONE YEAR:
■ Psalms 22–24

We may be able to relate to what the author of Psalm 119 had to say about the joy of reading and meditating on God's Word. But most of us have also experienced dry spells — times when we don't seem to get much from the Bible.

What can we do about those down times? Do we need to invest in a 20-volume set of commentaries, bury ourselves under a mound of theology books, or enroll in a Bible college or seminary? No, that isn't necessary.

Several years ago I heard about a six-point plan for getting something out of almost any passage of Scripture. It can make your Bible-reading time an opportunity to enjoy God and His message. Read a passage of Scripture and then ask yourself these questions:

- What did I like?
- What did I not like?
- What did I not understand?
- What did I learn about God?
- What should I do?
- What phrase can I take with me today?

This method can help to renew your appreciation for the Bible. Then you too will be able to say that God's Word is "the rejoicing of my heart" (Psalm 119:111). —Dave Branon

Give me the insight, Lord,
As I read Your Word today,
So I will truly understand
Your message and Your way. —Monroe

**THE BIBLE ISN'T A DRY BOOK
IF YOU KNOW ITS AUTHOR.**

HELP FOR THE HELPLESS

READ:
Hebrews 4:14-16

Let us therefore come boldly to the throne of grace, that we may obtain mercy and find grace to help in time of need. —Hebrews 4:16

THE BIBLE IN ONE YEAR:
■ Psalms 25–27

I sometimes ask people, "Where does it say in the Bible, 'God helps those who help themselves?'" Most say they're not sure, but the concept is so familiar that they think it must be somewhere in God's Word.

Actually, the Bible doesn't say that at all. It tells us just the opposite: God helps the helpless.

When you read the Gospels, you find that Jesus did not refuse to help the helpless. He did not withhold forgiveness and compassion from those who acknowledged their sin. He did not turn away from those who had no power to change. In fact, the people who distressed Him most were those who thought they didn't need any help at all.

God's thoughts are higher than ours (Isaiah 55:9), and He sees things differently than we do. We see our own ability to deal with problems; He shows us our weaknesses to teach us to rely on His strength. We take pride in our successes and begin to think we don't need God's help; He allows us to fail so He can teach us that true success comes through His grace.

Are you feeling helpless today? God's grace is available for those who recognize that they cannot help themselves. "Come boldly to the throne of grace" to find help in your time of need (Hebrews 4:16). — David Roper

> *Then boldly let our faith address*
> *The throne of grace and power;*
> *We shall obtain delivering grace*
> *In every needed hour.* — Watts

**GOD HELPS THOSE WHO KNOW
THEY ARE HELPLESS.**

Good Communicators

READ:
Ephesians 4:25–5:1

"Let each one of you speak truth with his neighbor," for we are members of one another.
—Ephesians 4:25

THE BIBLE IN ONE YEAR:
■ Psalms 28–30

A young boy and his stepfather had difficulty communicating with each other. The man was outgoing; the boy was quiet. The elder loved to fish; the youngster loved to read.

The stepfather, wanting to get close to the boy, took him on a fishing trip. The boy hated it but didn't know how to tell his stepfather directly. So he wrote him a note saying he wanted to go home. The man looked at it and stuck it in his pocket.

The fishing trip continued 4 more days. When they finally returned home, the boy shared his frustration with his mother and told her that his stepfather had paid no attention to his note. His mother said to him, "Son, your father can't read." The man had never shared this with the boy.

Good communication occurs not only when we know what we want to say, but also when we know the person to whom we are speaking. And to know one another requires a willingness to let others know our weaknesses and limitations.

Paul urged us as believers to speak truthfully with each other (Ephesians 4:25). He also admonished us to be "kind to one another, tenderhearted, forgiving one another" (v.32). That's Christlike love, and it provides the security in which good communication can thrive. — Haddon Robinson

We ought to speak the truth we feel
With careful thought for those who hear;
For truth and love must try to sense
What others feel, what others fear. — D. De Haan

**LISTEN TO UNDERSTAND,
THEN SPEAK WITH LOVE.**

BAD NEWS?

READ:
2 Peter 3:1-13

The day of the Lord will come . . . , in which the heavens will pass away with a great noise.
—2 Peter 3:10

THE BIBLE IN ONE YEAR:
■ Psalms 31–33

Some scientists tell us that in less than 10 million years the earth will be unable to sustain life because the sun will be too hot. This is depressing news for those who put all their hope in this world. It means that all of humankind's accomplishments will one day be wiped out.

For those who believe the Bible, though, this information is not surprising. We know that the earth in its present form will one day be destroyed "with fervent heat" (2 Peter 3:10). But that's not depressing news. On the contrary, we gladly anticipate the day when our sin-marred planet will be replaced by a world "in which righteousness dwells" (v.13). This expectation becomes for us a powerful incentive for "holy conduct and godliness" (v.11).

We also realize that our earthly lives have great significance, because through our prayers, our behavior, and our Christian witness we become partners with God as He works in the world. And one day, when He replaces our present cosmos with the perfect world, we will be given a place in our eternal home (John 14:2).

Because of our faith in Christ, we can be filled with joy and hope. The Lord wants to use our life in this world and He promises us a perfect world to come. — Herb Vander Lugt

Our earthly sight is limited,
The future we can't see;
Let come what may, one thing we know:
Our God will faithful be. — Hess

THE FUTURE IS BRIGHT IF CHRIST IS YOUR HOPE.

TASTE AND SAY!

READ:
Psalm 34:1-10

Oh, taste and see that the LORD is good; blessed is the man who trusts in Him!
—Psalm 34:8

THE BIBLE IN ONE YEAR:
■ Psalms 34–36

Do you believe God is good, even when life isn't? Mary did, and I gasped in amazement the day I heard her pastor share her story at her funeral.

Mary had been a widow — very poor, and housebound because of her ailments in old age. But like the psalmist, she had learned to praise God amid her hardships. Over the years she had come to savor with deep gratitude every good thing He sent her way.

Her pastor had occasionally visited her at home. Because of her crippling pain, it took her a long time to inch her way to the door to let him in. So he would call on the telephone and tell her that he was on his way and what time he would get there. Mary would then begin the slow, arduous journey to the door, reaching it about the time he arrived. Without fail, she would greet him with these triumphant words: "God is good!"

I've observed that those who speak most often about God's goodness are usually those with the most trials. They focus on the Lord's mercy and grace rather than on their troubles, and in so doing they taste His goodness. Mary's example not only challenges us to "taste and see," but also to taste and *say* that the Lord is good — even when life isn't. — Joanie Yoder

Though trials come, though fears assail
Through tests scarce understood,
One truth shines clear; it cannot fail—
My God is right and good. — Hager

**WHEN YOU TASTE GOD'S GOODNESS,
HIS PRAISE WILL BE ON YOUR LIPS.**

OUR UNSEEN HELPERS

READ:
Hebrews 1:5-14

Are [angels] not all
ministering spirits
sent forth to minister?
—Hebrews 1:14

THE BIBLE IN ONE YEAR:
■ Psalms 37-39

At one point in Martin Luther's stormy career, he received some discouraging news. But he responded by saying, "Recently I have been looking up at the night sky, spangled and studded with stars, and I found no pillars to hold them up. Yet they did not fall." Luther was encouraged as he reminded himself that the same unseen God who was upholding the universe was caring for him.

There is another unseen source of help from which God's children can take courage when facing a physical or spiritual crisis—angels! Those heavenly hosts are called "ministering spirits" (Hebrews 1:14), and they are instantly responsive to God's command. Little do we know what powerful protection and help they provide. When Jesus was enduring agony in Gethsemane, "an angel appeared to Him from heaven, strengthening Him" (Luke 22:43).

But you say, "I've never seen an angel." No need of that! It's enough to know that they do their quiet, protecting work beyond the realm of physical sight. They call no attention to themselves, lest we focus on them instead of Jesus. But their presence is real. Just knowing that these unseen helpers are on our side strengthens our trust in God, whom they faithfully serve. — Dennis De Haan

What ready help the Father gives
To struggling saints below!
He sends His heavenly ministers
To thwart our ancient foe. —D. De Haan

**THE ANGELS OF GOD ASSIST THE PEOPLE OF GOD
AS THEY DO THE WORK OF GOD.**

June 7

A PERSON IS THE PATHWAY

READ:
John 14:1-6

There is no other name under heaven given among men by which we must be saved. —Acts 4:12

THE BIBLE IN ONE YEAR:
■ Psalms 40–42

The pilot of a military plane was forced to parachute into a jungle in southeast Asia. How could he possibly find his way out? A local man saw what had happened and came to the pilot's rescue, slashing through the tangled underbrush. The frightened pilot cried out, "Where's the road? Where's the way out?" The rescuer shouted back, "No road! I'm the way! Follow me!" The pilot trusted the man, who led him through the jungle to safety.

Some people have a difficult time accepting similar words spoken by the Lord Jesus. He said, "I am the way, the truth, and the life. No one comes to the Father except through Me" (John 14:6). Critics call this teaching intolerant and divisive. But because the Son of God said it, and the Word of God records it, it is true no matter how much it is challenged. Faith in Jesus is the only way to eternal fellowship with God.

The pathway to God is not found by following a creed, developing moral character, or attending church. It's found by trusting Jesus to forgive our sin and reconcile us to the Father. When we open our hearts to the crucified and risen Savior, we are on the only pathway that will bring us home to God. — Vernon Grounds

Not all roads lead to God,
As many people claim;
There's only one true way —
Christ Jesus is His name. — Sper

NO ONE CAN BYPASS JESUS AND GET TO HEAVEN.

COMPANION AND GUIDE

READ:
John 16:5-15

When He, the Spirit of truth, has come, He will guide you into all truth.
—John 16:13

THE BIBLE IN ONE YEAR:
■ Psalms 43–45

Lisa Marino has a personal fitness coach who gives her daily advice and encouragement. But she's never seen him. As a participant in a program called "Life Practice," Lisa begins each day by sending a report of her diet, exercise, sleep, and stress to a Web site. Later, she receives an e-mail response from her coach. She says that the daily reporting helps keep her honest and focused on her fitness goals.

As Christians, we know the marvelous yet mysterious experience of having the Holy Spirit as our companion and guide — even though we can't see Him.

Jesus promised His disciples that when He left this earth He would send Someone else to be with them. "If I do not go away, the Helper will not come to you; but if I depart, I will send Him to you" (John 16:7).

The word translated "Helper" or "Comforter" means "called to one's side or aid." Bible scholar W. E. Vine says that it signifies Someone who can be to us what Christ was to His disciples.

Though He's invisible to our eyes, the Holy Spirit is with us every day, just as Jesus walked with His disciples on earth. He keeps us honest, focused, and encouraged so that we too can glorify Christ. — David McCasland

When Christ ascended in the clouds,
He sent the Spirit back
To comfort all who follow Him,
Providing what we lack. — Sper

**THE FATHER GAVE US THE SPIRIT
TO MAKE US LIKE HIS SON.**

ROUGH GOING

READ:
John 16:19-33

In the world you will
have tribulation; but
be of good cheer, I
have overcome the
world. —John 16:33

THE BIBLE IN ONE YEAR:
■ Psalms 46–48

There's a lake near our home in the mountains that is known for good fishing. To get there, I had to hike 2 miles up a steep ridge — a hard climb for an old-timer like me. But then I discovered that it's possible to drive within a half-mile of the lake. I spent most of a day driving several mountain roads until I found the one that got me the closest. Then I carefully mapped the road so I could find it again.

Several months later, I drove the road again. I came to a section that was much worse than I remembered — rocky, rutted, and steep. I wondered if I had missed a turn, so I stopped and checked my map. There, penciled alongside the stretch on which I was driving, were the words: "Rough and steep. Hard going." I was on the right road.

Jesus said that our life's journey will be rough going if we choose to follow Him. "In the world you will have tribulation" (John 16:33). So we shouldn't be surprised if our path becomes difficult, nor should we believe we've taken a wrong turn. We can "be of good cheer" because Jesus also said that in Him we can have peace, for He has "overcome the world" (v.33).

If you're following Christ and experiencing some bumpy times, take heart — you're on the right road! — David Roper

I know not if tomorrow's way
Be steep or rough;
But when Christ's hand is guiding me,
That is enough. — Anon.

**FOLLOWING JESUS IS ALWAYS RIGHT—
BUT NOT ALWAYS EASY.**

TRUTH: FRIEND OR FOE?

READ:
2 Chronicles 18:1-7

Have I therefore become your enemy because I tell you the truth?
—Galatians 4:16

THE BIBLE IN ONE YEAR:
■ Psalms 49–51

"Truth was my biggest enemy until it became my only friend," said Thelma, a former prostitute and drug addict.

People whose sin has pulled them down aren't the only ones who need to hear Thelma's testimony. Those whose sin has taken them to the heights of wealth and power also need to hear it.

After the truth came out about corruption in several major US corporations, a reporter said, "This isn't about executive salaries and perks; it's about truth."

Like corrupt executives, Israel's King Ahab was a rich and powerful person who got in trouble because he surrounded himself with advisers who told him the lies he wanted to hear rather than the truth he needed to know (2 Chronicles 18:4-7). His friends led him to a tragic dead end (vv.33-34).

Unlike Ahab, Thelma came to the point of realizing that lies were phony friends. In that moment, she turned and faced her biggest fear — truth — and found that what she was running from was actually what she was looking for: God. All her attempts to save herself with lies led to the brink of self-destruction; but when she turned to the God of all truth, He made her a new creation (2 Corinthians 5:17).

Have you made truth your friend or your foe?   —Julie Link

QUESTIONS TO PONDER
Have you surrounded yourself with friends who tell you the truth or lies? Is there a truth you're refusing to face? Have you turned to Christ, who is the truth?

**THOSE WHO LISTEN TO LIES
LOSE THE ABILITY TO HEAR THE TRUTH.**

A MATTER OF PRIDE

READ:
1 John 2:15-17

Do not love the world or the things in the world. If anyone loves the world, the love of the Father is not in him. —1 John 2:15

THE BIBLE IN ONE YEAR:
■ Psalms 52–54

I was at a conference to conduct a seminar. Other speakers were there as well, including a well-known Christian leader whose seminar was at the same time as mine. When the director of the conference announced the meetings, he urged as many people as possible to attend the well-known speaker's seminar, and he said, "It's such an honor to have him here."

I thought, *I probably spent as much time as he did getting my presentation ready. I took time away from my family to be here. And now the conference director tells everyone to go to the other seminar? What's that all about?*

I felt humiliated, hurt, and angry. But as I walked toward the room to start my seminar, the Holy Spirit convicted me that I was reacting in pride and envy. He also reminded me that He would direct the people He wanted to be there. I asked the Lord to forgive me for the "envy and self-seeking" in my heart (James 3:14).

Sometimes we experience spiritual setbacks because we are guilty of wrong thinking. We get caught up in worldly pride and self-centeredness (1 John 2:16). When this happens, we have some important spiritual work to do. We must repent, confessing our pride to God and asking for His forgiveness. —Dave Egner

Blessed Savior, make us humble,
Take away our sinful pride;
In ourselves we're sure to stumble,
Help us stay close by Your side. —D. De Haan

**UNLESS WE'RE HUMBLE,
WE'RE SURE TO STUMBLE.**

TROUBLE WITH PEOPLE

READ:
Psalm 56

In God I have put my trust; I will not be afraid. What can man do to me?
—Psalm 56:11

THE BIBLE IN ONE YEAR:
■ Psalms 55–57

Was David paranoid? Did he think the whole world was out to get him? You might get that impression as you read through some of his psalms. Look at a few of the statements he made:

- "Strangers have risen up against me, and oppressors have sought after my life" (Psalm 54:3).
- "There are many who fight against me" (56:2).
- "They lie in wait for my life; the mighty gather against me" (59:3).

Of course, during this time David was being hotly pursued by Saul and his men, so it's easy to see why he felt as he did. Nonetheless, his observations about people may echo the way we feel on occasions when others criticize and oppose us. Perhaps it's those with whom we work. They seem to disagree with us no matter what we do or say. Maybe it's family members who apparently enjoy irritating us. Or people at church who seem to be critical and faultfinding. We just feel as if everyone is against us.

If this describes your situation, it's time to do what David did. He declared, "In God I have put my trust; I will not be afraid. What can man do to me?" (56:11).

When you have trouble with people, turn to God. He understands. — Dave Branon

When people are cruel and attack you,
And hope for relief becomes dim,
Remember that Jesus has told you
To cast all your care upon Him. —Anon.

GOD IS STRONGER THAN OUR STRONGEST FOE.

FINDING SECURITY

READ:
Psalm 59

You have been my defense and refuge in the day of my trouble.
—Psalm 59:16

THE BIBLE IN ONE YEAR:
■ Psalms 58–60

After a man shot and killed two people at Los Angeles International Airport in 2002, some began insisting that armed guards be placed at every check-in area. Others said that individuals should be screened before entering an airport terminal. But a consultant on airport security said, "If you move the checkpoint, all you're going to do is push the problem to another part of the airport. There will always be a public area that is vulnerable to these kinds of attacks."

In a world where violence and terrorism may strike anytime, anyplace, where can we find security? Where can we be safe?

The Bible says that our security is not in human protection but in God Himself. The book of Psalms contains more than 40 references to taking refuge in the Lord, many of them from David's experience of being pursued by his enemies. In his prayers for help, he centered his hope in the Lord: "You have been my defense and refuge in the day of my trouble. To You, O my Strength, I will sing praises; for God is my defense, my God of mercy" (Psalm 59:16-17).

God doesn't guarantee to protect us from difficulty and physical harm, but He does promise to be our refuge in every situation. In Him we find real security. — David McCasland

> Though danger lurks on every side,
> In Christ our Lord we will abide;
> Our God is strong, our hope is sure —
> In Him alone we are secure! — Fitzhugh

**NO ONE IS MORE SECURE
THAN THE ONE WHO RESTS IN GOD'S HANDS.**

HEART
TO HEART

READ:
Psalm 62

Pour out your heart before Him; God is a refuge for us.
—Psalm 62:8

THE BIBLE IN ONE YEAR:
■ Psalms 61–63

We would expect King David to be extremely upset, because his enemies were scheming to dethrone him. Yet in Psalm 62 he testified that his soul was quietly confident before God. How was this possible in the midst of such turmoil? Verse 8 offers a clue — one I discovered for myself several years ago.

I had just returned home, weary, alone, and at my wit's end. As I began pouring out my woes before God, I suddenly stopped myself and said, "Father, forgive me. I'm treating You like a counselor!" But the torrent of words flowed on, followed by the same embarrassing apology. Then God's Spirit whispered deep within, "I am your Great Counselor."

But of course! Hadn't He, the Creator of my physical and spiritual makeup, also created the emotional part of me? How reasonable, then, to spread out my ragged feelings before Him. Then came His comforting, corrective counsel, ministered skillfully by the Holy Spirit through His Word. My problems didn't evaporate. But like David, I could rest in God alone. I was at peace again.

Never hesitate to pour out your heart to God. In your day of trouble, you'll find that prayer is the shortest route between your heart and God's. — Joanie Yoder

> *In the silence of my chamber*
> *I can with my Savior share*
> *All my worries and my troubles*
> *As I talk with Him in prayer.* — Anon.

GOD FILLS OUR HEART WITH PEACE
WHEN WE POUR OUT OUR HEART TO HIM.

WHAT WE REALLY NEED

READ:
Proverbs 3:13-26

Happy is the man who finds wisdom. . . . She is a tree of life to those who take hold of her.
—Proverbs 3:13, 18

THE BIBLE IN ONE YEAR:
■ Psalms 79–81

In a biting comment, one philosopher said of another that he was "the greatest of thinkers and the most petty of men." We admire individuals of high intelligence, but we certainly wouldn't want that statement to be said about us.

Better by far to be an ordinary person who by God's grace reflects Christ's character. Better not to be a mental giant who is spiritually petty.

Intelligence and knowledge are God's gifts, and we can admire them. But we must remember that a good heart and godly character are more to be desired than brainpower, and that love is the most praiseworthy of gifts (1 Corinthians 13:13).

Even though we may respect friends who are blessed with keen minds, we know that wisdom from the Lord is what we really need. In Proverbs 2–3, we are told to search for wisdom as for hidden treasures, and to realize that it is more valuable than silver, gold, or rubies (2:4; 3:14-15). Wisdom is called "a tree of life," which is a symbolic way of describing the blessings of being in a right relationship with God (3:18). A wise person can walk through life with confidence, assured of the Lord's approval (v.26).

Wisdom — that's what we really need. — Vernon Grounds

The blessings of the Lord are known
By those who will obey;
His wisdom, truth, and love are shown
To all who choose His way. — D. De Haan

YOU CAN GAIN KNOWLEDGE ON YOUR OWN, BUT WISDOM COMES FROM GOD.

THE COST OF NEGLECT

READ:
Proverbs 24:30-34

Keep your heart with all diligence, for out of it spring the issues of life. . . . Ponder the path of your feet.
—Proverbs 4:23, 26

THE BIBLE IN ONE YEAR:
■ Psalms 82–84

I read about a Detroit man who couldn't find his house. He had gone to the right address but all he found was an empty lot. Completely baffled, he asked the *Detroit Free Press* to help him figure out what was going on. A newspaper reporter learned that not only was the house gone, but the deed to the empty lot was in someone else's name.

What had happened? For one thing, a few years had passed since the homeowner had left the city without providing a forwarding address. In addition, he had failed to make arrangements for someone to keep the property in repair. So the house was torn down because a city ordinance called for the removal of neighborhood eyesores.

The homeowner's neglect illustrates the practical truth of Proverbs 24:30-34. Neglect leads to loss. This principle also applies to our daily walk with God. If we neglect our times of prayer and fellowship with the Lord, our relationship with Him will deteriorate and we will no longer experience His favor. We would never want that to happen, but we allow it when we become preoccupied with anything that comes between us and Christ.

We need to establish priorities that honor God. Then we'll avoid the loss that comes from neglect. — Mart De Haan

Unless we're occupied with Jesus
And seek to do His will each day,
We're sure to know the loss and sorrow
That comes when we neglect His way. —Anon.

**IF YOU SHIRK TODAY'S TASKS,
YOU INCREASE TOMORROW'S BURDENS.**

June 17

A Wish For The Aged

READ:
Psalm 71:9-18

Do not cast me off in the time of old age; do not forsake me when my strength fails.
—Psalm 71:9

THE BIBLE IN ONE YEAR:
■ Psalms 70–72

"As a white candle in a holy place, so is the beauty of an aged face." This line from a poem by Joseph Campbell applies to people who have served the Lord all their lives and are still bearing fruit in old age.

Behind the aged face of a long-time Christian are memories of family and friends. Wrinkles stand for earnest times of prayer, loving care, and decades of useful work. The beauty is no longer the skin-deep charm of youth but the time-honored loveliness of a life well-lived.

My wife ministers to some beautiful aged people like that as a nurse in a rest home. They are special people, like the man who gives her a weather report each night she works and the women who continue to serve God as prayer warriors.

But the elderly are not always appreciated. Unscrupulous people force them to live in wretched conditions. One politician has said that they should "die and get out of the way." Others suggest that they are an unnecessary burden. As Christians, we must resist this trend and work to reverse it. Many of these precious people feel rejected and abandoned.

Let's care for the aged and love them in Jesus' name. God can use us to encourage those who pray, "Do not cast me off in the time of old age." — Dave Branon

> *The older saints who trust God's Word*
> *Have trod the paths that you will walk;*
> *They've fought the battles you will fight —*
> *There's truth and wisdom in their talk.* — Branon

**KINDNESS TO THE ELDERLY
BRIGHTENS THEIR SUNSET YEARS.**

SOMETHING TO SAY

READ:
Isaiah 50:4-10

The Lord GOD has given Me the tongue of the learned, that I should know how to speak a word in season to him who is weary. —Isaiah 50:4

THE BIBLE IN ONE YEAR:
■ Psalms 73–75

I read that Albert Einstein was the featured speaker at a dinner given at Swarthmore College. When it came time for him to speak, he astonished everyone by standing up and announcing, "I have nothing to say." Then he sat down.

A few moments later he stood up and added, "In case I have something to say, I will come back and say it." Six months later he sent a message to the president of the college: "Now I have something to say." Another dinner was held and he gave his speech.

Perhaps you have had opportunities "to speak a word in season" to those who are weary (Isaiah 50:4), but you didn't feel as if you had anything to say. If so, follow the example of the Servant of the Lord, the promised Messiah, whom we read about in Isaiah 50:4-10. Because He listened and obeyed what He heard, He had a message to give to others.

Open God's Word with an eagerness to learn and do what He tells you to do. Think of the Lord as present and speaking to you, disclosing His mind and emotions and will. Meditate on His words till you know what He is saying.

Then, as the Servant discovered, in time God will give you "the tongue of the learned" (v.4). If you listen to the Lord, you'll have something worth saying. —David Roper

Instill within my heart, dear Lord,
A deep desire to know Your Word,
I want to learn to hear Your voice
And always make Your will my choice. —D. De Haan

OPEN YOUR EARS TO GOD
BEFORE YOU OPEN YOUR MOUTH TO OTHERS.

IS FAITHFULNESS ENOUGH?

READ:
Isaiah 6:8-13

I heard the voice of the Lord, saying: "Whom shall I send, and who will go for Us?"
—Isaiah 6:8

THE BIBLE IN ONE YEAR:
■ Psalms 76–78

A young missionary in Central America was tempted to give up. He wrote to friends and family, "I go about on fishing boats through the day. At night I sleep on piles of hides on the deck. The people do not seem to be interested in the gospel message I bring. Sometimes the adversary tempts me to discouragement in the face of seeming lack of success." But then he added, "I take courage and press on anew as I remember that God does not hold me responsible for success but for faithfulness."

The prophet Isaiah also may have been tempted to give up his difficult assignment. The Lord told him that the result of his efforts would be that the people would hear but not understand, and see but not perceive (Isaiah 6:9). Their hearts would be dull, their ears heavy, and their eyes shut (v.10).

Put yourself in the shoes of Isaiah or that missionary. Would you have pressed on or given up? Is faithfulness enough, or do you think your work must be recognized as successful before you feel satisfied in serving the Lord?

The prophet and the missionary did what God asked them to do. They preached God's Word and trusted in His purposes. You too can be a faithful servant. Do your best and leave the results in the hands of the Lord. — Albert Lee

Oh, let us be faithful to Jesus,
The faith we confessed let's renew,
And ask Him this question each morning:
"Lord, what will You have me to do?" — Pangborn

**THE WORLD CROWNS SUCCESS;
GOD CROWNS FAITHFULNESS.**

A PRAYING FATHER

READ:
Matthew 7:7-11

Hear my prayer, O LORD, give ear to my supplications! In Your faithfulness answer me. —Psalm 143:1

THE BIBLE IN ONE YEAR:
■ Psalms 64–66

A minister concluded his sermon one Sunday by saying, "If there's someone here who wants help in getting to know God, and you would like me to pray for you, please raise your hand." A young man stood up and said, "Please pray for me, sir. The burden of my sin is too heavy to bear."

After the service the minister talked with the man and led him to faith in Jesus. The young man had been wandering around the country for 8 years without contacting his parents, so he decided to write to them and tell them about the change in his life.

Several days later, a reply came from his mother: "My dear son, you must have accepted Jesus Christ at the same hour your father went home to heaven. He had been sick for a long time, and that day he was very restless. He tossed from side to side on his bed, crying out, 'Lord, please save my poor, wandering boy.' I'm sure that one of the reasons you became a Christian was Dad's unceasing intercession."

A praying father will "ask," "seek," and "knock" in behalf of his children, persistently trusting his wise heavenly Father to do what is best (Matthew 7:7-11).

Let's thank God today for faithful fathers who never stop praying for their children. — Henry Bosch

We thank You, Lord, for fathers true
Who always spoke to us of You;
Their great concern and tender care
Assured us of their constant prayer. — Bosch

A PRAYING FATHER REFLECTS THE LOVE OF OUR HEAVENLY FATHER.

Losing Dad

READ:
Genesis 49:28–50:3

**Joseph fell on his father's face, and wept over him, and kissed him.
—Genesis 50:1**

THE BIBLE IN ONE YEAR:
■ Psalms 67–69

Author Neil Chethik wrote a book about the way sons cope with the death of their dads. He commissioned a survey of 300 men and found that 65 percent said the death of their father affected them more than any other loss in their lives. Chethik said, "Each man, it seemed to me, experienced a significant reordering of his inner landscape."

One 48-year-old minister said: "When my father died, it was as if I had lived in . . . a house with a picture window looking out on a mountain range. Then one day I looked out the window, and one of the mountains was gone."

When Jacob died, Joseph experienced a great loss. We read that "Joseph fell on his father's face, and wept over him, and kissed him" (Genesis 50:1). The period of ceremony, mourning, and burial lasted more than 2 months.

For most of us, our fathers will die before we do. And we should feel free to grieve our loss, whether our memories are happy or painful.

God promises that one day "there shall be no more death, nor sorrow, nor crying" (Revelation 21:4). Until then, tears are God's gift for the cleansing of the soul when we must cope with losing Dad. — David McCasland

> *Lord, help us through our grief and loss —*
> *Through valleys deep when Dad is gone;*
> *Then heal our hearts, renew our joy,*
> *Grant us the strength to carry on.* — *Fitzhugh*

**IN EVERY DESERT OF GRIEF,
GOD HAS AN OASIS OF GRACE.**

JUST BE YOURSELF

READ:
Ephesians 4:1-16

Stir up the gift of God which is in you.
—2 Timothy 1:6

THE BIBLE IN ONE YEAR:
■ Psalms 85–87

S ome Christian groups exert pressure on their members to talk, act, or look alike. This must frustrate the people who are judged for not conforming. In trying to make them "fit," the group may be stifling their strongest and best gifts.

Here's a parable that illustrates the point: A rural village was located in an area inhabited by parrots. One day a falcon landed on a windowsill. The owner of the house caught it. The villagers had never seen such a bird. They decided to trim back its feathers, cut its talons, and file down its beak so it would be like the birds they were familiar with.

As followers of Christ, we are to imitate Him (1 Corinthians 11:1; 1 John 2:6). If we become more like Him, does that mean we all will begin to act alike? Yes and no. Yes, in that our behavior toward others and reactions to circumstances will increasingly become like those of Jesus. No, in that we are each given unique gifts and interests and abilities to develop and use for His glory (Ephesians 4:7).

Let's not be guilty of stifling our fellow Christians. Instead, let's allow for differences. God has made them unique and gifted them to fulfill His purposes. It's a shame to turn a falcon into a parrot. — Dave Egner

God builds His church with different stones,
He makes each one belong;
All shapes and sizes fit in place
To make the structure strong. — Sper

ALL CHRISTIANS HAVE THE SAME EMPLOYER—
THEY JUST HAVE DIFFERENT JOBS.

ON LOAN

READ:
Psalm 89:5-12

Command those who are rich . . . to trust . . . in the living God, who gives us richly all things to enjoy.
—1 Timothy 6:17

THE BIBLE IN ONE YEAR:
■ Psalms 88–90

I am surrounded every day by things that don't belong to me, yet I call them mine. For instance, I refer to the computer I am using to write this article as "my Mac." I talk about "my office," "my desk," and "my phone." But none of this equipment belongs to me. It's mine to use, but not mine to keep. When RBC Ministries "gave" it to me, we both knew what that meant: It was on loan.

This kind of situation is not unique to employer-employee relationships. That's the way it is with all of us and all of the things we call our own. When we speak of our family, our house, or our car, we are speaking of people and things God has allowed us to enjoy while here on earth, but they really belong to Him. Notice the psalmist's praise to God, "The heavens are Yours, the earth also is Yours" (Psalm 89:11).

Understanding who really holds the title to all we possess should change our thinking. Just as I am aware that RBC lets me use its equipment to help me do my work more efficiently, so also should we be aware that everything we have is given to us to serve the Lord.

Our time, talents, and possessions are all on loan from God so that we can do His work effectively. — Dave Branon

God's grace sustains the gift of life,
Its labor and reward;
What we possess is not our own —
It all comes from the Lord. — D. De Haan

ALL WE OWN IS REALLY ON LOAN—FROM GOD.

SOMEONE TO HOLD ON TO

READ:
Psalm 91

He is my refuge and my fortress; my God, in Him I will trust.
—Psalm 91:2

THE BIBLE IN ONE YEAR:
■ Psalms 91–93

In his book *The Fisherman and His Friends*, Louis Albert Banks tells of two men who were assigned to stand watch on a ship out at sea. During the night the waves from a raging storm washed one of them overboard. The sailor who drowned had been in the most sheltered place, while the one who survived was more exposed to the elements. What made the difference? The man who was lost had nothing to hold on to.

What a picture of the way some people are affected by the trials of life! When life is peaceful, they are very self-sufficient, but when the going gets rough they are swept off their feet. Because they have refused God's help and have nothing to hold on to, they are easily overwhelmed.

People who cling to the Lord, though, can weather the fiercest storms of adversity. They are often heard to say, "I don't know what I would do without the Lord." They know that the heavenly Father is always with them to strengthen, guard, and protect them.

Those who have put their hope in God have Someone they can rely on in every circumstance of life. They can say of the Lord, "He is my refuge and my fortress; my God, in Him I will trust" (Psalm 91:2). Can you? — Richard De Haan

He cannot fail, your faithful God,
He'll guard you with His mighty power;
Then fear no ill, though troubles rise,
His help is sure from hour to hour. — Bosch

GOD HAS NOT PROMISED TO KEEP US FROM
LIFE'S STORMS, BUT TO KEEP US THROUGH THEM.

PRAYER-MEETING BLUES

READ:
Psalm 102:1-17

Hear my prayer,
O LORD, and let my
cry come to You.
—Psalm 102:1

THE BIBLE IN ONE YEAR:
■ Psalms 94–96

Prayer meetings can get you down. No matter how much you look forward to gathering with friends to pray, the requests can be disheartening. A missionary is having health problems. A child has cancer. A couple from your Sunday school class is getting a divorce. The missionary appointee is having difficulty raising financial support. And you have struggles of your own. The more requests you hear, the more weary you grow.

But then a mighty prayer warrior begins to pray. With confidence, he thanks God for His absolute control over all things. With tears, he pleads with God to work in the lives of those for whom prayer is requested. With honesty, he acknowledges that we don't always understand what God is doing. Like the psalmist, he turns a time of complaining over man's problems into a time of praising God for His listening ear. Prayer turns to praise because one saint believes that the Lord hears "the prayer of the destitute, and shall not despise their prayer" (Psalm 102:17).

Are you struggling with difficulties in your own life or the overwhelming problems of dear friends and loved ones? Learn to hand them over to the everlasting God. That's how to drive away those prayer-meeting blues. — Dave Branon

Praise God's holy name forever!
There is none that can compare
To the blessing of His presence
When we meet with Him in prayer. — Anon.

**ALTHOUGH THE OUTLOOK MAY BE BLEAK,
THE UPLOOK IS ALWAYS BRIGHT.**

THE POWER OF OUR LIMITS

READ:
Exodus 4:10-12

Go, and I will be with
your mouth and teach
you what you shall
say. —Exodus 4:12

THE BIBLE IN ONE YEAR:
■ Psalms 97–99

When God called Moses to serve, he replied, "O my Lord, I am not eloquent, neither before nor since You have spoken to Your servant; but I am slow of speech and slow of tongue" (Exodus 4:10).

The language suggests that Moses may have had a speech impediment. Perhaps he stuttered. The Lord said to him, "Who has made man's mouth? Or who makes the mute, the deaf, the seeing, or the blind? Have not I, the LORD?" (v.11).

Our impairments, our disabilities, our handicaps are used by God for His own glory. His way of dealing with them may not be to remove them but to endow us with strength and use our limitations for good.

If our weaknesses cause us to seek God and rely on Him, they actually help us instead of hinder us. In fact, they become the best thing that could happen to us, because our growth in courage, power, and happiness depends on our relationship with the Lord and how much we are relying on Him.

Three times the apostle Paul pleaded with the Lord to remove his impediment, but the Lord answered, "My grace is sufficient" (2 Corinthians 12:9). Paul then gloried in his limitations, for he realized that they did not limit him. As he put it, "When I am weak, then I am strong" (v.10).   — David Roper

God uses weakness to reveal
His great sufficiency;
So if we let Him work through us,
His power we will see. — Sper

GOD'S STRENGTH IS BEST SEEN IN OUR WEAKNESS.

STANDING BEFORE GOD

READ:
2 Corinthians 5:1-11

**We must all appear before the judgment seat of Christ.
—2 Corinthians 5:10**

THE BIBLE IN ONE YEAR:
■ Psalms 100–102

During preparation for jury duty, I watched a videotape that said: "All across the state, jury panels are being assembled to sit in judgment of others, just as one day people may assemble to sit in judgment of us."

Being judged by a jury of my peers is possible, but standing before Almighty God is certain. Our works will be evaluated and our reward determined by the Lord.

All of us will be morally and spiritually audited. The Lord will review every entry in the ledger of our lives. Not only what we did on earth but also the reasons why we did it will be known and judged.

As believers in Jesus Christ, we have the assurance that when we die we will be "present with the Lord" (2 Corinthians 5:8). With that in mind, Paul wrote, "We make it our aim . . . to be well pleasing to Him. For we must all appear before the judgment seat of Christ, that each one may receive the things done in the body . . . whether good or bad" (vv.9-10).

Instead of cringing with fear, we can live with joy as we seek to please God and look forward to our heavenly reward. Let's strive to make sure our actions and motives will be found worthy, not worthless, on the day we stand before God. — David McCasland

> *To me it matters little*
> *If my life is long or short,*
> *If only at Christ's judgment seat*
> *I have a good report.* — Anon.

**OUR SALVATION DEPENDS ON WHAT CHRIST DID FOR US;
OUR REWARD DEPENDS ON HOW WE LIVE FOR HIM.**

HEADING HOME

READ:
2 Corinthians 5:1-8

We are confident, yes, well pleased rather to be absent from the body and to be present with the Lord.
—2 Corinthians 5:8

THE BIBLE IN ONE YEAR:
■ Psalms 103–105

It is possible for us to anticipate death with the gladness of school children when a day's classes are over. An unknown poet has written:

Someday the bell will sound,
Someday my heart will bound
As with a shout, that school is out,
And, lessons done, I homeward run.

It's a rare believer, though, who joyfully welcomes death. No doubt we may long to die if we are painfully and incurably sick, or if we are old, alone, and unable to enjoy the simple pleasures of life. Otherwise, though, we cling to life with a God-given instinct of self-preservation.

The Bible tells us that Jesus came to give us an abundant life here and now, as well as hereafter (John 10:10,28). And we can gladly recognize that God "gives us richly all things to enjoy" (1 Timothy 6:17).

Yet, we would be wise to balance our love for life with the truth reflected in the words of an old song: "This world is not my home." And indeed it isn't. We are aliens, pilgrims, and sojourners for a few fleeting years.

So, whether death seems far away or close at hand, we can be confident that if our faith is in the risen Christ we will leave this world to enter heaven's glory (2 Corinthians 5:8). One glad day we will be heading home. — Vernon Grounds

Home from the earthly journey,
Safe for eternity;
All that the Savior promised—
That is what heaven will be. —Anon.

NOTHING ON EARTH CAN COMPARE
TO BEING WITH CHRIST IN HEAVEN.

BEWARE OF QUICK FIXES

READ:
Psalm 106:1-15

**They soon forgot His works; they did not wait for His counsel.
—Psalm 106:13**

THE BIBLE IN ONE YEAR:
■ Psalms 106–108

S ome people pray only in a crisis. They have a "quick fix" mentality that sees God mainly as a problem solver. When merciful solutions come, He is courteously thanked, then more or less forgotten until the next crisis.

The story is told of a young rich girl, accustomed to servants, who was afraid to climb a dark stairway alone. Her mother suggested that she overcome her fear by asking Jesus to go with her up the stairs. When the child reached the top, she was overheard saying, "Thank You, Jesus. You may go now."

We may smile at that story, but Psalm 106 contains a serious warning against dismissing God from our lives — as if that were possible. Israel took the Lord's mercies for granted, and God called that rebellion (v.7). They developed malnourished souls because they chose to ignore Him (vv.13-15). What a lesson for us!

Anticipate great things from God, but don't expect Him to come at your beck and call. Instead, be at His beck and call, eager to fulfill His will.

Like the little rich girl, ask God to accompany you through life's dark passageways. But instead of dismissing Him when your special needs are met, cling to Him as if your life depended on it. It does! — Joanie Yoder

If we pray with sinful motives,
Then our heart is far from right;
We must seek to know God's bidding—
What is pleasing in His sight. — D. De Haan

GOD IS NOT A VENDING MACHINE.

EVERY INCH
OF ME

READ:
Acts 27:13-26

Take heart, men, for I
believe God that it will
be just as it was told
me. —Acts 27:25

THE BIBLE IN ONE YEAR:
■ Psalms 109–111

Shortly before Peter Doot died at age 92, he said, "I am six-foot-four, and every inch belongs to the Lord." I had known him for 65 years, and I'm sure what he said was true.

As a younger man, Peter had left a well-paying job so he could serve as an evangelist for his church. He made a profound impact on hundreds of lives, even though he had little formal training. When I was 19, he challenged me to witness and to preach the gospel in street-corner meetings.

What made Peter so effective? His way of life. Everybody could clearly see that God was his Master.

The same could be said about the apostle Paul. In Acts 27 we read that when he was a prisoner being taken to Rome, the ship on which he was sailing was being battered by a furious storm. The sailors had given up all hope. But when Paul spoke, everybody listened and was encouraged. Even the Roman centurion followed his instructions. Why? Because it was obvious that Paul was a godly man who was telling the truth. They had good reason to believe him when he spoke of "the God to whom I belong and whom I serve," and when he said there would be no loss of life (vv.22-23).

Let's yield ourselves to God so that we too can say, "Every inch belongs to the Lord." — Herb Vander Lugt

O loving Savior, here's my will —
With Yours, I pray, may it be one;
I long to know You more each day
So that Your will in me is done. —D. De Haan

GIVE YOUR ALL TO CHRIST;
HE GAVE HIS ALL FOR YOU.

What If It's True That The Creator Cares For Me?

We all long for meaningful relationships — to give and receive love, to care and to be cared for. Yet too many go through life without ever entering into a satisfying, significant relationship. Too many find their lives marked by an emptiness that fills them with profound sadness.

But it's not just the need for relationship that hounds us. It's the need for a meaningful relationship with our Creator.

French philosopher and mathematician Blaise Pascal declared that within every human being there exists a "God-shaped void" that only God Himself can fill.

The good news, according to the Bible, is this: God wants to fill that void in our lives, and He has worked out a plan to make it possible for us to have a relationship with Him. As amazing as it may seem, the Bible assures us that our Creator desires a relationship with us. To understand how we can have a personal relationship with this One who has an interest in us, consider the following points:

WHO THE CREATOR IS

In Colossians 1:16-17, the apostle Paul wrote:

> *By Him all things were created that are in heaven and that are on earth, visible and invisible, whether thrones or dominions or principalities or powers. All things were created through Him and for Him. And He is before all things, and in Him all things consist.*

Who created all things? In verse 15 He is identified as the "image of the invisible God." In verse 13 the writer is more specific. The Creator is "the Son of His love." According to the Bible, Jesus Christ is not only the Son of God, He is also the Creator of the universe! Let's consider other Scriptures that say the same thing:

- *All things were made through Him, and without Him nothing was made that was made (Jn. 1:3).*
- *He was in the world, and the world was made through Him (Jn. 1:10).*
- *Yet for us there is one God, the Father, of whom are all things, and we for Him; and one Lord Jesus Christ, through whom are all things, and through whom we live (1 Cor. 8:6).*
- *[God] has in these last days spoken to us by His Son, whom He has appointed heir of all things, through whom also He made the worlds (Heb. 1:2).*

The Bible is clear in declaring that our Creator came to us in the person we know as Jesus Christ.

WHAT THE CREATOR DID

The apostle John, in the first chapter of his gospel, wrote:

The Word became flesh and dwelt among us, and we beheld His glory, the glory as of the only begotten of the Father, full of grace and truth (v.14).

Every December, people in many parts of the world celebrate the birth of God's Son into the world. Most gift-givers, however, don't realize the significance of the event behind this holiday. Many of the celebrants might not even realize that, according to the original story, Jesus was born into our world as "the image of the invisible God" (Col. 1:15).

The idea that God was among us is more important than any of us can absorb. If it is true, then we can only scratch the surface of the thought that the little one bundled up in that crude stable manger was in fact our Creator. Yet this is the claim of the Bible:

- God was in a human body. Perhaps the most astounding miracle of all history is that God became a man. This is the amazing reality of Christmas: God came in human flesh!
- God lived among us. He came to fully engage in life. He walked on ground He Himself had created.
- God showed His goodness to us. Without seeing what God is like in human flesh, we could never realize how desperately we need Him.

God didn't just come, check things out, and then return to a better place. He lived here, placing Himself under the conditions, sufferings, and temptations we all live with.

HOW THE CREATOR LOVES

How has the Creator displayed the depth of His care and concern for us? In Revelation 1:5-6, the apostle John wrote:

> To Him who loved us and washed us from our sins in His own blood, and has made us kings and priests to His God and Father, to Him be the glory and dominion forever and ever. Amen.

From other Scriptures we learn more of what this love means. For example, He released us from our sins by giving His own life for us. This is the message of Hebrews 2:9.

> We see Jesus, who was made a little lower than the angels, for the suffering of death crowned with glory and honor, so that He, by the grace of God, might taste death for everyone.

Jesus removed the barrier that has kept us from enjoying a relationship with our Creator. According to the Bible, the Creator of the universe went to the cross and died for our sins so that we could be made right with God.

> In this the love of God was manifested toward us, that

God has sent His only begotten Son into the world, that we might live through Him (1 Jn. 4:9).

What a powerful thought — the Creator hanging on a cross, dying for people who were living on death row under the sentence of eventual judgment and death. He gave His life so that others could live, not by their own merits but by the merits of the perfect One who died in their behalf.

In the Old Testament, there were three offices in the leadership of the kingdom of Israel: king, prophet, and priest. Interestingly, the New Testament not only calls Jesus our Creator, but our King, our Prophet, and our Priest. Therefore we do not need any other mediator between God and us except Jesus Christ.

- *For there is one God and one Mediator between God and men, the Man Christ Jesus" (1 Timothy 2:5).*
- *Jesus said to him, "I am the way, the truth, and the life. No one comes to the Father except through Me" (Jn. 14:6).*
- *Having been justified by faith, we have peace with God through our Lord Jesus Christ, through whom also we have access by faith into this grace in which we stand, and rejoice in hope of the glory of God (Rom. 5:1-2).*
- *Seeing then that we have a great High Priest who has passed through the heavens, Jesus the Son of God, let us hold fast our confession. For we do not have a High Priest who cannot sympathize with our weaknesses, but was in all points tempted as we are, yet without sin. Let us therefore come boldly to the throne of grace, that we may obtain mercy and find grace to help in time of need (Heb. 4:14-16).*

These thoughts are not from just any book. They are from the Bible. They tell us that our Creator Himself died for our sins to restore the relationship that was broken in Eden. That's the essence of Jesus' words, "The Son of Man has come to seek and to save that which was lost" (Lk. 19:10). And He says to each of us, "Follow Me" (Lk. 9:23).

In his book *The Call*, author Os Guinness writes:

> We cannot find God without God. We cannot reach God without God. We cannot satisfy God without God—which is another way of saying that our seeking will always fall short unless God's grace initiates the search and unless God's call draws us to Him and completes the search.
>
> If the chasm is to be bridged, God must bridge it. If we are to desire the highest good, the highest good must come down and draw us so that it may become a reality we desire. From this perspective there is no merit in either seeking or finding. All is grace. The secret of seeking is not in our human ascent to God, but in God's descent to us. We start our searching, but we end up being discovered. We think we are looking for something; we realize we are found by Someone. As in Francis Thompson's famous picture, "the hound of heaven" has tracked us down (pp.13-14).

After his conversion from atheist to believer, C. S. Lewis looked back on his journey to faith in Christ and discovered that "God closed in on me." He wrote:

> Amiable agnostics will talk cheerfully about "man's search for God." To me, as I then was, they might as well have talked about the mouse's search for the cat (Surprised By Joy, p.179).

Yes, the seeking is real—but who seeks whom? The Creator of the universe is seeking you! To be sure, that's an imposing thought.

The great Christian prime minister of the Netherlands, Abraham Kuyper, declared,

> There is not one square inch of the entire creation

about which Jesus Christ does not cry out, "This is Mine! This belongs to Me!"

Why? Because He is the Creator, and He is merely claiming that which He Himself has made.

WHAT DOES THIS MEAN FOR US?

The Creator has shown that He really does care for us. Jesus is God in the flesh. He is our Creator and He seeks a personal relationship with us.

Have you responded to His sacrificial love with faith and accepted His invitation to everlasting life, forgiveness, and peace? Carefully consider what the Bible says:

For God so loved the world that He gave His only begotten Son, that whoever believes in Him should not perish but have everlasting life. For God did not send His Son into the world to condemn the world, but that the world through Him might be saved. He who believes in Him is not condemned; but he who does not believe is condemned already, because he has not believed in the name of the only begotten Son of God (Jn. 3:16-18).

Adapted from *What If It's True?* © 2001 RBC Ministries.
On the Web: www.discoveryseries.org/q0610

WHAT WOULD YOU DO?

READ:
Proverbs 19:17-22

**What is desired in a man is kindness.
—Proverbs 19:22**

THE BIBLE IN ONE YEAR:
■ Psalms 112–114

I will never forget being in the "big blackout" of November 9, 1965. This widespread power outage darkened eight states in the northeastern US, and portions of Ontario and Quebec in eastern Canada — covering 80,000 square miles and affecting 30 million people.

With no electric lights, candles were in great demand. An announcer on a New York radio station that stayed on the air because it had auxiliary power reported, "An interesting drama is being unfolded on our streets. The price of candles in many stores has doubled. On the other hand, some good-hearted merchants are offering their candles at half price, or even giving them away."

Some store owners let their concern for others in the hour of emergency outweigh their desire for personal gain. Others, however, took advantage of the situation and put their personal gain ahead of their concern for others. The very same circumstances produced both self-seeking opportunists and selfless philanthropists.

How would we react? Would we have pity on those in need and show kindness to them? (Proverbs 19:17,22). The words of Galatians 6:10 are the only fitting response: "As we have opportunity, let us do good to all." — Richard De Haan

Do a deed of simple kindness,
Though its end you may not see;
It may reach, like widening ripples,
Down a long eternity. — Norris

OPPORTUNITIES TO BE KIND ARE NEVER HARD TO FIND.

STRANGE TERRITORY

READ:
Joshua 3:1-13

You have not passed this way before.
—Joshua 3:4

THE BIBLE IN ONE YEAR:
■ Psalms 115–118

When my son Stephen was 8, he was invited to stay overnight at a cousin's house. It was his first time away from home and it all sounded like an exciting adventure. But when my wife and I took him there, he started getting that homesick feeling. With tears glistening in his eyes and his voice quivering, he said, "Mommy, I don't feel so good. I'd better go home with you."

My wife responded, "It's up to you, but I know you'd have a good time."

"But Mommy," Stephen whimpered, "they said they were going to climb a big hill tomorrow, and I've never been there before!"

We too can become fearful sometimes as we look ahead, because we've "never been there before." But just as the Lord took care of Joshua and Israel (Joshua 3), He will take care of us.

Perhaps right now you are anxious about some new and untried pathway on which the Lord is leading you. Then listen to God's Word and take courage: "I will never leave you nor forsake you" (Hebrews 13:5). "The LORD is my shepherd; I shall not want. . . . He leads me in the paths of righteousness for His name's sake" (Psalm 23:1,3).

Place your hand by faith in your heavenly Father's hand, and let Him lead the way. — Richard De Haan

I have promised you My presence —
With you everywhere you go;
I will never, never leave you
As you travel here below. — Rose

GOD DOES NOT ASK US TO GO
WHERE HE DOES NOT LEAD.

ARE YOU LISTENING?

READ:
1 Samuel 3:1-10

Speak, for Your
servant hears.
—1 Samuel 3:10

THE BIBLE IN ONE YEAR:
■ Psalm 119

One of the happiest memories of my childhood is that of my mother reading Bible stories to me at bedtime. Many of them made a great impression on me, especially the incident in the life of Samuel described in 1 Samuel 3. I can still hear my mother reciting the young boy's response to the call of God: "Speak, for Your servant hears" (v.10).

Like Samuel, we need to be willing to hear the voice of the Lord. We have this opportunity if in the midst of life's everyday activities we take time to prayerfully read and study the Bible. You see, God's Spirit communicates to us through the Word.

Thomas à Kempis (1379-1471) summed it up well when he wrote: "Blessed indeed are those ears which listen not for the voice sounding without, but for the truth teaching inwardly. Blessed are the eyes that are shut to outward things but intent on things inward. Blessed are they who are glad to have time to spare for God, and who shake off all worldly hindrances. Consider these things, O my soul, and hear what the Lord your God speaks."

How long has it been since you've asked the Lord to make your heart receptive to His Word? He wants to hear you say, "Speak, Lord, I'm listening." — Richard De Haan

By feeding on Your blessed Word, dear Lord,
I will no longer weak and childish be;
And as I listen to Your Spirit's voice,
May Christlike love and grace be seen in me. —Hess

**GOD SPEAKS THROUGH HIS WORD
TO THOSE WHO LISTEN WITH THEIR HEART.**

TRUE FREEDOM

READ:
Galatians 4:19–5:1

Stand fast therefore in the liberty by which Christ has made us free. —Galatians 5:1

THE BIBLE IN ONE YEAR:
■ Psalms 120–123

In 1776, the 13 British colonies in North America protested the limitations placed on them by the king of England and engaged in a struggle that gave birth to a brand-new republic. The infant nation soon adopted that now-famous document known as the Declaration of Independence.

Almost 2,000 years ago, the Lord Jesus cried out on the cross, "It is finished," proclaiming the believer's "declaration of independence." All of humanity was under the tyranny of sin and death. But Christ, the sinless One, took our place on Calvary and died for our sins. Having satisfied God's righteous demands, He now sets free for eternity all who trust in Him.

Paul wrote, "Christ has redeemed us from the curse of the law, having become a curse for us" (Galatians 3:13). Romans 8 assures us, "There is therefore now no condemnation to those who are in Christ Jesus . . . . For the law of the Spirit of life in Christ Jesus has made me free from the law of sin and death" (vv.1-2). Galatians 5:1 urges all who have been redeemed to "stand fast therefore in the liberty by which Christ has made us free."

I thank God for the freedom I enjoy as a US citizen. But above all, believers everywhere can praise Him for the freedom that is found in Christ! —Richard De Haan

Now are we free — there's no condemnation!
Jesus provides a perfect salvation;
"Come unto Me," O hear His sweet call!
Come — and He saves us once for all. —Bliss

OUR GREATEST FREEDOM IS FREEDOM FROM SIN.

PRETENDERS

READ:
Matthew 23:1-2,23-33

You also outwardly appear righteous to men, but inside you are full of hypocrisy and lawlessness.
—Matthew 23:28

THE BIBLE IN ONE YEAR:
■ Psalms 124–128

For 11 years a Massachusetts man kept his secret hidden from others. No one suspected that anything was wrong. Even at home his behavior appeared normal. He would sit down with the newspaper every night after dinner, and not even his wife knew of his problem.

But the day came when he couldn't take the strain of covering up any longer. After years of guarding his secret, he finally confessed — he couldn't read. He had been a pretender.

Many people put on a front in their spiritual lives. They appear to be Christians. They speak the language, join a church, and are careful to hide their sins. They act piously and try to make a good impression, and people assume that they are Christians. But deep down inside, these spiritual actors know they have never admitted their sinful condition to God and placed their trust in the Lord Jesus Christ as their only hope of salvation. Outwardly, they "appear righteous," but inwardly they are "full of hypocrisy and lawlessness" (Matthew 23:28).

Have you been faking it? You may fool others, but you can't fool God. He sees what's in your heart. Don't be a pretender. Receive God's Son as your Savior. Experience the real thing. — Richard De Haan

Though some may call you Christian
Because you act the part,
It's what God says that matters —
Does Christ live in your heart? — Bosch

**YOU CAN HAVE TONS OF RELIGION
WITHOUT AN OUNCE OF SALVATION.**

Mrs. Craig's Problem

READ:
Psalm 122

I was glad when they said to me, "Let us go into the house of the Lord." —Psalm 122:1

THE BIBLE IN ONE YEAR:
■ Psalms 129–132

Church attendance is a privilege. We recognize that some people cannot attend because of physical problems or other legitimate reasons. But those who can be in church should be. The singing, prayers, fellowship, and teaching of God's Word are just what we need for the week ahead.

The *Nashville Banner* reported that 81-year-old Ella Craig had perfect attendance in Sunday school for 20 years. That's 1,040 Sundays! The article then raised these questions:

1. Doesn't Mrs. Craig ever have company on Sunday to keep her away from church?
2. Doesn't she ever have headaches, colds, nervous spells, or tired feelings?
3. Doesn't she ever take a weekend trip?
4. Doesn't she ever sleep late on Sunday morning?
5. Doesn't it ever rain or snow on Sunday morning?
6. Doesn't she ever get her feelings hurt by someone in the church?

The article concluded by asking, "What's the matter with Mrs. Craig?" The answer? Nothing at all. But if we are not in church on Sunday when we can be, there is something wrong with us! We need to take a lesson from Mrs. Craig. — Richard De Haan

Each week if we make it our goal
On Sunday to nourish our soul,
God's help for the tasks that we face
We're sure to receive by His grace. — D. De Haan

WEAK EXCUSES KEEP SOME PEOPLE FROM CHURCH WEEK AFTER WEEK.

DYING FOR ENCOURAGEMENT

READ:
Deuteronomy 3:23-29

**Command Joshua, and encourage him and strengthen him.
—Deuteronomy 3:28**

THE BIBLE IN ONE YEAR:
■ Psalms 133–136

In Deuteronomy 3 we read that Moses encouraged Joshua as he was about to assume leadership of the Israelites. No doubt Joshua was filled with fear and a feeling of inadequacy to fill Moses' shoes. The Lord therefore told Moses to encourage Joshua.

All of us need a word of encouragement from time to time to spur us on when we are facing a major new challenge. But we also need words of appreciation and commendation as we carry out our daily responsibilities, whether at home or at work.

When a corporate accountant committed suicide, an effort was made to find out why. The company's books were examined, but no shortage was found. Nothing could be uncovered that gave any clue as to why he took his life — that is, until a note was discovered. It simply said: "In 30 years I have never had one word of encouragement. I'm fed up!"

Many people crave some small sign of approval. They need a word of recognition, a caring smile, a warm handshake, and an honest expression of appreciation for the good we see in them or in their work.

Every day let's determine to encourage (not flatter) at least one person. Let's do our part to help those around us who are dying for encouragement. — Richard De Haan

It may seem insignificant
To say a word or two;
But when we give encouragement,
What wonders it can do! — K. De Haan

**A WORD OF ENCOURAGEMENT CAN MAKE THE
DIFFERENCE BETWEEN GIVING UP OR GOING ON.**

GOD IS LISTENING

READ:
Psalm 139

**There is not a word on my tongue, but behold, O LORD, You know it altogether.
—Psalm 139:4**

THE BIBLE IN ONE YEAR:
■ Psalms 137–139

When Scottish theologian John Baillie taught at Edinburgh University, he made it a practice to open his course on the doctrine of God with these words: "We must remember, in discussing God, that we cannot talk about Him without His hearing every word we say. We may be able to talk about others behind their backs, but God is everywhere, yes, even in this classroom. Therefore, in all our discussions we must be aware of His infinite presence, and talk about Him, as it were, before His face."

The knowledge that the Lord is everywhere should have an impact on what we say. David, thinking of the everywhere-present God, declared, "There is not a word on my tongue, but behold, O LORD, You know it altogether" (Psalm 139:4).

Lies, gossip, unkind remarks, off-color jokes, angry words, vulgar comments, and disrespectful use of the Lord's name should never come from our lips. Rather, we should speak only those things that God approves of. Our desire should be the same as David's passionate prayer in Psalm 19, "Let the words of my mouth and the meditation of my heart be acceptable in Your sight, O LORD, my strength and my Redeemer" (v.14).

Remember, God is listening. — Richard De Haan

*From others we can hide some things
We've thought and said and done;
We cannot hide them from the Lord,
He knows them, every one.* — Cooper

**EVERY WORD WE SAY ON EARTH
IS HEARD IN HEAVEN.**

SOME TALK ABOUT TALK

READ:
Psalm 141

**Set a guard, O LORD, over my mouth; keep watch over the door of my lips.
—Psalm 141:3**

THE BIBLE IN ONE YEAR:
■ Psalms 140–144

A man attended a meeting where the guest lecturer was extremely long-winded. When the listener could stand it no longer, he got up and slipped out a side door. In the corridor he met a friend who asked, "Has he finished yet?"

"Yes," the man replied, "he's been through for a long time, but he's not aware of it! He simply won't stop!"

The idea of coming to the point and saying something worthwhile is also good counsel for us as we talk with others each day. If we are honest with ourselves, we must admit that some of our conversation is nothing more than careless talk. The Lord Jesus warned, "For every idle word men may speak, they will give account of it in the day of judgment" (Matthew 12:36).

Pause a minute and think about what your usual conversation is like. What is the subject of most of your discussions? Do you talk too much and not give opportunity for others to speak? Is your speech profitable to others? And above all, do your words glorify the Lord?

God can enable you to speak words that build up others and don't just fill the air. Today, make the words of David your prayer: "Set a guard, O LORD, over my mouth; keep watch over the door of my lips" (Psalm 141:3). — Richard De Haan

How easy to use many words
When really we've nothing say!
But when we are yielded to God,
Our words will bless hearts every day. — D. De Haan

**IF YOUR MIND GOES BLANK,
DON'T FORGET TO TURN OFF THE SOUND.**

NOT ENOUGH STARS!

READ:
Psalm 147

Oh, give thanks to the
LORD, for He is good!
For His mercy endures
forever.
—1 Chronicles 16:34

THE BIBLE IN ONE YEAR:
■ Psalms 145–147

"I like to play with the stars," a little girl told her pastor one day when he came to visit her. She was confined to bed because of a severe spinal deformity, and her bed was positioned so that she had a good view of the sky. She wanted it that way so she could see the stars. "I wake up a lot at night and can't get back to sleep," she told the minister, "and that's when I play with the stars."

Her pastor, curious about what she meant by that, asked, "How do you play with the stars?" The child answered, "I pick out one and say, 'That's Mommy.' I see another and say, 'That's Daddy.' And I just keep on naming the stars after people and things I'm thankful for — my brothers and sisters, my doctor, my friends, my dog." And on and on she went, until at last she exclaimed, "But there just aren't enough stars to go around!"

Do you ever feel that way when you think about the many blessings God has showered on you? Of course, you could never name all your physical, spiritual, temporal, and eternal blessings. But from time to time, it's good to remember with gratitude His many gifts. As you do, like that little girl, you'll feel like exclaiming, "There just aren't enough stars to go around!" — Richard De Haan

Thanks, O God, for boundless mercy
From Thy gracious throne above;
Thanks for every need provided
From the fullness of Thy love! — Storm

THANKFULNESS BEGINS WITH A GOOD MEMORY.

HYMNS
OF PRAISE

READ:
Psalm 149

Sing to the LORD a new song, and His praise in the assembly of saints. —Psalm 149:1

THE BIBLE IN ONE YEAR:
■ Psalms 148–150

Music is one of those good things in life we take for granted. Yet, as is so often the case, sinful man has taken this good gift from God and used it to serve evil purposes. In our day we're especially aware of its misuse and of the shameful lyrics that so often are a part of it. Good music, however, is a blessing from the Lord. It's a soothing tonic for troubled hearts. It can motivate us to live for Christ, and through it we can lift our hearts in praise to the Lord. Without music, we would be greatly deprived.

An old Jewish legend says that after God had created the world He called the angels to Himself and asked them what they thought of it. One of them said, "The only thing lacking is the sound of praise to the Creator." So God created music, and it was heard in the whisper of the wind and in the song of the birds. He also gave man the gift of song. And throughout all the ages, music has blessed multitudes of people.

Singing God's praises honors the Lord, edifies our brothers and sisters in Christ, and brings us joy. As we join with other Christians in singing, it should be with a renewed appreciation of music. So let us join voices with fellow believers and lift our hearts in hymns of praise whenever we have the privilege. — Richard De Haan

Bless the Lord and sing His praises,
Bless the Lord now, O my soul;
Join the song all heaven raises,
Let the anthem loudly roll! — Peterson

HEARTS IN TUNE WITH GOD WILL SING HIS PRAISES.

LIFE'S FINAL DEADLINE

READ:
Luke 12:16-21

Prepare to meet your God. —Amos 4:12

THE BIBLE IN ONE YEAR:
■ Proverbs 1–3

W e're all confronted with deadlines. Bills must be paid, licenses renewed, tax returns filed — the list goes on and on.

One deadline, though, is of supreme importance. It's one we all will face. The Bible says, "It is appointed for men to die once, but after this the judgment" (Hebrews 9:27).

Except for believers who are living when Jesus returns (1 Thessalonians 4:16-17), everyone will die. And all people from the beginning of history will stand before God in judgment. How foolish to neglect the preparation necessary for this inevitable accounting!

In Luke 12, Jesus told a parable of a rich man who planned to build bigger barns to store all his earthly goods so he could live out his days in pleasure and ease. But God unexpectedly announced, "Fool! This night your soul will be required of you" (Luke 12:20). His ultimate deadline had arrived.

Are you ready to meet God? If you've never received Christ as your personal Savior, do so without delay. Believe that He shed His blood on the cross to forgive your sins, and that He conquered death by rising from the grave. Ask Him to save you. Then you can face life's final deadline with confidence. — Richard De Haan

Life is uncertain,
Death is sure;
Sin the cause,
Christ the cure. — Anon.

**IF YOU BELIEVE THAT JESUS LIVES,
YOU DON'T NEED TO FEAR DEATH.**

GETTING RID OF THE PASTOR

READ:
1 Timothy 5:17-25

Let the elders who rule well be counted worthy of double honor.
—1 Timothy 5:17

THE BIBLE IN ONE YEAR:
■ Proverbs 4–7

A Christian leader told about some church members who came to him for advice. They wanted to know of a way to get rid of their pastor. Sensing that they were not being fair, he gave them these suggestions:

1. Look your pastor straight in the eye while he is preaching and say "Amen!" once in a while. He'll preach himself to death.

2. Pat him on the back and tell him his good points. He'll work himself to death.

3. Rededicate your life to Christ and ask your minister for a job to do. He'll die of heart failure.

4. Get the church to pray for him. Soon he'll become so effective that a larger church will take him off your hands.

If your pastor faithfully preaches God's Word and tries to live an exemplary life, do all you can to support and encourage him. Of course, no pastor is perfect, and sometimes a loving rebuke may be needed (1 Timothy 5:20). But a pastor carries a big responsibility (Hebrews 13:17), and a faithful man of God is worthy of respect and generous financial support (1 Timothy 3:1; 5:17-18).

By the way, when did you last say to your pastor, "I'm grateful for you and all you've done for me"? — Richard De Haan

We give the help that pastors need
For burdens they must bear
When we express our thanks to them
And hold them up in prayer. — D. De Haan

**A PASTOR LEADS BEST
WHEN HIS PEOPLE GET BEHIND HIM.**

July 14

NO VACANCY

READ:
Ephesians 6:5-9

He who is slothful in
his work is a brother
to him who is a great
destroyer.
—Proverbs 18:9

THE BIBLE IN ONE YEAR:
■ Proverbs 8—11

Fred, a clerk in a retail store, was rude to the customers and lazy. On several occasions his boss was about to fire him. But he didn't follow through because of his concern for Fred's wife and children, who would suffer from his dismissal.

One day a regular customer stopped in and noticed that Fred wasn't there. He asked the manager about him and was told that he had taken another job. The customer asked, "Are you planning to replace him?" The manager replied, "No, it isn't necessary. Fred didn't leave a vacancy."

Fred's work was of such poor quality that the business was better off without him. That should never be true of any employee, especially a Christian.

The apostle Paul told servants to be obedient to their masters "with goodwill doing service, as to the Lord, and not to men" (Ephesians 6:7).

God expected Christian servants in Paul's day to work diligently for their masters, and we too should give our employers an honest day's work. It's the right thing to do, and it strengthens our witness for Christ.

One good way to test the value of your work is to ask yourself this question: If I left my job, would it create a vacancy? — Richard De Haan

I ask You, Lord, for strength to do
The task You have assigned;
And help me work with diligence —
With all my heart and mind. — Fasick

**SOME PEOPLE STOP LOOKING FOR WORK
WHEN THEY GET A JOB.**

GIVERS AND TAKERS

READ:
Proverbs 14:15-21

... let him labor,
working with his
hands what is good,
that he may have
something to give
him who has need.
—Ephesians 4:28

THE BIBLE IN ONE YEAR:
■ Proverbs 12–14

S ome young children were talking about what they wanted to be when they grew up. When it was Jimmy's turn to speak, he didn't mention one of the more common professions like doctor, lawyer, policeman, and fireman. What he wanted to be was a philanthropist. When the other kids asked him to explain, he replied, "I heard they're the guys who have all the money."

Jimmy was only partially right. According to the dictionary, a philanthropist is "one who loves and seeks to benefit mankind." Simply having a lot of money, then, doesn't make one a philanthropist. In fact, a poor person who "loves and seeks to benefit mankind" out of his limited resources is more of a philanthropist than a person of great wealth who is a miser and gives grudgingly — even though the amount of his charitable gifts is large.

The apostle Paul encouraged takers to become givers. He said, "Let him who stole steal no longer, but rather let him labor . . . that he may have something to give him who has need" (Ephesians 4:28). That kind of giving will give joy to the giver (Proverbs 14:21).

Regardless of our income or vocation, we can all be philanthropists. — Richard De Haan

It's not what you'd do with a million
If riches should e'er be your lot,
But what you are doing at present
With the dollar and quarter you've got. — Anon.

**GOD GIVES US ALL WE NEED,
SO WE CAN GIVE TO THOSE IN NEED.**

A NEW LOCATION

READ:
Philippians 1:12-26

For to me, to live is Christ, and to die is gain.
—Philippians 1:21

THE BIBLE IN ONE YEAR:
■ Proverbs 15–18

A bank in Binghamton, New York, had some flowers sent to a competitor who had recently moved into a new building. There was a mixup at the flower shop, and the card sent with the arrangement read, "With our deepest sympathy."

The florist, who was greatly embarrassed, apologized. But he was even more embarrassed when he realized that the card intended for the bank was attached to a floral arrangement sent to a funeral home in honor of a deceased person. That card read, "Congratulations on your new location!"

A sentiment like that is appropriate for Christians, because they move to a wonderful new location when they die. They go to be with Christ, and the sorrows and heartaches of this earthly existence are gone forever. Near the end of his life, Paul said that to be with Christ is "far better" than to remain on earth (Philippians 1:23).

Yes, separation is painful, but as Christians we do not grieve as those who have no hope. Rather, we can rejoice, even with tear-filled eyes, because our loved ones have taken up a new residence in heaven.

Whenever believers in Christ die, it would be appropriate for us to say to them (if we could), "Congratulations on your new location!" — Richard De Haan

Someday my earthly house will fall —
I cannot tell how soon 'twill be;
But this I know — my All in All
Has now a place in heaven for me. —Crosby

DON'T DRIVE YOUR STAKES TOO DEEP—
WE'RE MOVING IN THE MORNING.

REVERSE THE TREND

READ:
Proverbs 15:1-7

A soft answer turns
away wrath.
—Proverbs 15:1

THE BIBLE IN ONE YEAR:
■ Proverbs 19–21

Researchers at Kenyon College conducted a test in cooperation with the US Navy. The purpose was to discover how the tone of the voice affected sailors when they were given orders. The experiments revealed that the way a person was addressed determined to a large extent the kind of response he would make.

For example, when an individual was spoken to in a soft voice, he would answer in a similar manner. But when he was shouted at, his reply came back in the same sharp tone. This was true whether the communication was given face-to-face, over the intercom, or by telephone.

This study reminds me of Proverbs 15:1, which states, "A soft answer turns away wrath, but a harsh word stirs up anger." What we say and how we say it not only makes a difference in the reaction we'll receive, but it also determines whether conflict or peace will result. Many arguments could be avoided and tense situations relaxed if we practiced the truth of this verse.

The next time someone speaks to you in a harsh or angry tone, reverse the trend by expressing meekness, quietness of spirit, and loving concern. What a difference a soft answer can make in our relationships! — Richard De Haan

So many folks use words that are harsh,
When angry, they speak their mind;
But Christ would have us reverse this trend
With words that are always kind. — D. De Haan

**TO GET OUT OF A HARD SITUATION,
TRY A SOFT ANSWER.**

THE PATHETIC PELICAN

READ:
Galatians 6:6-10

He who sows to his flesh will of the flesh reap corruption.
—Galatians 6:8

THE BIBLE IN ONE YEAR:
■ Proverbs 22–24

Pelicans, with their huge beaks, are strange-looking birds. But I saw one that was especially weird. Its beak was crisscrossed, as if someone had pulled the upper and lower parts in opposite directions. He was a pathetic sight!

Remembering that pelicans zoom headfirst from a considerable height into schools of fish to obtain their meals, I wondered if this particular bird had seen such a tempting catch that he dove into water that was too shallow for him and hit bottom. I don't know if this is what happened, but it made me think about the consequences and sometimes permanent effects of bad choices.

Many people today carry with them the scars of sin. Although it is true that "if we confess our sins, He is faithful and just to forgive us our sins and to cleanse us from all unrighteousness" (1 John 1:9), physical and emotional problems often remain. Those who live a reckless and unrestrained life may bear the marks of their destructive lifestyle to their dying day, even though in later years they are marvelously saved.

When you're tempted to sin, remember the pelican with the mangled beak. God will forgive sin when you confess it, but the consequences may last a lifetime. — Richard De Haan

The bounty of God's matchless grace
Is greater than our sinful deeds,
Yet from the evil that we sow
There may remain a crop of weeds. — D. De Haan

FORBIDDEN FRUIT TASTES SWEET
BUT ITS AFTERTASTE IS BITTER.

A STORM IS COMING!

READ:
2 Peter 3:1-15

The heavens will pass away with a great noise. —2 Peter 3:10

THE BIBLE IN ONE YEAR:
■ Proverbs 25–28

Several years ago in Florida, I watched the ominously black sky as a howling wind drove the rain in stinging sheets across angrily churning baywaters. A hurricane was approaching! All day long, radio and TV stations gave urgent instructions on how to guard against the destructive winds and surging tides of the impending storm.

As residents were frantically preparing for the storm, I asked myself, "Why do people take the warnings issued by the weather bureau so seriously, yet stubbornly refuse to hear God's warnings?" In His Word, God has told us that a much greater disaster will come upon the entire world. The Bible says, "The day of the Lord will come as a thief in the night, in which the heavens will pass away with a great noise, and the elements will melt with fervent heat; both the earth and the works that are in it will be burned up" (2 Peter 3:10).

Yes, that dreadful day is coming. But there is a sure way of escaping God's judgment. It's found in Christ. Those who have placed their faith in Him enjoy His peace here on earth and are assured of spending eternity with Him in heaven.

Are you prepared? If not, accept the Lord Jesus as your Savior today (Romans 10:9-13). — Richard De Haan

Eternity apart from God
Awaits all those who say
That there is not a hell to shun
Or future judgment day. — Sper

TO REJECT GOD'S DELIVERANCE IS TO INVITE DESTRUCTION.

A SERMON FROM NATURE

READ:
Proverbs 29:15-17

A child left to himself brings shame to his mother.
—Proverbs 29:15

THE BIBLE IN ONE YEAR:
Proverbs 29–31

I'll never forget seeing a mother wren angrily dive at my father when I was a boy. He had placed a number of wren houses around the yard and was always happy when his tenants returned each year to raise their families. One of his birdhouses was made with a hinged cover so that Dad could lift the top and look into the nest.

One day, wanting to see a new family that had just hatched, my father approached the birdhouse— but not without a severe scolding from Mother Wren. How she told him off! Disregarding her warning, my father was just about to lift the lid when this furious little mother flew full speed right down on top of his head. She gave him such a vicious peck that it drew blood!

Do we as Christian parents have that much concern for our children? Are we diligent in protecting them from the evil that could bring them spiritual injury? Are we teaching them about the threats of the world, the flesh, and the devil? (1 John 2:14-16). Do we know their friends? Do we monitor the TV programs they are watching?

Our children need our attention, guidance, and care (Proverbs 29:15). May God help us to guard them from spiritual harm. — Richard De Haan

God gives us children for a time
To train them in His way,
To love them and to teach them how
To follow and obey. — Sper

THE CHARACTER OF YOUR CHILDREN TOMORROW DEPENDS ON WHAT YOU PUT INTO THEIR HEARTS TODAY.

LOAD LIMIT

READ:
1 Corinthians 10:1-13

God is faithful, who will not allow you to be tempted beyond what you are able.
—1 Corinthians 10:13

THE BIBLE IN ONE YEAR:
■ Ecclesiastes 1–3

We've all seen load-limit signs on highways, bridges, and elevators. Knowing that too much strain can cause severe damage or complete collapse, engineers determine the exact amount of stress that various materials can safely endure. Posted warnings tell us not to exceed the maximum load.

Human beings also have their load limits, which vary from person to person. Some people, for example, can bear the pressure of trial and temptation better than others; yet everyone has a breaking point and can take only so much.

At times, circumstances and people seem to be pushing us beyond what we can bear. But the Lord knows our limitations and never allows any difficulties to enter our lives that exceed our strength and ability to endure. This is especially true when we're enticed by sin. According to 1 Corinthians 10:13, "God is faithful, who will not allow you to be tempted beyond what you are able."

So when trials and temptations press down on you, take courage. Remember, your heavenly Father knows the limits of your ability to stand up under life's pressures. Draw on His strength; no temptation will ever be greater than that! —Richard De Haan

When sorrows assail us or terrors draw nigh,
His love will not fail us, He'll guide with His eye;
And when we are fainting and ready to fail,
He'll give what is lacking and make us prevail. —Anon.

IF YOU YIELD TO GOD,
YOU WON'T GIVE IN TO SIN.

DARE TO BE A DANIEL

READ:
Daniel 6:1-10

**Daniel purposed in his heart that he would not defile himself.
—Daniel 1:8**

THE BIBLE IN ONE YEAR:
■ Ecclesiastes 4–6

The examples of people like Daniel in the Bible encourage us and show us how to live. We still need "Daniels" today — men and women who have convictions and the courage to stand for them even when it involves sacrifice or unpopularity.

My father, Dr. M. R. De Haan, was just such a man. Oh, he wasn't perfect. He was human. He had his faults. Some people even thought of him as stubborn. But he was a man of the Book, the Word of God. He was a man of conviction. And he was a man of courage.

My father went home to be with the Lord on December 13, 1965. Yet I can recall his words to me on one occasion as if he said them only yesterday. Accenting his statement by pounding his fist on his desk, he said, "Richard, I don't care if the whole world differs with me. I must do what's right. I must act according to my convictions!"

Of course, we must be careful to make sure our beliefs are properly grounded. But once we are certain of that, we should be like Daniel, who not only had convictions but the courage to stand for them (Daniel 1:8).

Today, when you are tempted to compromise your principles, don't give in. Dare to be a Daniel! — Richard De Haan

The life that counts must toil and fight,
Must hate the wrong and love the right,
Must stand for truth, by day, by night —
This is the life that counts. — Anon.

**YOU WON'T FALL FOR WHAT'S WRONG
IF YOU STAND FOR WHAT'S RIGHT.**

OPEN WIDE

READ:
Psalm 81

I am the Lord your God . . . ; open your mouth wide, and I will fill it. —Psalm 81:10

THE BIBLE IN ONE YEAR:
■ Ecclesiastes 7–9

As a boy, I was always thrilled to discover a newly constructed robin's nest. It was fascinating to watch for the eggs and then to wait for those featherless little creatures with bulging eyes and gaping mouths to break out of their shells. Standing at a distance, I could see their heads bobbing unsteadily and their mouths wide open, expecting Mother Robin to give them their dinner.

As I recall those childhood scenes, I think of God's promise: "I am the LORD your God . . . ; open your mouth wide, and I will fill it" (Psalm 81:10). In spite of this gracious offer to ancient Israel, the people ignored God, and He "gave them over to their own stubborn heart, to walk in their own counsels" (v.12). If they had accepted God's offer, "He would have fed them also with the finest of wheat; and with honey from the rock" (v.16).

So too God longs to give us spiritual food. And He will satisfy our spiritual hunger as we study His Word, worship with others, listen to faithful Bible teachers, read literature with good biblical content, and daily depend on Him.

If we refuse God's provisions, we will suffer spiritual malnutrition and fail to grow. But if we open our mouth wide, we can be sure that God will fill it. — Richard De Haan

> *The Savior can satisfy fully*
> *The heart that the world cannot fill;*
> *His presence will sanctify wholly*
> *The soul that is yielded and still.* — Smith

**TO HAVE A FULFILLING LIFE,
LET GOD FILL YOU.**

SAY IT NOW!

READ:
Romans 16:1-16

Greet Priscilla and
Aquila, . . . to whom
. . . I give thanks.
—Romans 16:3-4

THE BIBLE IN ONE YEAR:
■ Ecclesiastes 10–12

An unknown author has penned these thought-provoking words:

I would rather have one little rose
From the garden of a friend
Than to have the choicest flowers
When my stay on earth must end.

I would rather have a pleasant word
In kindness said to me
Than flattery when my heart is still,
And life has ceased to be.

I would rather have a loving smile
From friends I know are true
Than tears shed 'round my casket
When to this world I bid adieu.

Bring me all your flowers today,
Whether pink, or white, or red;
I'd rather have one blossom now
Than a truckload when I'm dead.

Recalling the good qualities of deceased friends or relatives at their funeral is appropriate, but how much better to give sincere praise to them while they are still living. It may be the encouragement they desperately need.

As the apostle Paul closed his letter to the Romans, he publicly commended those who had helped and encouraged him in the work of the gospel. He not only greeted them by name, but he also expressed his gratitude for what they had done (16:1-15). What an example for all of us to follow!

Do you owe someone a word of thanks or appreciation? Don't put it off. Say it today. Tomorrow may be too late! — Richard De Haan

---

YOU CAN'T SPEAK A KIND WORD TOO SOON,
FOR YOU NEVER KNOW HOW SOON IT WILL BE TOO LATE.

LOOKING TO JESUS

READ:
John 14:15-24

Let us run with
endurance the race
that is set before us,
looking unto Jesus,
the author and finisher
of our faith.
—Hebrews 12:1-2

THE BIBLE IN ONE YEAR:
■ Song of Solomon 1–4

Leslie Dunkin told about a dog he had when he was a boy. His father would occasionally test the dog's obedience. He would place a tempting piece of meat on the floor and give the command, "No!" The dog, who must have had a strong urge to go for the meat, was placed in a most difficult situation—to obey or disobey his master's command.

Dunkin said, "The dog never looked at the meat. He seemed to feel that if he did, the temptation to disobey would be too great. So he looked steadily at my father's face." Dunkin then made this spiritual application: "There is a lesson for us all. Always look up to the Master's face."

Yes, that's good advice. God, of course, will not tempt us to do wrong (James 1:13). We do encounter many temptations, though, and if we keep our eyes fixed on the Lord Jesus we will be able to overcome them. When confronted by enticements that could easily overwhelm us, we need to look to Christ and follow His direction. "Seeing" Him and "hearing" Him as He is revealed in the Scriptures will give us the discernment to know what's right, and the desire and strength to obey Him.

Are you battling temptation? Keep your eyes fixed on the Lord Jesus. He will give you victory. — Richard De Haan

> *The only way to overcome*
> *Temptations that we face*
> *Is just to focus on the Lord,*
> *Who strengthens by His grace.* — Sper

**TO MASTER TEMPTATION,
KEEP YOUR EYES ON THE MASTER.**

A CHURCHLESS CHRISTIAN

READ:
Hebrews 10:19-25

**Let us consider one another . . . , not forsaking the assembling of ourselves together.
—Hebrews 10:24-25**

THE BIBLE IN ONE YEAR:
■ Song of Solomon 5–8

Nowhere in the Bible does it say we must have our names on a church membership roll to be saved. That doesn't mean, however, that joining with other believers in a local church is not vital to our spiritual growth. Gathering regularly for worship and instruction encourages love for others, good works, and mutual accountability (Hebrews 10:24-25).

I read an interesting article some time ago that compared a Christian without a church to . . .

- a student who won't go to school
- a soldier without an army
- a citizen who won't vote
- a sailor without a ship
- a child without a family
- a drummer without a band
- a ballplayer without a team
- a honeybee without a hive
- a scientist who does not share his findings with his colleagues

If you have been neglecting one of God's greatest provisions for your spiritual growth, find a church that believes and teaches God's Word and start attending faithfully. Take time to get to know others and let them get to know you. Ask God to help you find ways to serve others.

Don't be a churchless Christian. — Richard De Haan

I love Thy church, O God!
I prize her heavenly ways —
Her sweet communion, solemn vows,
Her hymns of love and praise. — Dwight

**SEVEN DAYS WITHOUT CHURCH
MAKES ONE WEAK.**

HOPE FOR THE WORLD

READ:
Isaiah 2:1-5

. . . looking for the blessed hope and glorious appearing of our great God and Savior Jesus Christ.
—Titus 2:13

THE BIBLE IN ONE YEAR:
■ Isaiah 1–3

PEACE TALKS FALL APART AGAIN. UNEMPLOYMENT RATE RISES. TORNADO RIPS THROUGH TOWN.

These newspaper headlines selected at random tend to lead us to despair. There just doesn't seem to be any hope for this world. And yet, according to the Scriptures, the dream of abolishing war is not merely wishful thinking. The idea of prosperity for all is more than a political gimmick. The Bible tells us that the eventual taming of nature is a certainty.

The hope for this world, however, is not to be found in human efforts but in the return of Jesus Christ. He alone can solve the problems that are baffling mankind.

The prophet Isaiah said that someday "nation shall not lift up sword against nation, neither shall they learn war anymore" (Isaiah 2:4). This glorious prospect will become a reality when the Lord Jesus Himself returns as "King of kings and Lord of lords" (1 Timothy 6:15) to set up His kingdom of peace and righteousness. We are to be "looking for the blessed hope and glorious appearing of our great God and Savior Jesus Christ" (Titus 2:13). Because we have this hope, we can be optimistic even in the deepening gloom of this age.

Keep looking up! — Richard De Haan

Lift up your heads, pilgrims aweary,
See day's approach now crimson the sky;
Night shadows flee, and your Beloved,
Awaited with longing, at last draweth nigh. —Camp

THE ONLY HOPE FOR WORLD PEACE
IS THE COMING OF THE PRINCE OF PEACE.

THE WRONG STANDARD

READ:
Isaiah 6:1-5

**Woe is me, for I am undone! . . . My eyes have seen the King, the LORD of hosts.
—Isaiah 6:5**

THE BIBLE IN ONE YEAR:
■ Isaiah 4–6

A little boy announced, "I'm like Goliath. I'm 9 feet tall." "What makes you say that?" asked his mother. The child replied, "Well, I made a ruler and measured myself with it, and I am 9 feet tall!"

Many people fail to see their need of salvation because they measure themselves by a faulty standard. By looking at their peers and comparing their behavior with others who have done worse than they have, they come to the conclusion that they are not so bad after all. But such feelings of pride are demolished when people compare themselves with a perfect standard of righteousness.

How do we measure up in God's sight? When the prophet Isaiah saw the Lord in all His glory, he exclaimed, "Woe is me, for I am undone! Because I am a man of unclean lips, . . . for my eyes have seen the King, the LORD of hosts" (Isaiah 6:5). According to Romans 3:23, we all have sinned and fall short of God's glory. That's why everyone needs to be forgiven.

If you're measuring your morality against that of others, you are using the wrong standard of measurement. But if you recognize how far you fall short in the sight of God, reach out in faith to Jesus today and receive His gift of forgiveness. — Richard De Haan

By God's Word at last my sin I learned —
Then I trembled at the law I'd spurned,
Till my guilty soul imploring turned
To Calvary. —Newell

**IF WE COULD EARN OUR SALVATION,
CHRIST WOULD NOT HAVE DIED TO PROVIDE IT.**

BEWARE!

READ:
2 Corinthians 11:1-15

Take heed that you
not be deceived.
—Luke 21:8

THE BIBLE IN ONE YEAR:
■ Isaiah 7–9

An acquaintance of mine was "taken in" by a smooth-talking salesman who stopped at his place of business. The man displayed some attractive jewelry that he said he had purchased at a tremendous discount. He was especially proud of some very expensive-looking watches that had a well-known name on the dials.

My friend was impressed and bought several watches. But after the salesman left, he examined his "bargains" more carefully. He was surprised to discover that the trademark was not that of a famous brand after all. Two letters in the name were different, but the print was so small he hadn't noticed it before. The watch straps were not genuine leather but "genuine lizard," and on the back of the cases were the words "Swiss base metal."

The incident reminded me of what the Savior said in Luke 21:8, "Take heed that you not be deceived." Even as some in the business world cleverly pervert the facts and victimize their customers, there are also false teachers in the church who distort the truth. They use biblical terminology and appear to be orthodox. But beware! They are evil and will lead you astray. Be firmly grounded in the Word of God and you won't be "taken in" by deception. — Richard De Haan

O grant us grace, Almighty Lord,
To read and mark Your holy Word,
Its truths with meekness to receive,
And by its holy precepts live. — Beddome

EXAMINE ALL TEACHING IN THE LIGHT OF GOD'S WORD.

A STONE
OR BREAD?

READ:
Matthew 7:7-11

What man is there among you who, if his son asks for bread, will give him a stone?
—Matthew 7:9

THE BIBLE IN ONE YEAR:
■ Isaiah 10–12

No loving father would give a stone or a snake to his hungry son if he asked for a piece of bread or a fish. Jesus used the absurdity of that analogy in Matthew 7 to underscore the heavenly Father's readiness to give good things to His children when they ask Him. He wanted them to have complete confidence in the Father's provision for their spiritual needs.

Sometimes, however, it may seem as if the Lord has given us "stones" instead of "bread." But in His wisdom, He actually is working through our circumstances to give us something far better than what we requested. An unknown author expressed it this way:

I asked for health that I might do greater things;
I was given infirmity that I might do better things.
I asked God for strength that I might achieve;
I was made weak that I might learn to obey.
I asked for riches that I might be happy;
I was given poverty that I might be wise.
I asked for power and the praise of men;
I was given weakness to sense my need of God.
I asked for all things that I might enjoy life;
I was given life that I might enjoy all things.
I got nothing I asked for but everything I hoped for;
In spite of myself, my prayers were answered—
I am among all men most richly blessed.

Yes, God always gives us what's best for us. —Richard De Haan

---

WE MAY ASK AMISS, BUT GOD ANSWERS ARIGHT.

I Got A Ticket

READ:
Colossians 3:1-9

Do not lie to one
another, since you
have put off the old
man with his deeds.
—Colossians 3:9

THE BIBLE IN ONE YEAR:
■ Isaiah 13–15

W hen I arrived home from a trip, I announced to my wife, "I got a ticket when I was driving through Indiana." She was about to give me a good scolding, but then I said, "Wait a minute! I can explain everything."

I told her that I had been traveling on the Indiana Toll Road. Everyone who enters it receives a "ticket." It's not handed out because of a traffic violation, but it's used to determine the amount of toll to be paid on the basis of the distance traveled.

This incident reminded me that it's possible to tell a lie while making a true statement. It's done by using words that have a double meaning, or by making incomplete statements to leave an erroneous impression.

People often tell half-truths and use certain terms that are intended to mislead others. When selling a used TV, for example, the seller may emphasize the great picture quality but neglect to tell the buyer that the volume control doesn't work properly. Then, he can later rationalize and say, "I told the truth. I told him the picture was great. He didn't ask me about the sound." This is just another form of lying.

Instead of stretching or bending the truth to serve our own agenda, let's heed the words of Scripture: "Do not lie to one another" (Colossians 3:9). —Richard De Haan

With our minds we can conceive
Of truthful words that can deceive;
Although we claim the truth was meant,
In truth, a lie was our intent. —D. De Haan

**THE MOST DECEPTIVE LIARS ARE THOSE
WHO LIVE ON THE EDGE OF TRUTH.**

KEEP TALKING ABOUT JESUS

READ:
1 Corinthians 15:51-57

Jesus said to her, "I am the resurrection and the life. He who believes in Me, though he may die, he shall live." —John 11:25

THE BIBLE IN ONE YEAR:
■ Isaiah 16–18

Pastor Eloy Pacheco said at a funeral for a believer that Jesus is the only lasting source of comfort. Afterward a woman came up to him and said, "You preachers are all alike. All you talk about is Jesus, Jesus, Jesus!"

"That's true," he replied kindly. "What comfort do you have to offer the grieving family?"

She was speechless for a few moments, and then she said, "You're right. At least you have Jesus."

Sooner or later someone dear to us will die, and we'll want to be comforted. A hug, a kind deed, shared tears, and the presence of a friend may ease sorrow's pain just a bit. But these gestures won't answer our most urgent questions: What's beyond the grave? Where is the person now? Will we be reunited in heaven? How can I have the assurance of eternal life?

For the answers to those questions, we must look to Jesus Christ. He is the One who defeated sin and death by dying on the cross for us and rising from the grave (1 Corinthians 15:1-28,57). Because He lives, all who put their faith in Him will live forever with Him (John 11:25).

When a believer in Christ dies, we who are left behind can find comfort and confidence in Him. So let's keep talking about Jesus. — Dennis De Haan

We have hope, for Christ has risen,
Death was conquered by God's Son;
May we gently share that message
With some hurting, grieving one. —D. De Haan

IN LIFE AND IN DEATH, OUR ONLY HOPE IS JESUS.

HIS PAIN

READ:
Judges 10:6-16

They put away the foreign gods from among them and served the LORD. And His soul could no longer endure the misery of Israel.
—Judges 10:16

THE BIBLE IN ONE YEAR:
■ Isaiah 19–21

The Old Testament book of Judges is a somewhat depressing account of God's people locked in a recurring cycle of rebellion, punishment, repentance, and deliverance. After every divine intervention, the process was repeated. It was always their pain that caused God's people to call on Him: "The children of Israel said to the LORD, 'We have sinned! Do to us whatever seems best to You; only deliver us this day, we pray'" (Judges 10:15).

Six times in Judges they cried out to God, and each time He came to their rescue. But the Lord Himself was also in pain. In a remarkable statement, the Bible says of Almighty God, "His soul could no longer endure the misery of Israel" (v.16).

The misery we suffer because of our spiritual rebellion will always cause pain to the Lord. As the prophet Isaiah wrote: "In all their affliction He was afflicted" (Isaiah 63:9).

God's suffering reached its zenith when His Son Jesus Christ went to the cross to die for our sin. We will never fully understand what it meant for the intimacy of the Father and the Son to be broken (Matthew 27:46-50).

It's good to ponder the pain of God even as we praise Him for the marvel of our salvation. — David McCasland

Your love, O God, would spare no pain
To conquer death and win;
You sent Your only Son to die
To rescue us from sin. — D. De Haan

SIN BRINGS PAIN—TO US, AND TO GOD.

BROKEN STATUES

READ:
Daniel 2:36-45

The court shall be seated, and they shall take away his dominion, to consume and destroy it forever.
—Daniel 7:26

THE BIBLE IN ONE YEAR:
■ Isaiah 22—24

In Moscow stands the New Tretyakov Gallery, a museum that displays art and artifacts from the days of the former Soviet Union. Scattered along the banks of the Moscow River near the museum are statues of once-powerful leaders that have been smashed and disfigured. Images of Stalin and Lenin have their noses knocked off and their heads separated from their bodies.

These gloomy scenes bring to mind the dream of King Nebuchadnezzar in Daniel 2. He saw a statue with a glorious head of gold, a chest and arms of silver, a torso of bronze, legs of iron, and feet of iron and clay (vv.31-33). It portrayed the succession of four great ruling nations of the world. From history we know they were Babylon, Medo-Persia, Greece, and Rome. Then a stone "cut out of the mountain without hands" (v.45) rolled down and smashed the statue to smithereens. This pictured God's judgment of those four kingdoms and His supremacy over all the earth.

One day God will judge the nations of the world, and their monuments will lie in ruins. No matter how powerful the nation, all will crumble beneath the outpouring of God's holy wrath. We can be confident that Jesus Christ, the King of kings, will rule the world in righteousness, justice, and peace. What a glorious prospect! — Dave Egner

Now evil prospers, falsehood reigns,
And darkness dims the light;
But soon the day will come when Christ
Returns to set things right. —Sper

NATIONS RISE AND FALL,
BUT CHRIST'S KINGDOM STANDS FOREVER.

WHAT WILL LAST?

READ:
2 Corinthians 4:16-18

**The things which are seen are temporary, but the things which are not seen are eternal.
—2 Corinthians 4:18**

THE BIBLE IN ONE YEAR:
■ Isaiah 25–27

I have a friend who was denied a doctorate from a prestigious West Coast university because of his Christian worldview. As he was approaching the conclusion of his studies, his advisor invited him to come into his office and informed him that his dissertation had been rejected.

My friend's first thought was of thousands of dollars and 5 years of his life taking flight, and his heart sank. But then he thought of the words of the hymn by Rhea Miller: "I'd rather have Jesus than silver or gold, I'd rather be His than have riches untold; . . . I'd rather have Jesus than anything this world affords today." And then my friend laughed—for he realized that nothing of eternal value had been lost.

How we respond to loss is all a matter of perspective. One person is absorbed with the permanent; the other with the passing. One stores up treasure in heaven; the other accumulates it here on earth. One stays with a difficult marriage because heaven is on ahead; another moves out and looks for happiness in another mate. While one believes that happiness is found in being rich and famous, Christ's followers are willing to suffer poverty, hunger, indignity, and shame because of "the glory that will be revealed" (1 Peter 5:1).

Wouldn't you "rather have Jesus"? — David Roper

I'd rather have Jesus than men's applause,
I'd rather be faithful to His dear cause;
I'd rather have Jesus than worldwide fame,
I'd rather be true to His holy name. — Miller

**LIVING ONLY FOR TEMPORARY GAIN
LEADS TO ETERNAL LOSS.**

August 5

UNEXPECTED GRIEF

READ:
2 Corinthians 1:3-11

**Blessed be the God and Father of our Lord Jesus Christ, the Father of mercies and God of all comfort.
—2 Corinthians 1:3**

THE BIBLE IN ONE YEAR:
■ Isaiah 28–30

Since 1988, I've enjoyed writing several *Our Daily Bread* articles each month. I've felt blessed to dig into Scripture, observe life, and provide spiritual help in this publication.

But on June 6, 2002, I found myself unable to offer help. On the last day of her junior year of high school, our 17-year-old daughter Melissa was killed in a car accident.

In one horrible instant, everything we knew about God and the Bible and heaven was put to the test. We needed the Christian community to guide us toward hope as we stood at the funeral of a beloved young woman who had touched so many lives with her smile, her godliness, her love of life, and her care for others.

For many weeks, I couldn't write. What could I say? How could I find words to help others when my family — when I — needed so much?

Now, months later as I begin to write again, I can say that God has not changed. He is still our loving heavenly Father, the "God of all comfort" (2 Corinthians 1:3). He is still the source of hope in the face of unexpected grief. I write of Him with a renewed sense of my need for His touch, His love, His strength. Broken, I write of the only One who can make us whole. — Dave Branon

I have been through the valley of weeping,
The valley of sorrow and pain;
But the God of all comfort was with me,
At hand to uphold and sustain. — Anon.

**WHEN GOD PERMITS TRIALS,
HE ALSO PROVIDES COMFORT.**

Eyes Of Compassion

READ:
Luke 10:25-37

A certain Samaritan,
as he journeyed,
came where he was. And
when he saw him,
he had compassion.
—Luke 10:33

THE BIBLE IN ONE YEAR:
■ Isaiah 31–33

As Francisco Venegas, a school custodian in Colorado, watched the children on the playground, he saw a 9-year-old girl fall off a bench for no apparent reason. Another time he noticed her face twisted in a strange expression. Sensing that something was wrong, Francisco reported what he had seen to the school office.

A few days later, the girl had a seizure and was rushed to the hospital. The information that Francisco provided led doctors to perform a brain scan, and they found a tumor. Successful surgery and recovery followed.

Many people have called Francisco Venegas a "good samaritan," a name drawn from a story Jesus told about three people who saw a man in need. The first two "passed by on the other side" (Luke 10:31-32). But the third, a Samaritan, showed compassion (vv.33-35).

Compassion cannot see someone in need without helping. It accepts the consequences of getting involved because it cannot bear to turn away. Compassion comes from a heart that is tender toward God and fellow travelers on the road of life.

Jesus' story of the Good Samaritan ends with a command for each of us: "Go and do likewise" (v.37). Jesus sees everyone through eyes of compassion, and He calls us to do the same. — David McCasland

> *When you see someone in need,*
> *Love demands a loving deed;*
> *Don't just say you love him true,*
> *Prove it by the deeds you do.* —Sper

COMPASSION IS LOVE IN ACTION.

August 7

OBSOLETE

READ:
Isaiah 35

**The ransomed of the LORD . . . shall obtain joy and gladness, and sorrow and sighing shall flee away.
—Isaiah 35:10**

THE BIBLE IN ONE YEAR:
■ Isaiah 34–36

Pastor and author Joseph Parker (1830-1902) commented about the closing words of Isaiah 35:10, "Sorrow and sighing shall flee away." He said, "Looking through the dictionary, you will occasionally come across a word marked 'obsolete.' The time is coming when the two words *sorrow* and *sighing* shall be obsolete. The things which mar life here and now will then belong to the past."

Human existence has been marked by tragedy, heartache, disappointment, and evil. It's comforting to know that the time is coming when sorrow and death will pass away, and God Himself will wipe all tears from our eyes. Then we will experience the truth that "the former things have passed away" (Revelation 21:4).

Are you burdened today by some seemingly insurmountable problem? Are you lonely, heartbroken, and disappointed? If you are a child of God, dwell on this reassuring thought: "The sufferings of this present time are not worthy to be compared with the glory which shall be revealed in us" (Romans 8:18). A brighter day is coming when words such as *sighing*, *death*, and *tears* will all be obsolete.

So don't be downhearted, beloved child of God. Keep looking up! — Richard De Haan

> *God's tomorrow is a day of gladness,*
> *And its joys shall never fade;*
> *No more weeping, no more sense of sadness,*
> *No more foes to make afraid.* — *Ackley*

HEAVEN—NO PAIN, NO NIGHT, NO DEATH, NO TEARS.

LITTLE NICKS — BIG TROUBLE!

READ:
Galatians 5:16-26

A little leaven leavens the whole lump.
—Galatians 5:9

THE BIBLE IN ONE YEAR:
■ Isaiah 37–39

We couldn't figure it out. My son and I had purchased an old powerboat for fishing and couldn't make it run properly. We were unable to get it up to speed, and it shuddered when we tried to go faster. We figured that the trouble was with the fuel system, so we adjusted the carburetor and changed the fuel filter. But that still didn't solve the problem.

When we took the boat out of the water, my son found the cause of the trouble. One of the propeller fins had a ³/₄-inch (2 cm) nick in it. *That can't be it,* I thought. *That nick is too small.* But when we installed a new propeller, what a difference it made! We had been slowed down by a tiny nick.

A similar problem is often at work in our lives as Christians. Sinful practices like those described in Galatians 5:16-21 have their roots in the seemingly insignificant thoughts and attitudes of the heart (Matthew 5:28; 15:18-19). If we ignore or tolerate these "little" sins, they will eventually grow, corrupting more of our thoughts and actions — even harming people around us. Just as a little yeast leavens a whole lump of dough (Galatians 5:9), so also a "little" sin can eventually weaken our service for Christ and the ministry of His church.

Remember, little nicks can cause big trouble. — Dave Egner

One little sin, what harm can it do?
Give it free reign and soon there are two.
Then sinful deeds and habits ensue —
Guard well your thoughts, lest they destroy you. — D. De Haan

---

LITTLE SINS WON'T STAY LITTLE.

CALVARY'S DEEPEST PAIN

READ:
Matthew 26:36-46

The LORD has laid on Him the iniquity of us all. —Isaiah 53:6

THE BIBLE IN ONE YEAR:
■ Isaiah 40–42

After washing His disciples' feet and celebrating the Passover with them, Jesus led them into a familiar garden and "began to be sorrowful and deeply distressed" (Matthew 26:37). Going a bit farther with Peter, James, and John, He said, "My soul is exceedingly sorrowful, even to death. Stay here and watch with Me" (v.38).

Then, walking a short distance away, Jesus "fell on His face" before God, saying, "O My Father, if it is possible, let this cup pass from Me; nevertheless, not as I will, but as You will" (v.39). He did this three times (v.44).

How do we account for such a surge of emotional turmoil? Only by understanding the "cup" that Jesus asked His Father to take from Him. He was about to bear "the iniquity of us all" (Isaiah 53:6). That "cup" was filled with the sins of the whole world.

The agony of Gethsemane would culminate on the cross in His heart-wrenching cry: "My God, My God, why have You forsaken Me?" (Matthew 27:46). Jesus' physical pain was nothing compared with Calvary's deepest pain — the awful reality of being abandoned by His Father. God made Jesus "to be sin for us" (2 Corinthians 5:21), so the Father had to turn away from Him.

Praise God for His great love for us! — Herb Vander Lugt

> *"Man of Sorrows," what a name*
> *For the Son of God who came*
> *Ruined sinners to reclaim!*
> *Hallelujah! What a Savior! — Bliss*

**CHRIST BRAVED THE SHADOW OF ETERNAL DEATH
TO BRING US THE SUNSHINE OF ETERNAL LIFE.**

KEEP ON ROWING

READ:
1 Corinthians 3:18–4:1

Let a man so consider us, as servants of Christ and stewards of the mysteries of God.
—1 Corinthians 4:1

THE BIBLE IN ONE YEAR:
■ Isaiah 43–45

I once saw a cartoon depicting a group of shackled prisoners standing on a dock, waiting for a Roman galley that was pulling into port. "That's a great ship," one mused. "I wonder what makes it go?"

The sketch reminded me of the words of the apostle Paul: "Let a man so consider us, as servants of Christ" (1 Corinthians 4:1). Paul used an unusual Greek word for servants. Literally, it means "under-rowers," and in that day it referred to the slaves that pulled the oars in Roman warships.

What a striking word picture! The great apostle, who could have asserted his authority, considered himself a mere galley slave in the hold of the ship with the rest of God's people, pulling on an oar with everyone else.

This is different from our usual concept of leadership. We tend to think of a regally dressed captain standing on the deck of a great sailing vessel, "calling the shots" and controlling the ship.

The Lord Jesus is our true Captain. The direction in which a church or any other ministry goes, the speed with which it develops, and the size to which it grows is His prerogative. Our task, no matter what our position or work, is to keep our eyes on Jesus and to keep on rowing. —David Roper

The Master needs what you have to offer,
No matter if you think it's small;
His work on earth is done through His children,
So give Him your best, give your all. —Hess

LEADERS DON'T ATTAIN GREATNESS BY GIVING ORDERS, BUT BY SERVING OTHERS.

THE HYPOCRITE EXCUSE

READ:
Galatians 2:11-18

The rest . . . also
played the hypocrite
with him.
—Galatians 2:13

THE BIBLE IN ONE YEAR:
■ Isaiah 46–48

I have a neighbor who can't stand hypocrites. In fact, he tells me that he stopped going to church because he saw too many hypocrites there.

He's not alone. That's one of the most popular reasons people give for rejecting Christianity. My neighbor is right — there are too many hypocrites in the church.

The problem of hypocrisy, though, is not the issue to pursue with people who reject the gospel. The key is *validity*. Does the presence of hypocrites in the church invalidate the gospel message?

In today's Bible reading, Paul accused Peter of hypocrisy (Galatians 2:13). Did that invalidate the gospel Peter preached? Some people may think so, perhaps because they expect Christians to be perfect. What might surprise them, however, is that Jesus Himself warned against and condemned hypocrisy (Matthew 6:1-18; 23:13-33). He hates it more than they do.

That brings us to a key point: The validity of Christianity is not based on imperfect Christians but on the perfect Christ. Therefore, if a person could show that Jesus was a hypocrite, he would have an argument. But that's impossible. Jesus was sinless and without fault (John 8:46; Hebrews 4:15).

Jesus is the answer to the hypocrite excuse. — Dave Branon

> Lord, help me make my witness clear,
> And labor faithfully,
> So friends and neighbors turn to Christ
> Through what they hear from me. — Anon.

**INSTEAD OF LOOKING AT HYPOCRITES,
LOOK AT JESUS.**

SELF-PITY OR REJOICING?

READ:
Philippians 4:1-8

Rejoice in the Lord always. Again I will say, rejoice!
—Philippians 4:4

THE BIBLE IN ONE YEAR:
■ Isaiah 49–51

Temperament seems to be something that each of us is born with. Some of us have upbeat dispositions, while others play the music of life in a minor key. Yet how we respond to life's trials also affects our overall disposition.

For example, Fanny Crosby lost her sight when she was only 6 weeks old. She lived into her nineties, composing thousands of beloved hymns. On her 92nd birthday she cheerfully said, "If in all the world you can find a happier person than I am, do bring him to me. I should like to shake his hand."

What enabled Fanny Crosby to experience such joy in the face of what many would term a "tragedy"? At an early age she chose to "rejoice in the Lord always" (Philippians 4:4). In fact, Fanny carried out a resolution she made when she was only 8 years old: "How many blessings I enjoy that other people don't. To weep and sigh because I'm blind, I cannot and I won't."

Let's remember that "the joy of the LORD is [our] strength" (Nehemiah 8:10). Let's also take comfort in the teachings of Jesus, who in John 15:11 said, "These things I have spoken to you, that My joy may remain in you, and that your joy may be full." When faced with the choice of self-pity or rejoicing, let's respond with rejoicing. — Vernon Grounds

Be this the purpose of my soul,
My solemn, my determined choice:
To yield to God's supreme control,
And in my every trial rejoice. —Anon.

RATHER THAN COMPLAIN ABOUT THE THORNS ON ROSES, BE THANKFUL FOR ROSES AMONG THE THORNS.

CLOSE THE GATE

READ:
Isaiah 54:1-10

"With everlasting kindness I will have mercy on you," says the LORD, your Redeemer.
—Isaiah 54:8

THE BIBLE IN ONE YEAR:
■ Isaiah 52–54

After a round of golf, a British statesman and his friend walked through a field in which cows were grazing. The men were so absorbed in conversation that they forgot to close the gate when they left the fenced area.

The statesman happened to notice the open gate, however, and went back to close it. Then he told his friend that this little incident reminded him of a doctor who was dying and was asked by a minister whether there was anything he wanted to say before he slipped away. "No," the doctor replied, "except that through life I think I have always closed the gates behind me." The dying man had learned to put failures and disappointments behind him so they wouldn't rob him of his joy and peace.

As Christians, we should learn that lesson well. When we sin, we can "close the gate" to nagging guilt by confessing our sin to our merciful Lord and accepting His forgiveness (Isaiah 54:7-10; 1 John 1:9). Or, if we have a misunderstanding with someone, rather than allowing the irritation to fester, we should go to that person and make things right (Matthew 18:15).

Let's close the gate to the failures and disappointments of the past — then move on! — Richard De Haan

> Look not back to yesterday,
> So full of failure and regret;
> Look ahead and seek God's way —
> Sins confessed you must forget. — D. De Haan

**TO ENJOY THE FUTURE,
ACCEPT GOD'S FORGIVENESS FOR THE PAST.**

THE PRICE OF FOOD

READ:
Isaiah 55

Why do you spend money for what is not bread, and your wages for what does not satisfy? —Isaiah 55:2

THE BIBLE IN ONE YEAR:
■ Isaiah 55–57

A hummingbird near Bingham Canyon, Utah, was seen pressing its bill against the biggest red "flower" in town. No one knows for sure how long it took for the bird to realize you can't get nectar out of a traffic light!

National Wildlife magazine also told about a red-tailed hawk in North Carolina that was seen swooping down in an attempt to carry off a large tomcat. The cat fought back with such fury that the hawk barely escaped with its life.

This kind of foolishness is not just for the birds. Expending a lot of energy to feed our souls with food that doesn't satisfy is something all of us know about. Sometimes we're merely left empty, while at other times we are nearly consumed by the things we pursue. This is why the Lord's words in Isaiah 55 are so relevant. He asks, "Why do you spend money for what is not bread, and your wages for what does not satisfy?"

God doesn't just leave us with the question. He goes on to assure us that our heart's deepest longing can be fulfilled — in Him alone (vv.1-7). There is strength in feeding on mercy rather than revenge, truth rather than falsehood, and peace rather than conflict. That's why we must choose Christ over religion, and the Bible over tradition. When we eat right, we'll discover that the Lord is good (v.2). — Mart De Haan

Now none but Christ can satisfy,
None other name for me;
There's love and life and lasting joy,
Lord Jesus, found in Thee. — McGranahan

**THERE'S A LONGING IN EVERY HEART
THAT ONLY JESUS CAN SATISFY.**

UNLIKELY SERVANTS

READ:
Judges 6:11-16

**God has chosen the foolish things of the world to put to shame the wise.
—1 Corinthians 1:27**

THE BIBLE IN ONE YEAR:
■ Isaiah 58–60

We often hear people say things like: "I'm only a housewife." "I'm only a janitor." "I'm only an average student."

Underestimating one's usefulness to God is nothing new. In Old Testament times, for example, when God looked for someone to conquer the troublesome Midianites, He chose unimpressive Gideon, calling him a "mighty man of valor" (Judges 6:12). Gideon responded, "How can I save Israel? Indeed my clan is the weakest in Manasseh, and I am the least in my father's house" (v.15). But God persisted, saying, "Have I not sent you? . . . Surely I will be with you" (vv.14-16).

Gideon became God's man for the task, because there's no such thing as a "nobody" in His eyes. The Lord gave Gideon just 300 men to help him, rather than thousands (7:1-7), so that God alone would receive the glory.

The apostle Paul also taught that God chooses and uses things that the world calls foolish, weak, lowly, and despised. He shames the wise and the mighty so "that no flesh should glory in His presence" (1 Corinthians 1:29).

If you feel that you're "only a nobody," review God's call to Gideon. The Lord wants to use you more than you ever thought possible. — Joanie Yoder

Gladly take the task God gives you,
Let His work your pleasure be;
Answer quickly when He calls you,
"I am willing, Lord, use me." — Darch

**GOD USES ORDINARY PEOPLE
TO CARRY OUT HIS EXTRAORDINARY PLAN.**

CONSIDER THE POOR

READ:
Psalm 41:1-3

**Blessed is he who considers the poor; the LORD will deliver him in time of trouble.
—Psalm 41:1**

THE BIBLE IN ONE YEAR:
Isaiah 61–63

You may have heard of the blessings Jesus spoke of in His Sermon on the Mount (Matthew 5:1-10). Here's a "blessing" from the Old Testament that is less well-known: "Blessed is he who considers the poor" (Psalm 41:1).

The Hebrew word translated "considers" means "to take thought for others." The word translated "poor" means "those in need."

There are many people around us who are poor — in love, in hope, and in the knowledge of God. Even though we cannot solve all their problems, we can show them that we care.

We may not have lots of money, but we can give of ourselves. We can let needy people know that we're thinking of them. We can listen as they tell their stories. We can treat them with courtesy and respect. We can pray for them. We can write letters of encouragement. We can tell them about Jesus. If we can do nothing else, we can love them.

Think about those who live only for themselves, always trying to get ahead, looking for the next thing to make them happy. Compare them with people who give themselves to others. Which ones possess inner calm, strength, and joy?

The place of God's blessing is easily entered: Consider the poor. — David Roper

Not in having or receiving,
But in giving, there is bliss;
He who has no other pleasure
Ever may rejoice in this. — Anon.

GIVING IS THE TRUE MEASURE OF LOVE.

August 17

BARREN BUT NOT BITTER

READ:
Luke 1:5-17

They were both righteous before God . . . . But they had no child.
—Luke 1:6-7

THE BIBLE IN ONE YEAR:
■ Isaiah 64–66

Barrenness, whether physical or spiritual, can lead to bitterness in some of God's people. It can develop in the heart of a disappointed couple who cannot have a child. It can also occur when people serve God and see no results.

A missionary couple who served diligently for many years with no visible fruit asked in frustration, "Have we wasted our lives?" A young pastor and his wife labored 5 years for a thankless, unresponsive congregation, pouring out their lives for their people. "Do they even care?" the woman asked.

Zacharias and Elizabeth, mentioned in Luke 1, are a model for anyone who is facing physical or spiritual barrenness. The aged couple had an impeccable reputation, having faithfully and obediently served the Lord for many years (v.6). They had prayed for children, but none came. Yet instead of becoming bitter, they kept serving and obeying the Lord. In His time, God honored Zacharias and Elizabeth with a son named John, the one who would prepare the way for the Messiah (vv.13-17).

To avoid developing a bitter spirit in your life, faithfully serve and obey the Lord in the place where He has called you. Trust God to bless you in His time, in His way, and according to His plan. — Dave Egner

Lord, keep me from being bitter
When things don't go my way,
And grant me Your grace and wisdom
To do Your will today. —Fitzhugh

BE FAITHFUL—AND LEAVE THE RESULTS WITH GOD.

CAUGHT RED-HANDED

READ:
Jeremiah 2:4-19

**The prophets . . .
walked after things
that do not profit.**
—Jeremiah 2:8

THE BIBLE IN ONE YEAR:
■ Jeremiah 1–2

A small plane loaded with cocaine valued at $20 million was intercepted by federal agents as it flew over the Florida coast. Suddenly, bales of cocaine began falling out of the sky. One dropped in a church parking lot. Another hit a housetop. Several others came down in the Everglades.

When the plane landed at a small airstrip near Homestead Air Force Base, four bundles of cocaine were still on board. Two men were arrested and charged with offenses that could put them behind bars for the rest of their lives. What irony! Something they thought was so profitable suddenly became so condemning.

The Israelites and their leaders also went after what they thought would be profitable for them — they followed foreign gods (Jeremiah 2:5). But the Lord told them they were going after "things that do not profit" (v.8), and their own sin was condemning them (v.19). When intercepted by God, they stood accused not only by Him but also by their own actions. They could not elude the eyes of the Lord nor escape His justice.

We all stand guilty before the Lord and in need of His forgiveness (Romans 3:23). But because He loved us enough to send His Son to die in our place, we can find — before it is too late — the mercy no human court can offer. — Mart De Haan

Sin-laden soul with your shame and disgrace,
Jesus stands ready your sin to erase;
Gladly He suffered and died in your place —
Why not receive His forgiveness and grace? — D. De Haan

**THE WAGES OF SIN IS DEATH,
BUT THE GIFT OF GOD IS ETERNAL LIFE.** — Romans 6:23

A Ray Of Hope

READ:
1 Thessalonians 4:13-18

I do not want you to be ignorant, brethren, concerning those who have fallen asleep, lest you sorrow as others who have no hope.
—1 Thessalonians 4:13

THE BIBLE IN ONE YEAR:
■ Jeremiah 3–5

It was to be an exciting summer for our family. We had many activities planned, including a trip to Florida to help our daughter Julie begin her teaching career.

Instead, the summer of 2002 began with tragedy. When our teenage daughter Melissa was killed in an automobile accident on the last day of school, our summer of hope turned into a nightmare.

Right away, I began to pray that the loss of our bright, athletic, friendly daughter could have a positive impact on teenagers — first among her friends and then in ever-widening ways.

Toward the end of the summer, we did take that Florida trip to get Julie started, heavy-hearted as we were. As she began teaching, Julie never forgot the desire to see Melissa's life change the lives of others. She told her classes about her sister and her faith.

One day, a student talked to Julie after class. "I'm scared," she said, "because I'm not a Christian like Melissa was." Julie then led her to faith in Jesus Christ. I imagined Melissa rejoicing in heaven.

The summer of 2002 didn't turn out as planned, but we were thankful to see some fruit of a life well-lived. Even in our sorrow, God gave us this ray of hope. — Dave Branon

Lord, give us grace to trust You when
Life's burdens seem too much to bear;
Dispel the darkness with new hope
And help us rise above despair. — Sper

**EVEN IN LIFE'S DARKEST HOUR,
CHRISTIANS HAVE THE BRIGHTEST HOPE.**

JESUS IS GREATER

READ:
Luke 11:14-23

He who is in you is greater than he who is in the world.
—1 John 4:4

THE BIBLE IN ONE YEAR:
■ Jeremiah 6–8

Chinese communities in Southeast Asia and some villages in China celebrate the month-long Ghosts Festival. It is believed that during this time the spirits of the dead return to earth to roam among the living. So people burn joss sticks (incense) and phony money, prepare feasts, and perform in street theaters — all to keep the spirits happy.

As a child growing up in Singapore, I was taught to fear those ghosts. One year I had a fever during the festival, and I was told that I must have bumped into some and offended them.

Now that I know what the Bible says about Jesus' power over the real spirit world of Satan and his demons, I have been freed from my former fears. Because I have placed my faith in Christ as my Lord and Savior, I realize that I don't need to try to appease or fight evil spirits by myself.

Jesus showed His power over the spirit world as He cast out demons (Luke 11:14-23). When He died on the cross for us and rose from the grave, Jesus triumphed over Satan and sealed his doom (Colossians 2:15; Revelation 20:10). The Bible assures followers of Christ, "He who is in you is greater than he who is in the world" (1 John 4:4).

We need not fear the devil or demons. Our Lord Jesus is greater! — Albert Lee

And though this world, with devils filled,
Should threaten to undo us,
We will not fear, for God has willed,
His truth to triumph through us. — Luther

THE POWER OF SATAN IS NO MATCH
FOR THE POWER OF JESUS.

ON WEARING WHITE

READ:
Colossians 3:8-14

**Put on tender mercies,
kindness, humility,
meekness,
longsuffering.
—Colossians 3:12**

THE BIBLE IN ONE YEAR:
■ Jeremiah 9–12

When I was growing up, wearing white in the US after Labor Day was a serious fashion blunder. So even though I love white clothes, every year I dutifully start putting them away at the end of August.

Late one year, while following a Bible-reading schedule, I came to Ecclesiastes 9:8, which states, "Let your garments always be white." I smiled, imagining for a moment that the author was giving permission to wear white all year. But Solomon was not talking about fashion. He was instructing us to find joy in everything we do and to express it in ways that show faith in God even at times when life doesn't seem to make sense.

One way we can do this is to observe the "fashion advice" of the apostle Paul. First-century Christians in Colosse had become confused. They were overly concerned with man-made rules, so Paul reminded them of the holy laws of God and gave them these instructions: "Put on tender mercies, kindness, humility, meekness, longsuffering" (Colossians 3:12).

These are the commands of an infinite God, not the rules of finite humans. So if we put on these "clothes" every day, we'll never be out of season. — Julie Link

*Help us, O Lord, to live our lives
So people clearly see
Reflections of Your loving heart,
Your kindness, purity.* — Sper

CHRISTLIKENESS IS ALWAYS IN SEASON.

WHEN YOU SAY, "I'M SORRY"

READ:
Hosea 6:1-6

Godly sorrow produces repentance leading to salvation, not to be regretted.
—2 Corinthians 7:10

THE BIBLE IN ONE YEAR:
■ Jeremiah 13–16

With tears in his eyes a man said to me, "I told my wife I was sorry, but she says she won't continue to live with me. First John 1:9 says that God forgives us when we confess our sins. Please talk to her and tell her that if God forgives, she should too."

I knew this man had "repented" several times before, only to revert to his abusive behavior. So I said, "No, I'm not going to tell her that. In your case, saying 'I'm sorry' isn't enough." His wife insisted that he receive counseling and give evidence of a genuine change before returning home. She was right.

Just saying "I'm sorry" is not enough for God either. The leaders of Israel, in the face of trouble brought on by their sin, thought that merely returning to prescribed sacrificial offerings would solve their problems. But God rejected that kind of "repentance." It was as fleeting as "a morning cloud" and "the early dew" that fades away with the first rays of sunlight (Hosea 6:4).

Merely saying "I'm sorry" is no different than the empty rituals of the Israelites. God said, "I desire mercy and not sacrifice, and the knowledge of God more than burnt offerings" (v.6). He meant that repentance must result in a change of heart and a change in behavior. That's "godly sorrow" (2 Corinthians 7:10). — Herb Vander Lugt

Repentance is to leave the sin
That we had loved before,
And showing we are grieved by it
By doing it no more. — Anon.

REPENTANCE MEANS HATING SIN ENOUGH TO TURN FROM IT.

THE DIVIDED HEART

READ:
Hosea 7:8-12

Teach me Your way,
O LORD; I will walk in
Your truth; unite my
heart to fear Your
name. —Psalm 86:11

THE BIBLE IN ONE YEAR:
■ Jeremiah 17–20

The Israelites of Hosea's day were trying to worship both pagan idols and the one true and living God. So the prophet Hosea used three colorful figures of speech to describe their divided hearts.

First, they were like a half-baked cake — palatable neither to God nor the pagans (7:8). Second, they were like a proud man who can't see the signs of his aging — they were unaware of their spiritual decline (vv.9-10). Third, they were like a senseless dove — flying from one pagan nation to another in a vain quest for help (v.11).

Today, we as Christians are often afflicted with the same divided-heart syndrome. We believe on Jesus but are reluctant to commit every area of our lives to Him. We go to church but don't want to live out our faith each day if it deprives us of worldly success or pleasure. A divided heart, though, results in some serious consequences. First, we don't please God or attract non-believers to Christ. Second, it may take a crisis to show us our true spiritual decline. And third, we live unfulfilled lives, even though we flit from one worldly pleasure to another.

Let's pray each day, "Teach me Your way, O LORD; I will walk in Your truth; unite my heart to fear Your name" (Psalm 86:11). — Herb Vander Lugt

An undivided heart, O Lord,
Is what we need each day,
For we are prone to compromise
And wander from Your way. — D. De Haan

A DIVIDED HEART MULTIPLIES OUR PROBLEMS.

SPARE CHANGE?

READ:
1 Corinthians 12:12-27

God composed the body, having given greater honor to that part which lacks it.
—1 Corinthians 12:24

THE BIBLE IN ONE YEAR:
■ Jeremiah 21–23

A Washington, DC, couple invited friends to bring their loose change to a party to benefit a charity fund. From what people had at home in boxes, cookie jars, plastic bags, and a few old socks, they brought coins totaling more than $1,500.

Few individuals have more than $30 in change around the house, but Americans together have an estimated $7.7 billion in loose change just lying around. And researchers say that's typical of people in many other countries of the world.

To me, it's a wonderful illustration of the collective wealth and worth of the family of all believers in Jesus Christ. The Bible often refers to the church as "the body of Christ" and says that "all the members of that one body, being many, are one body" (1 Corinthians 12:12).

Every person, therefore, is essential and valuable as part of the whole. By ourselves, we may sometimes feel insignificant, unneeded, and of little value, like so much spare change. But as individual parts that make up the whole, each of us is needed (vv.15-22).

All people are unique individuals, but as Christians we are also indispensable parts of the body of Christ, and of greater value than we can ever know. — David McCasland

Help us, Lord, to work together
With the gifts that You bestow;
Give us unity of purpose
As we serve You here below. — Sper

**THERE ARE NO UNIMPORTANT MEMBERS
IN THE BODY OF CHRIST.**

CHRIST-CENTERED FAITH

READ:
Colossians 2:1-10

As you therefore have received Christ Jesus the Lord, so walk in Him.
—Colossians 2:6

THE BIBLE IN ONE YEAR:
■ Jeremiah 24–26

Some Christians try to live from one dramatic mountaintop experience to another. Their relationship with the Lord is based on their feelings at the moment. They go from Bible conferences to seminars to Bible studies, trying to maintain an emotional high.

Author Creath Davis, referring to his early Christian life, wrote, "I felt that if something spectacular was not transpiring, my faith was weakening. As a result, I missed most of what was going on in the valleys, waiting to get back to the mountain."

What's an effective antidote for a feelings-centered faith? According to the apostle Paul in Colossians 2, being Christ-centered is the answer. Having received Christ Jesus by faith, we are instructed to continue to "walk in Him" by faith (v.6) through both the highs and lows of life. By walking in close fellowship with Him each day, we become "rooted and built up in Him and established in the faith" (v.7). We grow steadily into maturity as we focus on Christ and what He has done for us, and not on our feelings.

Mountaintop experiences can be beneficial, but nothing is more profitable than an ongoing, Christ-centered life of faith. —Joanie Yoder

> With faith in Christ we walk each day,
> Accepting all that comes our way;
> So let us view each task at hand
> As being His divine command. —D. De Haan

TRUE FAITH NEEDS NO FEELINGS TO REST UPON.

GESTURES OF LOVE

READ:
Romans 12:9-16

Be kindly affectionate
to one another with
brotherly love . . .
and weep with those
who weep.
—Romans 12:10,15

THE BIBLE IN ONE YEAR:
■ Jeremiah 27–29

Cards. Hundreds and hundreds of cards. Our mail carrier must have thought we were going for a world record. They came by the stack — day after day after day.

It was just one of the many ways we knew that people cared for us as our family endured the painful first weeks after our teenage daughter Melissa died in a car accident.

But it wasn't just the cards that provided assurance of loving support. Food came in so fast we nearly filled up the freezer. Flowers filled every corner of the house, especially sunflowers — Melissa's favorite.

People sent pictures of her, blankets with verses, memorial gifts to her school, and books — lots of helpful books on trusting God with a broken heart. Then there were the e-mails, phone calls, and personal words of hope and help. Promises of prayer. Offers to do anything we needed. All from friends following God's prompting.

Our aching hearts were lifted by these deeds too numerous to list but too beautiful to forget. The love behind these expressions carried us through days heavy with sorrow.

Look for people in need and follow the Lord's leading. Help heal their brokenness with gestures of love (Romans 12:10-15). Encourage them for God's glory. — Dave Branon

It was only a brief little note,
Or a word that was prayerfully spoken,
Yet not in vain, for it soothed the pain
Of a heart that was nearly broken. — Anon.

A LITTLE KINDNESS CAN MAKE A BIG DIFFERENCE.

MORE THAN A CONTRACT

READ:
Romans 8:14-17

The Spirit Himself bears witness with our spirit that we are children of God, and if children, then heirs. —Romans 8:16-17

THE BIBLE IN ONE YEAR:
■ Jeremiah 30–32

We are all accustomed to contracts. We are often required to sign them, whether we're closing a business deal, taking out a bank loan, buying a car, leasing an apartment, or purchasing a major appliance. Contracts, formal or informal, specify what happens if one of the parties fails to live up to an agreement.

When we put our trust in Christ for salvation, however, we do more than sign a contract. We enter into a binding relationship with God whereby He makes us His children by the new birth and by adoption (1 Peter 1:23; Ephesians 1:5). Because of this close family relationship, we are permanent heirs of an eternal inheritance reserved in heaven for us (1 Peter 1:4).

Contracts can be broken if one of the parties fails to keep his part of the promise. Fortunately for us, our eternal destiny is based on more than some legal agreement we make with God. Rather, we are secure because of our family relationship with Him. If a youngster fails to show up for dinner, the parent's obligation isn't canceled. The parent starts a search for the child. One member's failure doesn't cancel the relationship.

How thankful we can be that eternal life is based on our relationship with God through Christ. — Haddon Robinson

We're members of God's family,
We're children of the King;
Because we've put our faith in Christ,
To us He'll always cling. — Sper

WE ARE HEIRS OF GOD NOT MERELY BY CONTRACT, BUT BY BIRTHRIGHT.

PRICELESS LETTERS

READ:
Ephesians 3:1-12

When you read, you
may understand my
knowledge in the
mystery of Christ.
—Ephesians 3:4

THE BIBLE IN ONE YEAR:
■ Jeremiah 33–36

If you have a letter from Mark Twain in your attic, it could be worth a lot of money. A personal, 9-page letter written to his daughter in 1875 sold for $33,000 back in 1991. Ordinary correspondence from the author of *Tom Sawyer* usually brings $1,200 to $1,500 a page. Experts say that even though Twain wrote 50,000 letters during his lifetime, demand is still strong for these personal notes from one of America's favorite authors.

You probably don't have any correspondence from Mark Twain, but chances are you own a priceless collection of letters. Twenty-one of the 27 books in the New Testament are letters written to encourage and instruct Christians. They contain the priceless revelation of Jesus Christ.

In his letter to the Ephesians, Paul wrote, "By revelation He made known to me the mystery . . . of which I became a minister" (3:3,7). He had received a message from God and was told to preach it to the world (v.8). The letters we hold in our hands today contain God's special revelation to us.

To every Christian, the value of the New Testament letters is not their cash value, but the wisdom they bring to an open heart — wisdom from God Himself. — David McCasland

> *Exceeding great and precious*
> *Are the promises of God,*
> *Inscribed in golden letters*
> *In the pages of His Word.* — Cockrell

**IF YOU WANT LIFE-CHANGING MAIL,
OPEN YOUR BIBLE AND READ A LETTER FROM GOD.**

FRETTING IS A WASTE

READ:
Psalm 90:10-17

**Teach us to number our days, that we may gain a heart of wisdom.
—Psalm 90:12**

THE BIBLE IN ONE YEAR:
■ Jeremiah 37–39

The older we get, the shorter life seems. Author Victor Hugo said, "Short as life is, we make it still shorter by the careless waste of time."

There's no sadder example of wasted time than a life dominated by fretting. Take, for example, an American woman whose dream of riding a train through the English countryside came true. After boarding the train she kept fretting about the windows and the temperature, complaining about her seat assignment, rearranging her luggage, and so on. To her shock, she suddenly reached her journey's end. With deep regret she said to the person meeting her, "If I'd known I was going to arrive so soon, I wouldn't have wasted my time fretting so much."

It's easy to get sidetracked by problems that won't matter at life's end — difficult neighbors, a tight budget, signs of aging, people who are wealthier than you. Moses acknowledged the brevity of life and prayed, "Teach us to number our days, that we may gain a heart of wisdom" (Psalm 90:12).

Instead of fretting, feed on God's Word and apply it to yourself. Strive to grow in God's wisdom every day. Stay focused on eternal values. Make it your goal to greet your waiting Savior one day with a heart of wisdom, rather than a heart of care. — Joanie Yoder

Day by day and with each passing moment,
Strength I find to meet my trials here;
Trusting in my Father's wise bestowment,
I've no cause for worry or for fear. — Berg

WORRY CASTS A BIG SHADOW BEHIND A SMALL THING.

AN ETERNAL FUTURE

READ:
John 5:24-29

He who hears My word and believes in Him who sent Me has everlasting life, and . . . has passed from death into life. —John 5:24

THE BIBLE IN ONE YEAR:
■ Jeremiah 40–42

Some countries are very old. Their history stretches far into the distant past. Others are fairly new to the world map. Yet, while all nations are destined to disappear, every human soul is destined to live eternally.

This prompted C. S. Lewis to say, "If we had foolish unchristian hopes about human culture, they are now shattered. If we thought we were building up a heaven on earth, if we looked for something that would turn the present world from a place of pilgrimage into a permanent city satisfying the soul of man, we are disillusioned, and not a moment too soon."

Civilizations will fall, but the human soul will live on forever. And because every individual will one day stand and face God's judgment (Hebrews 9:27), the most important question is how each of us will spend the endless ages stretching before us. Will we be with God in indescribable glory and joy? Or will we be exiled from God, lost forever in a condition too horrible for language to describe?

What a responsibility rests on believers! We must tell people that the only way to spend eternity in God's presence is to accept His offer of forgiveness and reconciliation (John 5:24). By God's grace, we can begin rejoicing in eternal life with Him right now! — Vernon Grounds

There is a place reserved in heaven
For all who have believed;
Eternal life is freely given
When humbly it's received. — Sper

**WHEN YOU OPEN YOUR HEART TO JESUS,
HEAVEN IS OPEN TO YOU.**

THE REAL JESUS

READ:
Matthew 16:13-20

**You are the Christ, the Son of the living God.
—Matthew 16:16**

THE BIBLE IN ONE YEAR:
■ Jeremiah 43–46

Who is Jesus? Observing the ways He is portrayed these days, it's almost impossible to recognize Him as the Jesus of the Bible. Some groups add to what the Bible says about Him, while others diminish Him to simple humanity, claiming that He was merely a wise teacher or a master moralist. Some would like to make Him disappear altogether.

But this is nothing new. It's been happening for nearly 2,000 years. This reminds me of Thomas Jefferson, who wrote the US Declaration of Independence. He went through the New Testament Gospels with scissors and cut out all references to Jesus' deity and the supernatural. This is known as *The Jefferson Bible*. Even recently, people have approached the Gospels in similar ways.

When Jesus asked His 12 disciples what people were saying about who He was, some answers were Elijah, Jeremiah, and John the Baptist, but these answers were all inadequate. Peter was correct when he said, "You are the Christ, the Son of the living God" (Matthew 16:16).

Don't be deceived by fuzzy, watered down, or false descriptions of Jesus that you read, see, or hear about. Stick to the Bible. When people try to minimize His identity, tell them in no uncertain terms who the real Jesus is! — Dave Egner

All glory to Jesus, begotten of God,
The great I AM is He;
Creator, sustainer — but wonder of all,
The Lamb of Calvary! — Peterson

TO KNOW JESUS IS TO KNOW GOD.

PEOPLE OVER PROFITS

READ:
Colossians 3:22–4:1

**Masters, give your bondservants what is just and fair, knowing that you also have a Master in heaven.
—Colossians 4:1**

THE BIBLE IN ONE YEAR:
■ Jeremiah 47–49

When Truett Cathy started his first restaurant in 1946, it was closed on Sundays to give his employees time to be with their families and to attend church. It's still true today of the more than 1,000 Chick-fil-A fast-food outlets franchised by his company.

Cathy's slogan is: "Put people and principles before profit." It's a motto each of us can make our own, whether we give orders or take them on the job.

The apostle Paul had a word for employers and employees in Colossians 3:22–4:1. He said we need to remember that we have a Master in heaven (4:1), and we are to work from our hearts to please Him, not just the person watching us (3:22-24).

Truett Cathy strives to remain true to biblical principles in his business. Larry Julian, author of *God Is My CEO*, a book about Cathy and other business leaders, says: "God doesn't promise a tangible return on investments, but He promises the fruits of the Spirit, love and peace and joy, on a personal level. Cathy is not only experiencing peace and joy and love in his life personally, but he's also making a difference to his foster children, his own children and grandchildren, and his employees. He's leaving a legacy on how you can do things the right way."

That's an example we can take to work. — David McCasland

Lord, teach me how to love and work,
That everything I do
May be to someone in its turn
A service good and true. — Anon.

**WHEN PEOPLE ARE MORE IMPORTANT THAN PROFITS,
EVERYONE PROFITS.**

A WEEPING WORLD

READ:
Lamentations 3:1-9,24

"The LORD is my portion," says my soul, "therefore I hope in Him!"
—Lamentations 3:24

THE BIBLE IN ONE YEAR:
■ Jeremiah 50—52

A mother was told that her son had been killed in an accident on the job. In that moment, her life was flooded with tears. In another family, a sudden heart attack snatched away a husband, leaving a wife to face life alone. More tears! We live in a weeping world.

The book of Lamentations was written by Jeremiah, who is called the weeping prophet. The citizens of Judah had been taken into captivity (1:3); Jerusalem lay in ruins (2:8-9); the people were destitute (2:11-12); their suffering was horrible beyond belief (2:20); and the prophet wept continually (3:48-49). Yet Jeremiah still affirmed the mercies, the compassions, and the faithfulness of God. From deep within him, his soul was saying, "The LORD is my portion, therefore I hope in Him!" (3:24).

What realism in those tear-saturated words! It's the reality that weeping and lamentations do not necessarily reflect a weak faith or a lack of trust in God. Some of us may think that a Christian must feel joyful even when the heart is breaking — or at least try to appear that way. But Jeremiah's experience refutes that. Tears are a natural part of a Christian's life. But thank God, one day in Glory our blessed Savior will wipe them all away (Revelation 21:4). — Dennis De Haan

Christian, when your way seems darkest,
When your eyes with tears are dim,
Go to God your Father quickly,
Tell your troubles all to Him. — Anon.

THE SOUL WOULD HAVE NO RAINBOW IF THE EYES HAD NO TEARS.

A REASON FOR HOPE

READ:
Lamentations 3:19-33

His compassions
fail not. They are
new every morning;
great is Your
faithfulness.
—Lamentations 3:22-23

THE BIBLE IN ONE YEAR:
■ Lamentations 1–5

It's one of the saddest stories of the Bible, yet it inspired one of the most hopeful hymns of the 20th century.

The prophet Jeremiah witnessed unimaginable horrors when the Babylonians invaded Jerusalem in 586 BC. Solomon's temple was reduced to ruins, and with it went not only the center of worship but also the heart of the community. The people were left with no food, no rest, no peace, no leader. But in the midst of suffering and grief, one of their prophets found a reason for hope. "Through the LORD's mercies we are not consumed," wrote Jeremiah, "because His compassions fail not. They are new every morning; great is Your faithfulness" (Lamentations 3:22-23).

Jeremiah's hope came from his personal experience of the Lord's faithfulness and from his knowledge of God's promises in the past. Without these, he would have been unable to comfort his people.

This hope of Lamentations 3 is echoed in a hymn by Thomas Chisholm (1866–1960). Although suffering sickness and setbacks throughout his life, he wrote "Great Is Thy Faithfulness." It assures us that even in times of great fear, tragic loss, and intense suffering we can find comfort and confidence as we trust in God's great faithfulness. — Julie Link

Great is Thy faithfulness, O God my Father,
There is no shadow of turning with Thee;
Thou changest not, Thy compassions they fail not;
As Thou hast been, Thou forever wilt be. — Chisholm

THE BEST REASON FOR HOPE IS GOD'S FAITHFULNESS.

EATING WORDS

READ:
Ezekiel 2:7–3:4

**Son of man, eat what you find; eat this scroll, and go, speak to the house of Israel.
—Ezekiel 3:1**

THE BIBLE IN ONE YEAR:
■ Ezekiel 1–3

I read about an Australian woman who developed a craving for paper. She began her unusual diet as a child, and as she grew older she ate as many as 10 tissues and a half page of the newspaper every day. The woman had also consumed small quantities of blotting paper, sheets from exercise books, and petty cash vouchers.

Of course, there's no relationship between that woman's strange habit and the symbolic actions of the prophet Ezekiel. His eating of a scroll was meant to illustrate a spiritual exercise that all of us should engage in. If we are to declare God's truth with meaning and power, we must take time to let it fill our hearts. We need to feel the implications of what God has said. We are to let His Word become a vital part of us so that we can't talk about it glibly as uninvolved, detached students, but as those who have personally "tasted" it.

The actual words and thoughts of God are revealed in the Bible. Don't just read them and repeat them. Think them. Feel them. Ask the Lord to clarify them, to make them a part of your experience, and to teach you.

Yes, today's Bible reading contains a profound principle: We must "eat" the Word before we speak it. Maybe then we won't have to eat our own words later on. — Mart De Haan

Lord, teach us from Your holy Word
The truth that we must know;
And help us share the joyous news
Of blessings You bestow. — D. De Haan

**LET GOD'S WORD FILL YOUR MIND, RULE YOUR HEART,
AND GUIDE YOUR TONGUE.**

BECOMING A MENTOR

READ:
2 Timothy 1:13–2:2

The things that you have heard from me . . . , commit these to faithful men who will be able to teach others also. —2 Timothy 2:2

THE BIBLE IN ONE YEAR:
■ Ezekiel 4–7

According to Homer's *Odyssey*, when King Odysseus went off to fight in the Trojan war, he left his son Telemachus in the hands of a wise old man named Mentor. Mentor was charged with the task of teaching the young man wisdom.

More than 2,000 years after Homer, a French scholar and theologian by the name of François Fénelon adapted the story of Telemachus in a novel titled *Télémaque*. In it he enlarged the character of Mentor. The word *mentor* soon came to mean "a wise and responsible tutor"—an experienced person who advises, guides, teaches, inspires, challenges, corrects, and serves as a model.

Second Timothy 2:2 describes spiritual mentoring, and the Bible gives us many examples. Timothy had Paul; Mark had Barnabas; Joshua had Moses; Elisha had Elijah.

But what about today? Who will love and work with new Christians and help them grow spiritually strong? Who will encourage, guide, and model the truth for them? Who will call young believers to accountability and work with God to help mold their character?

Will you become one whom God can use to impart wisdom and to help others grow toward maturity? —David Roper

THINKING IT OVER
Who has helped you to grow in your faith?
How did that person help you? By teaching, example,
or friendship? To whom can you be a mentor?

GOD TEACHES US SO THAT WE CAN TEACH OTHERS.

THE NAME

READ:
Philippians 2:5-11

You shall call His name JESUS, for He will save His people from their sins.
—Matthew 1:21

THE BIBLE IN ONE YEAR:
■ Ezekiel 8–11

If you were to select some of the most influential figures in the whole sweep of the ages, men and women who have affected millions of lives, what names would be on your list? I think one name that would appear on all our lists, without exception, would be the name of Jesus.

Reynolds Price, writing about "Jesus of Nazareth" in *Time* magazine (December 1999), declared that "a serious argument can be made that no one else's life has proved remotely as powerful and enduring as that of Jesus." So when this Man, born in an obscure village two millennia ago, declared, "I am the light of the world" (John 8:12) and "My words will by no means pass away" (Luke 21:33), He was making predictions that history has verified.

Jesus has undeniably been the world's most influential Person, but has He impacted your life personally? Do you put Him in the same class as other influential figures, or has He transformed your life? Unlike all other notable people who eventually died, Jesus is still miraculously alive.

Is Jesus your Savior and constant companion? If He isn't, He can be. Call on His name in faith and invite Him into your life. Then the name of Jesus will become to you the most precious of names. — Vernon Grounds

> *No other name can save me,*
> *No other name beside,*
> *But Jesus Christ the risen Lord,*
> *The One they crucified.* — Brandt

**WHAT YOU DECIDE ABOUT JESUS
WILL DETERMINE YOUR DESTINY.**

WHY THEY ARE GRAND

READ:
Titus 2:1-5

**Older women . . . [are to] admonish the young women to love their husbands, to love their children.
—Titus 2:3-4**

THE BIBLE IN ONE YEAR:
■ Ezekiel 12–14

Grandparents are great bridge-builders. My grandparents, farmers on both sides of the family, were children of the 19th century and relayed an important heritage of both history and faith through the years.

Today, my children benefit from their grandparents' faith because they can see that my wife and I have personally accepted the faith modeled for us. And our children have seen and heard their grandparents' testimonies of faith for themselves.

In a sense, it seems strange that grandparents can have such far-reaching influence. After all, they can be separated in age from their grandchildren by 40 to 70 years. Yet they have an uncanny ability to bridge that generation gap — sometimes even better than parents can.

Older Christians, including grandparents, have a unique responsibility and opportunity — that of example and instruction — which either directly or indirectly keeps the heritage of faith alive from generation to generation.

Let's be thankful for the strong heritage of faith, love, and family that grandparents can leave to those who come after them. And grandparents should seize every opportunity of relating to their grandchildren, so that their faith will become the faith of their children's children. — Dave Branon

> *I do not ask for mighty words*
> *To leave them all impressed,*
> *But grant my life may ring so true*
> *My family will be blessed.* — Anon.

THE RICHEST INHERITANCE A GRANDPARENT CAN LEAVE IS A GODLY EXAMPLE.

September 8

NO MORE EXCUSES

READ:
Ezekiel 18:1-18

The soul who sins shall die.
—Ezekiel 18:4

THE BIBLE IN ONE YEAR:
■ Ezekiel 15–18

When salmon travel hundreds of miles up rivers and streams to spawn, they are acting on instinct. They are in a sense being driven by an uncontrollable force.

I read about a young convict who thinks that human conduct is similar to that of the salmon. Referring to the murders he committed and to his own fate, he said, "Things just happen." He thinks some kind of force was responsible for his pulling the trigger and killing two people. But he is wrong. Man is free and cannot blame his sinful actions on an uncontrollable force such as instinct.

More than 2,500 years ago, some Israelites were using a similar excuse for their sin. They quoted a well-known proverb that placed the blame for their sins on their ancestors (Ezekiel 18:2). But God told them they were wrong. He said that a good man will not be punished for the sins of a wicked son. Nor will a godly son be punished for the sins of his evil father.

Make no mistake. No matter what your situation, you are responsible for what you do. Stop offering excuses for your sins. Instead, acknowledge your guilt to God and accept the forgiveness He offers (Psalm 32:5). That's the first step in exercising your individual responsibility. — Herb Vander Lugt

Our actions are accountable
In God's just court above,
So we must face this certain fact:
We need His pardoning love. — Branon

THERE'S NO EXCUSE FOR EXCUSING SIN.

LIVING WITH GRACE

READ:
1 Peter 5:5-11

**Be clothed with humility, for "God resists the proud, but gives grace to the humble."
—1 Peter 5:5**

THE BIBLE IN ONE YEAR:
■ Ezekiel 19–21

Kevin Rogers, pastor of a church in Canada, has likened the grace of God to an imaginary secretary who compels him to treat other people as God does. Rogers writes: "Grace is my secretary, but she won't let me obey my Day-Timer. She lets the strangest people into my workspace to interrupt me. Somehow she lets calls get through that I would prefer to leave for a more convenient time. Doesn't Grace know that I have an agenda? Some days I wish that Grace weren't here. But Grace has an amazing way of covering my mistakes and turning the office into a holy place. Grace finds good in everything, even failures."

By God's grace—His unmerited love and favor—we have been forgiven in Christ. God tells us that instead of relating to others from a position of superiority, we must put others ahead of ourselves. We should wear the clothes of humility because He "resists the proud, but gives grace to the humble" (1 Peter 5:5).

When "the God of all grace" (v.10) controls our lives, He can transform interruptions into opportunities, mistakes into successes, pride into humility, and suffering into strength. That's the amazing power of God. That's the evidence of His grace! — David McCasland

THINKING IT THROUGH
How have you seen grace at work in your life lately?
In what areas of life do you see a need for grace?
To whom can you demonstrate God's grace today?

**WHEN YOU KNOW GOD'S GRACE,
YOU'LL WANT TO SHOW GOD'S GRACE.**

WHEN IT'S HARD TO PRAY

READ:
Romans 8:26-27

**There is not a word on my tongue, but behold, O LORD, You know it altogether.
—Psalm 139:4**

THE BIBLE IN ONE YEAR:
■ Ezekiel 22–24

The Bible tells us that God knows our every thought and every word on our tongue (Psalm 139:1-4). And when we don't know what to pray for, the Holy Spirit "makes intercession for us with groanings which cannot be uttered" (Romans 8:26).

These biblical truths assure us that we can have communication with God even without a word being spoken, because He knows the intentions and desires of our heart. What a comfort when we are perplexed or in deep distress! We don't have to worry if we can't find the words to express our thoughts and feelings. We don't have to feel embarrassed if sometimes our sentences break off half-finished. God knows what we were going to say. We don't have to feel guilty if our thoughts wander and we have to struggle to keep our minds focused on the Lord.

And for that matter, we don't have to worry about a proper posture in prayer. If we are elderly or arthritic and can't kneel, that's okay. What God cares about is the posture of our heart.

What a wonderful God! No matter how much you falter and stumble in your praying, He hears you. His heart of infinite love responds to the needs and emotions of your own inarticulate heart. So keep on praying! — Vernon Grounds

> *Prayer is the soul's sincere desire,*
> *Unuttered or expressed,*
> *The motion of a hidden fire*
> *That trembles in the breast.* — *Montgomery*

**PRAYER DOES NOT REQUIRE ELOQUENCE
BUT EARNESTNESS.**

HOUSEHOLD SECURITY

READ:
Deuteronomy 6:4-9

Whoever trusts in the LORD shall be safe.
—Proverbs 29:25

THE BIBLE IN ONE YEAR:
■ Ezekiel 25–27

After the United States was attacked by terrorists on September 11, 2001, President Bush called on Congress to create a Department of Homeland Security. The job of this agency is to do everything possible to keep citizens safe.

Our individual households also need a plan for "homeland security" if we are to keep others from endangering our children. But in a world of easy access to harmful outside forces, how do we do that? Here are some suggestions for household security:

1. Take charge of the media. Instead of allowing makers of TV programs, movies, and CDs to dictate what you watch and hear, use biblical guidelines to evaluate the language and morality of what your children see and what they listen to.

2. Check out their friends. The standards of your children's friends may not match yours. Make your home a haven where their friends are welcome. It'll help you get to know them.

3. Build shields. By teaching your children biblical principles and encouraging their faith, you'll help them to be discerning and to build inner shields that will protect them from the dangers they face.

How good is your household security? — Dave Branon

Our children need a home where love
Provides security,
Where what is taught is not confused
By what they hear and see. — Sper

THE BEST SAFEGUARD FOR THE YOUNGER GENERATION IS A GOOD EXAMPLE BY THE OLDER GENERATION.

NICE IS NOT THE POINT

READ:
Romans 3:21-28

**. . . justified freely by His grace through the redemption that is in Christ Jesus.
—Romans 3:24**

THE BIBLE IN ONE YEAR:
■ Ezekiel 28–30

Your two closest neighbors are Ernestine Quibbles and George Smiley. Ernestine has a sharp tongue and is quick to inform you when your kids' soccer ball goes into her yard. George, the nicest man you've ever met, is always friendly. He loves to play ball with your boys. He gives you vegetables from his garden, and he helps you whenever you need it.

Wouldn't it be nice if Mrs. Quibbles would become a believer in Christ? If God were to work in her life, she might become as nice as Mr. Smiley. It's obvious that she needs the Lord, so you pray for her. It never occurs to you to pray for Mr. Smiley too.

But could it be that we're missing something here? Jesus did not die on the cross merely to make difficult people nice. Every person, difficult or nice, needs salvation. He came to pay the penalty for our sins by His sacrificial death (Romans 5:6-8). He offers forgiveness to all who place their trust in Him (3:28). Once people are born again, they should become nicer people — but that is not the Lord's primary purpose for saving them.

Mrs. Quibbles and Mr. Smiley both need the Lord. Without Him, they are lost and need His salvation (just as you and I do). That's why Jesus came — to offer us new life from above. — Dave Egner

*The goal was reached, the price was paid
To ransom all of Adam's race;
Our guilt and sin on Christ were laid,
And now He saves us by His grace.* — Anon.

**WE ALL NEED SALVATION,
WHETHER WE'RE NICE OR NOT.**

"GOD MAKES NO MISTAKES"

READ:
Romans 12:14-21

Do not be overcome by evil, but overcome evil with good.
—Romans 12:21

THE BIBLE IN ONE YEAR:
■ Ezekiel 31–33

A few days after arriving on the campus of Texas A&M University in 1984, Bruce Goodrich was awakened at 2 a.m. Upperclassmen roused him out of bed to initiate him into the Corps of Cadets, a military-style training program.

Bruce was forced to exercise and run several miles in hot and humid conditions. When he eventually collapsed, he was told to get up and keep going. He collapsed again, went into a coma, and died later that same day. The students who mistreated Bruce were put on trial and charged with causing his death.

Bruce's father wrote a letter to the administration, faculty, and student body. He didn't excuse the cruel injustice of what happened to his son, but he said: "I would like to take this opportunity to express the appreciation of my family for the great outpouring of concern and sympathy from Texas A&M University and the community over the loss of our son Bruce. . . . We harbor no ill will . . . . [He] is now secure in his celestial home. When the question is asked, 'Why did this happen?' perhaps one answer will be, 'So that many will consider where they will spend eternity.'"

Trusting in the sovereignty of God can turn outrage into compassion and hatred into concern. — Haddon Robinson

The Lord can turn a tragedy
Into an opportunity
To show us that eternity
Must never be ignored. —Sper

NO TRAGEDY IS BEYOND GOD'S SOVEREIGNTY.

SUFFERING'S REWARD

READ:
Romans 5:1-5

We also glory in tribulations, knowing that tribulation produces perseverance.
—Romans 5:3

THE BIBLE IN ONE YEAR:
■ Ezekiel 34–36

A young Christian went to an older believer and asked, "Will you pray that I may be more patient?" So they knelt together and the man began to pray, "Lord, send this young man tribulation in the morning; send him tribulation in the afternoon; send him —" Just then the young believer blurted out, "No, not *tribulation*! I asked for *patience*." "I know," said the wise Christian, "but it's through tribulation that we learn patience."

The word *perseverance* in today's Scripture can mean the ability to remain steadfast under difficulties without giving in. John A. Witmer wrote, "Only a believer who has faced distress can develop steadfastness. That in turn develops character."

When the apostle Paul told the Christians in Rome that "tribulation produces perseverance" (Romans 5:3), he was speaking from personal experience. He had suffered beatings, whippings, stoning, shipwreck, and persecution. Yet he remained steadfast in his faith and did not shrink from his responsibility to preach the gospel.

If you are facing a difficult test, praise God! Under His wise control, everything that happens to us — whether pleasurable or painful — is designed to develop Christlike character. That's why we can glory in tribulation. — Richard De Haan

> Looking back, I clearly see
> All the grief that had to be
> Left me when the pain was o'er
> Richer than I'd been before. — Anon.

HE WHO WAITS ON THE LORD WILL NOT BE CRUSHED BY THE WEIGHTS OF ADVERSITY.

ARE YOU WEARY?

READ:
2 Corinthians 4:1-10

Since we have this ministry, as we have received mercy, we do not lose heart.
—2 Corinthians 4:1

THE BIBLE IN ONE YEAR:
■ Ezekiel 37–39

I read a story about a pastor of a small, rural church in Scotland. He had been forced out by his elders, who claimed they saw no fruit from his ministry. The village in which the pastor served was a difficult place. People's hearts were cold and hostile to the truth. During the time the pastor served, there had been no conversions and no baptisms. But he did recall one positive response to his preaching.

When the offering plate was passed during a service, a young boy placed the plate on the floor, stood up, and stepped into it. When asked to explain, he replied that he had been deeply touched by the minister's life, and while he had no money to give he wanted to give himself wholly to God.

The boy who stepped into the plate was Bobby Moffat, who in 1817 became a pioneer missionary to South Africa. He was greatly used of God to touch many lives. And it all started with that small church and the faithful work of that unappreciated pastor.

Perhaps you see no fruit from your work for the Lord. Remain faithful! Do not lose heart, but ask God to strengthen you with His power (2 Corinthians 4:1,7). In His time and in His way, He will produce a harvest if you do not give up (Galatians 6:9). — David Roper

Keep me faithful, keep me grateful,
This my earnest plea each day!
Keep me serving, keep me telling
Of His love while yet I may! — Thiesen

A FRUITFUL HARVEST
REQUIRES FAITHFUL SERVICE.

A BAD HABIT

READ:
Exodus 17:1-7

**They tempted the LORD, saying, "Is the LORD among us or not?"
—Exodus 17:7**

THE BIBLE IN ONE YEAR:
■ Ezekiel 40–42

M ost people have a bad habit or two. Some habits are just irritating, such as talking too much or too fast. Others are much more serious.

Consider, for example, the bad habit developed by the people of ancient Israel. They had just been delivered from slavery (Exodus 14:30), and they ought to have been thankful. Instead, they started to complain to Moses and Aaron, "Oh, that we had died by the hand of the LORD in the land of Egypt!" (16:3).

We read in Exodus 17 that their complaining escalated into a quarrel. In reality, their complaint was with God, but they picked a fight with Moses because he was the leader. They said, "Why is it you have brought us up out of Egypt, to kill us and our children and our livestock with thirst?" (v.3). The people even began questioning if God was really with them (v.7). Yet He always met their needs.

If we're honest, we would have to admit that we sometimes complain when God isn't coming through for us the way we want. We accuse Him of being absent or disinterested. But when our heart is concerned with God's purposes rather than our own, we will be patient and trust Him to provide all that we need. Then we won't develop the bad habit of complaining. — Albert Lee

Those Christians who with thankful hearts
Praise God throughout the day
Won't tend to grumble and complain
When things don't go their way. — *Branon*

**TO CONQUER THE HABIT OF COMPLAINING,
COUNT YOUR BLESSINGS.**

September 17

LEARNING TO GIVE

READ:
Luke 19:1-10

Zacchaeus stood and said to the Lord, "Look, Lord, I give half of my goods to the poor." —Luke 19:8

THE BIBLE IN ONE YEAR:
■ Ezekiel 43–45

Many people in affluent countries have become burdened by the accumulation of material goods they no longer need or use. But they have a hard time getting rid of things that clog their homes and businesses. After five moves in four years, one woman said, "You know how much stuff I brought with me to each place? I've asked myself, 'Where was your brain when you moved all this stuff?'" She then hired a professional organizer to help her learn to let go of things.

People cling to their possessions for many different reasons. It seems that Zacchaeus struggled with this problem because he was greedy (Luke 19:1-10). But the story of this wealthy tax collector who climbed a tree to see Jesus culminated in a complete change of heart when Zacchaeus said, "Look, Lord, I give half of my goods to the poor" (v.8). He then promised, "If I have taken anything from anyone by false accusation, I restore fourfold." Jesus responded by saying, "Today salvation has come to this house" (v.9).

The new spiritual freedom that Zacchaeus found could be observed as he turned from getting to giving. His relaxed grip revealed a renewed heart.

Is it true of us as well?   — David McCasland

Speak to us, Lord, till shamed by Thy great giving,
Our hands unclasp to set our treasures free;
Our wills, our love, our dear ones, our possessions
All gladly yielded, gracious Lord, to Thee. — Anon.

**WE HAVEN'T LEARNED TO LIVE
UNTIL WE'VE LEARNED TO GIVE.**

TRUTH IS LIBERATING

READ:
John 8:28-36

You shall know the truth, and the truth shall make you free.
—John 8:32

THE BIBLE IN ONE YEAR:
■ Ezekiel 46–48

A Christian friend shared several problems with me over the phone. He was particularly concerned about his frustration and anger. But talking seemed to help. The next day he e-mailed this message to me: "After our talk, I read my Bible notes and found several pages that spoke to me. But what helped me most was the realization that Christianity really is the truth. I suppose that for a Christian this should be obvious. But for me it was a revelation that Jesus in fact is the Son of God and He loves me." He added, "Just knowing the truth was very liberating. Suddenly, all the frustration and anger left me."

Writer Os Guinness tells about a young, searching Christian who exclaimed, "I always knew the Christian faith was true, but I never realized it was *this* true!"

As these believers searched for greater understanding of the gospel, they rediscovered what Jesus promised: "You shall know the truth, and the truth shall make you free" (John 8:32).

Do you need a fresh realization of truth in your life? Then spend time searching the Scriptures (the written truth), and earnestly seek Jesus Christ (the living truth). Soon the old, familiar truth of Jesus and His love will become refreshingly new to you and will make you free indeed. — Joanie Yoder

> *Our selfish ways imprison us —*
> *We cry out to be free;*
> *But if we will obey God's Word,*
> *We'll find true liberty.* — Sper

THE TRUTH OF CHRIST IS THE ONLY PATH TO FREEDOM.

TESTED AND TRUE

READ:
Daniel 3:8-18

Let it be known to you, O king, that we do not serve your gods, nor will we worship the gold image which you have set up.
—Daniel 3:18

THE BIBLE IN ONE YEAR:
■ Daniel 1–3

A young nurse was assisting a surgeon for the first time. As he was completing the operation, she told him he had used 12 sponges, but she could account for only 11. The doctor curtly replied that he had removed them all from inside the patient. The nurse insisted that one was missing, but the doctor declared he would proceed with sewing up the incision.

The nurse, her eyes blazing, said, "You can't do that! Think of the patient!" The doctor smiled and, lifting his foot, showed the nurse the twelfth sponge, which he had deliberately dropped on the floor. "You'll do fine!" he said. He had been testing her.

Daniel's three friends faced a different kind of test (Daniel 3), but they too would not budge. They knew their refusal to worship the image might result in their death, yet they never wavered. They proved they were true to God by standing firm.

The Lord still permits trials and temptations to enter the lives of His children. The challenge may come as an opportunity to gratify the lusts of the flesh, or as a series of disheartening circumstances. Whatever form it takes, we must not yield. Rather, we must stand for what is right and trust God to supply the grace we need (1 Corinthians 10:13).

Are you "tested and true"? — Herb Vander Lugt

Yield not to temptation, for yielding is sin —
Each victory will help you some other to win;
Fight manfully onward, dark passions subdue,
Look ever to Jesus, He will carry you through. — Palmer

**A GEM CANNOT BE POLISHED WITHOUT FRICTION,
NOR CAN WE BE PERFECTED WITHOUT TRIAL.**

Pigeon Walk

READ:
Daniel 6:1-10

He knelt down on his knees three times that day, and prayed and gave thanks before his God, as was his custom. —Daniel 6:10

THE BIBLE IN ONE YEAR:
■ Daniel 4–6

H ave you ever wondered why a pigeon walks so funny? It's so it can see where it's going. A pigeon's eyes can't focus as it moves, so the bird actually has to bring its head to a complete stop between steps in order to refocus. It proceeds clumsily — head forward, stop, head back, stop.

In our spiritual walk with the Lord, we have the same problem as the pigeon: We have a hard time seeing while we're on the go. We need to stop between steps — to pause and refocus on the Word and the will of God. That's not to say we have to pray and meditate about every little decision in life. But certainly our walk with the Lord needs to have built into it a pattern of stops that enable us to see more clearly before moving on.

Daniel's practice of praying three times a day was an essential part of his walk with God (Daniel 6:10). He knew there's a certain kind of spiritual refocusing that we can't do without stopping. His stops gave him a very different kind of walk — one that was obvious to those around him.

What about us? At the risk of being thought of as different, as Daniel was, let's learn this valuable lesson from the pigeon: "Looking good" isn't nearly as important as "seeing well." — Mart De Haan

There is a blessed calm at eventide
That calls me from a world of toil and care;
How restful, then, to seek some quiet nook
Where I can spend a little time in prayer. — Bullock

TIME IN CHRIST'S SERVICE REQUIRES TIME OUT FOR RENEWAL.

REPENTING AND REJOICING

READ:
Psalm 51

Let the wicked forsake his way . . . ; let him return to the LORD, and He will have mercy on him. —Isaiah 55:7

THE BIBLE IN ONE YEAR:
■ Daniel 7–9

A Christian woman asked another believer how he was doing. With a broad smile he replied, "Repenting and rejoicing, sister!"

I believe this man was walking in a spirit of repentance — daily confessing and turning from sins and rejoicing in God's forgiveness.

Because honest repentance involves sorrow, we may forget that repenting leads to rejoicing. When we first repent and become new believers, we experience great joy. But if we then choose to live with unconfessed sin, our joy is lost.

David believed his joy could be restored. After pouring out his prayer of repentance to God, he made this humble plea: "Restore to me the joy of Your salvation" (Psalm 51:12). As David turned back to the Lord, his sense of purpose returned: "Then I will teach transgressors Your ways, and sinners shall be converted to You" (v.13). Through his faith in a forgiving and merciful God, David began rejoicing again in his salvation (vv.14-15).

Do you sometimes lose the joy of your salvation because you fail to deal with your sins? If you'll confess them, God will forgive you (1 John 1:9). He'll restore your joy and help you overcome sins that trouble you. That's what it means to be a "repenting and rejoicing" Christian. — Joanie Yoder

> *When we confess our sins to God,*
> *We're washed as white as snow,*
> *And He keeps on forgiving us*
> *Each time to Him we go.* — Sper

**CONVICTION MAKES US SAD—
CONFESSION MAKES US GLAD.**

September 22

SILENT SERMON

READ:
Colossians 3:12-17
Hebrews 10:24-25

Let the word of Christ dwell in you richly in all wisdom, teaching and admonishing one another.
—Colossians 3:16

THE BIBLE IN ONE YEAR:
■ Daniel 10–12

How important is our fellowship in the local church? Let me answer that question by telling a story.

A minister was concerned about the absence of a man who had normally attended services. After a few weeks, he decided to visit him. When the pastor arrived at the man's home, he found him all alone, sitting in front of a fireplace. The minister pulled up a chair and sat next to him. But after his initial greeting he said nothing more.

The two sat in silence for a few minutes while the minister stared at the flames in the fireplace. Then he took the tongs and carefully picked up one burning ember from the flames and placed it on the hearth. He sat back in his chair, still silent. His host watched in quiet reflection as the ember flickered and faded. Before long it was cold and dead.

The minister glanced at his watch and said he had to leave, but first he picked up the cold ember and placed it back in the fire. Immediately it began to glow again with the light and warmth of the burning coals around it.

As the minister rose to leave, his host stood with him and shook his hand. Then, with a smile on his face, the man said, "Thanks for the sermon, pastor. I'll see you in church on Sunday." — David Roper

Lord, help us see how much we need each other
As we walk along the Christian way;
In fellowship with sister and with brother,
You will keep us growing day by day. — Hess

THE WARM FELLOWSHIP OF THE CHURCH
WILL KEEP YOUR HEART FROM GROWING COLD.

COMMITTED TO SERVE

READ:
Ruth 1:1-18

Wherever you go,
I will go; . . . your
people shall be my
people, and your
God, my God.
—Ruth 1:16

THE BIBLE IN ONE YEAR:
■ Hosea 1–4

The best-known words of Ruth are most often heard at weddings, even though they were spoken by a grieving young widow to her mother-in-law, Naomi. She said, "Wherever you go, I will go; and wherever you lodge, I will lodge; your people shall be my people, and your God, my God" (Ruth 1:16).

Ruth had no legal or cultural responsibility to Naomi, who also was a widow and had no means of support. No one would have blamed Ruth for staying with her own people in Moab where the chances of remarriage were greater.

Naomi even urged Ruth to stay, but Ruth was determined to go with her to Judah, and to follow her God. Ruth's unselfish devotion was considered worthy of praise. Boaz, Ruth's future husband, told her, "It has been fully reported to me, all that you have done for your mother-in-law since the death of your husband . . . . The LORD repay your work" (2:11-12).

Promises spoken at a wedding are full of hope and meaning, but Ruth's words have survived the centuries because of her unwavering commitment to God and a person in need. She points us to the value of loving sacrifice for the Lord, and to His rich blessing on all who give themselves unselfishly to others. — David McCasland

Searching to know life's true meaning?
You'll find it in only one way:
Serving the Lord with commitment
And living for others each day. — Branon

**A LIFE FILLED WITH LOVE FOR THE LORD
AND FOR OTHERS IS A FULFILLING LIFE.**

A CIRCLE OF COMPASSION

READ:
2 Corinthians 1:1-4
Philippians 2:1-4

Rejoice with those who rejoice, and weep with those who weep.
—Romans 12:15

THE BIBLE IN ONE YEAR:
■ Hosea 5–7

Following the death of our 17-year-old daughter in a car accident in June 2002, each member of our family handled the loss differently. For my wife, among the most helpful sources of comfort were visits from moms who had also lost a child in an accident.

Sue found strength in their stories, and she wanted them to tell her how God had been faithful in their lives, despite the deep sorrow that comes with losing a precious child.

Soon Sue became part of a circle of compassion, a small group of moms who could weep, pray, and seek God's help together. That cadre of grieving moms formed a bond of empathy and hope that provided encouragement in the face of her daily sorrow.

Each person grieves uniquely, yet we all need to share our hearts, our burdens, our questions, and our sadness with someone else. That's why it's vital that we find others with whom to discuss our pain and sorrow.

In our relationship with Christ, we find encouragement, consolation, love, fellowship, affection, and mercy (Philippians 2:1). God comforts us so that we can comfort others (2 Corinthians 1:4). So let's "rejoice with those who rejoice, and weep with those who weep" (Romans 12:15). Then others will find a circle of compassion too. — Dave Branon

A heartfelt tear can show our love
As words can never do;
It says, "I want to share your pain—
My heart goes out to you." — D. De Haan

WE MUST LEARN TO WEEP
BEFORE WE CAN DRY ANOTHER'S TEARS.

IT'S STILL RELEVANT

READ:
Psalm 19:7-11

. . . having been born again . . . through the Word of God which lives and abides forever. —1 Peter 1:23

THE BIBLE IN ONE YEAR:
■ Hosea 8–10

It's estimated that every year 300,000 new books are published worldwide. What a torrent of print! Yet one volume, the Bible, stands out above all the others.

How do we explain the appeal of this ancient book? The answer is simple. It is God's Word, given in human language, and it tells us about our Creator and His purposes for the world. But it also gives us the most accurate understanding of mankind's perplexing nature and why we behave the way we do.

Harvard professor Robert Coles has interviewed hundreds of people in many different societies. When asked what he had learned from his research on human nature, Dr. Coles pointed to the Bible on his desk and said, "Nothing I have discovered about the makeup of human beings contradicts in any way what I learn from the Hebrew prophets . . . and from Jesus and the lives of those He touched."

The writings of others and our own experience can teach us much about why we behave as we do. But only the Bible tells us that our sinful heart is the heart of our problem, and that we can be changed from within by trusting Jesus.

Yes, the Bible is still relevant. Are you growing in your love for this ancient book? — Vernon Grounds

Your heart and conscience cannot guide,
For they're deceived by sin inside;
But if you want to see what's true,
The Word of God will mirror you. —Hess

**THE BIBLE IS A MIRROR THAT LETS US SEE
OURSELVES AS GOD SEES US.**

PEOPLE GOD CAN USE

READ:
1 Timothy 6:17-19

Be rich in good works, ready to give, willing to share.
—1 Timothy 6:18

THE BIBLE IN ONE YEAR:
■ Hosea 11–14

E vangelist Franklin Graham wrote, "If we want to become the type of people that God can use anytime, anywhere, anyplace, we must offer ourselves, our homes, our kitchens, and our living rooms as outposts for the kingdom of God." People who practice these words are fulfilling Paul's challenge to "be rich in good works, ready to give, willing to share" (1 Timothy 6:18).

Years ago, our family sensed that the Lord was placing this same challenge before us. Believing that He desired greater access to our lives, our possessions, and our time, we prayerfully said yes to Him.

Soon we encountered a desperate drug addict and opened our home to him. Several families joined us in helping others who needed to come to Christ and come off drugs. Eventually we established a Christian rehabilitation center — a ministry that continues today. To equip us for this ministry, God used our own painful experiences. Our own troubles helped us identify with others, and enabled us to guide them to depend on Jesus for salvation and every daily need.

God also wants to use you, your possessions, and even your pain, to equip you for a life that's rich in giving and sharing. Have you said yes to Him? — Joanie Yoder

Give me a heart sympathetic and tender,
Jesus, like Thine, Jesus, like Thine,
Touched by the needs that are surging around me,
And filled with compassion divine. — Anon.

COMPASSION IS NEEDED
TO HEAL THE HURTS OF OTHERS.

September 27

HAPPY NEW YEAR!

READ:
Joel 2:12-17

Rend your heart, and not your garments; return to the LORD your God, for He is gracious and merciful.
—Joel 2:13

THE BIBLE IN ONE YEAR:
■ Joel 1–3

R osh Hashanah, the Jewish New Year, is regarded as the anniversary of the day that God created the world. The celebration begins with a blast of the shofar (ram's horn) to announce that the God who created the world is still the One ruling it. The blowing of the horn also begins a 10-day period of self-examination and repentance leading to Yom Kippur, the Day of Atonement (Leviticus 23:23-32; Numbers 29:1-6).

The prophet Joel urged people not to just go through the motions of repentance, but to turn from their sins and obey God (Joel 2:13). In his day, tearing garments was a sign of sorrow for sin. It made a good show, but it didn't impress God. He was more concerned with their hearts.

Especially interesting is the basis for Joel's appeal. It wasn't only to avoid God's wrath, but also to enjoy God's grace, compassion, and love. Sometimes we think of God as being heavy-handed with punishment and tight-fisted with mercy. The words of Joel remind us that the opposite is true. The Lord is slow to punish and eager to forgive.

There's no better way to celebrate God's creation than to let Him re-create your heart through faith in Jesus the Messiah and turn your desires toward Him. — Julie Link

When I tried to cover my sin,
My guilt I could not shake;
But when I sought Your mercy, Lord,
My sin I did forsake. — Hess

CONFESSION IS THE KEY THAT OPENS THE DOOR TO FORGIVENESS.

WINDTALKERS

READ:
2 Peter 1:19-21

Prophecy never came by the will of man, but holy men of God spoke as they were moved by the Holy Spirit. —2 Peter 1:21

THE BIBLE IN ONE YEAR:
■ Amos 1–3

Their contribution to victory in World War II was enormous, but few people even knew about them. In 1942, the US Army recruited and trained 29 young Navajo Indians and sent them to a base surrounded in secrecy. These people, who were called "windtalkers," had been asked to devise a special code in their native language that the enemy couldn't break. They succeeded, and the code was never broken. It secured and greatly speeded up war communications. For 23 years after the war, that secret code remained classified in case it might be needed again.

By contrast, the Bible was not sent down to us in some unbreakable code impossible to understand. Although it contains rich imagery, vivid metaphors, and the record of magnificent visions, it was written by human authors to give people the message of God's love and salvation.

That message is clear and unmistakable. The biblical writers were moved by God's Spirit to record exactly what He wanted us to know. For centuries people have been freed from their sin and guilt by believing His message.

We owe a great debt to the windtalkers. We owe an even greater debt to the writers of Scripture, who received God's Word and wrote it down. So let's read it often. — Dave Egner

When reading God's Word, take special care
To find the rich treasures hidden there;
Give thought to each line, each precept clear,
Then practice it well with godly fear. — Anon.

MANY WHO HAVE BEEN BLIND TO THE TRUTH HAVE FOUND THAT READING THE BIBLE IS A REAL EYE-OPENER.

September 29

IN PARTNERSHIP WITH GOD

READ:
Matthew 6:5-15

**Your Father knows the things you have need of before you ask Him.
—Matthew 6:8**

THE BIBLE IN ONE YEAR:
■ Amos 4–6

A man had transformed an overgrown plot of ground into a beautiful garden and was showing a friend what he had accomplished. Pointing to a bed of flowers, he said, "Look at what I did here." His companion corrected him, "You mean, 'Look at what God and I did here.'" The gardener replied, "I guess you're right. But you should have seen the shape this plot was in when He was taking care of it by Himself."

We chuckle at the man's reply, but it expresses a wonderful spiritual truth—we are co-workers with God. This applies to every area of life, including prayer. It answers a question that naturally comes to mind when we reflect on Jesus' statements in Matthew 6. He said we don't need to pray on and on with vain repetitions like the pagans, because our Father knows what we need before we ask (Matthew 6:7-8).

The question is, then, why pray? The answer is simple and comforting. God has graciously chosen to give us the privilege of being His partners in both the physical and spiritual areas of life. Through prayer we work with Him in defeating the powers of evil and in bringing about the fulfillment of His loving purposes in the world. Partners with God — what a privilege! What an incentive to pray! — Herb Vander Lugt

Although God knows our every need,
His work He wants to share;
He takes us into partnership
By calling us to prayer. — D. De Haan

GOD'S WORK IS DONE BY THOSE WHO PRAY.

HE CAN BE TRUSTED

READ:
Psalm 84

**O LORD of hosts, blessed is the man who trusts in You!
—Psalm 84:12**

THE BIBLE IN ONE YEAR:
■ Amos 7–9

I was sitting in my chair by the window, staring out through fir and spruce trees to the mountains beyond, lost in thought. I looked down and saw a young fox, staring up at my face. She was as still as a stone.

Days before, I had seen her at the edge of the woods, looking nervously over her shoulder at me. I went to the kitchen for an egg, and rolled it toward the place I had last seen her. Each day I put another egg on the lawn, and each day she ventured out of the trees just long enough to pick it up. Then she would dart back into the woods.

Now she had come on her own to my door to get an egg, convinced, I suppose, that I meant her no harm.

This incident reminded my wife of David's invitation: "Oh, taste and see that the LORD is good" (Psalm 34:8). How do we start doing that? By taking in His Word. As we read and reflect on His compassion and lovingkindness, we learn that He can be trusted (84:12). We lose our dread of getting closer to Him. Our fear becomes a healthy respect and honor of Him.

You may at times distrust God, as the fox was wary of me at first. But give Him a chance to prove His love. Read about Jesus in the Gospels. Read the praises to God in the Psalms. Taste and see that He is good! — David Roper

O taste and see that God is good
To all that seek His face;
Yea, blest the man that trusts in Him,
Confiding in His grace. — Psalter

NO ONE IS BEYOND THE REACH OF GOD'S LOVE.

CUT OFF?

READ:
Psalm 31:14-24

You heard the voice
of my supplications
when I cried out to
You. —Psalm 31:22

THE BIBLE IN ONE YEAR:
■ Obadiah, Jonah

During Antarctica's 9-month winter, the continent is engulfed in darkness and the temperature sinks to -115° F (-82° C). Flights are halted from late February to November, leaving workers at scattered research stations isolated and virtually cut off from outside help. Yet, during 2001, two daring rescue missions penetrated the polar winter and airlifted people with serious medical conditions to safety.

We all feel helpless and cut off at times. It may seem that not even God can hear or answer our cries for help. The psalmist David said in a time of trouble, "I am cut off from before Your eyes" (Psalm 31:22). But David discovered that the Lord had not forgotten him, and he rejoiced, "You heard the voice of my supplications when I cried out to You" (v.22).

What circumstances make you feel helpless or hopeless today? Poor health, broken relationships, a family member in great need? In Jesus Christ, God has pierced the dark winter of our world in a daring rescue through His redeeming love. He is therefore able to reach us and calm our fears in the most desperate circumstances.

We are never cut off from the mighty power and sustaining peace of God. — David McCasland

The Lord is near to all who call;
He promised in His holy Word
That if we will draw near to Him,
Our faintest heartcry will be heard. —Hess

GOD'S HELP IS ONLY A PRAYER AWAY.

GOD'S TREASURE CHEST

READ:
Psalm 119:9-16

I have rejoiced in the way of Your testimonies, as much as in all riches.
—Psalm 119:14

THE BIBLE IN ONE YEAR:
■ Micah 1–4

Most of us wouldn't ignore a dollar lying on the ground. We would gladly pick it up and put it in our pocket. Yet we often ignore the Bible, a treasure chest overflowing with God's precious promises. David, the likely author of Psalm 119, recorded the rich blessings he experienced as he studied God's Word and stored it in the pocket of his heart. No wonder British pastor Charles H. Spurgeon referred to it as "David's pocket book."

David not only rejoiced in God's Word, but he also used it as a personal safeguard against sin. He said to God, "Your Word I have hidden in my heart, that I might not sin against You" (v.11). But David did more than memorize it. He saturated his heart with its truth, using these methods: He meditated on God's precepts, contemplated His ways, and delighted himself in the Lord's teachings (vv.15-16). Therefore he could say, "I will not forget Your Word" (v.16), for we don't easily forget what we treasure in our hearts.

When you read *Our Daily Bread*, take time to read the Scripture verses. The Bible, God's treasure chest, is the basis for all these articles. Use them to help you hunt for precious gems in God's Word. Like David, hide them in your heart so that you'll remember them and rejoice. — Joanie Yoder

> *My Bible to me is a treasure house,*
> *Where I can always find*
> *Whatever I need from day to day*
> *For heart and soul and mind.* — Anon.

**RICH TREASURES OF GOD'S TRUTH
CAN BE DISCOVERED IN HIS WORD.**

Racing Toward The Goal

READ:
1 Corinthians 9:24-27

**Do you not know that those who run in a race all run, but one receives the prize? Run in such a way that you may obtain it.
—1 Corinthians 9:24**

THE BIBLE IN ONE YEAR:
■ Micah 5-7

When my son began his sophomore year of high school, he also began his second year of cross-country running. Steve started the year fighting for a spot on the varsity team, which was not an easy task.

It meant running miles and miles and miles. It meant lifting weights. It meant getting extra rest and eating right (well, some of the time). And it meant running his heart out at races.

His times gradually improved. Then he pulled a muscle and had to start over. But he didn't quit. Finally he gained a spot on the varsity. And by the time they ran in the regional meet, he was the third fastest runner on the team.

Having goals in life can give us the purpose and drive to accomplish something truly valuable. This principle is especially helpful in our lives as believers in Christ. As we run the Christian race, our goal is to "run in such a way" that we may win an imperishable crown — an eternal reward from our Savior (1 Corinthians 3:12-14; 9:24-25). This requires personal discipline, hard work, and continual improvement. It includes a Spirit-enabled commitment to do our very best for the Lord.

That takes perseverance, an all-out effort, and a push to become increasingly like Christ. But running that way is worth it, for the prize will last forever. — Dave Branon

Run the straight race through God's good grace,
Lift up your eyes and seek His face;
Life with its way before us lies,
Christ is the path and Christ the prize. — Monsell

**GREAT ACHIEVEMENT REQUIRES
GREAT PERSEVERANCE.**

Life's Uncertainty

READ:
James 4:13-17

**You do not know what will happen tomorrow.
—James 4:14**

THE BIBLE IN ONE YEAR:
■ Nahum 1–3

Life's one certainty is its sheer uncertainty. As Scripture reminds us, we "do not know what will happen tomorrow" (James 4:14). Real estate developer Larry Silverstein can bear witness to the truth of that text. Though he owned impressive property in New York City, he was, according to his own testimony, obsessed by the desire to add the great Twin Towers of the World Trade Center to his holdings. His wish came true. Six weeks before those two imposing skyscrapers were destroyed by terrorists, he had obtained a 99-year lease worth $3.2 billion for that majestic center.

Sadly, the fulfillment of our dreams can sometimes turn into nightmares. This reminds us not only of the uncertainty of life, but also of the need to align our desires with God's will. Experience teaches us that if we allow presumption to run our lives, the fulfillment of our own compulsive dreams may turn to dust and ashes.

There are legitimate desires, to be sure, but the book of James tells us how to approach them. Instead of presuming that our plans and dreams will be fulfilled, we ought to say, "If the Lord wills, we shall live and do this or that" (4:15).

When we submit our plans to God's will, we can enjoy His peace in the midst of life's uncertainty. — Vernon Grounds

*Our life is uncertain, our path is unclear,
Yet we have no cause to falter or fear
If plans that we make our dreams to fulfill
Are born out of love for God and His will.* — D. De Haan

**WRITE YOUR PLANS IN PENCIL,
THEN GIVE GOD THE ERASER.**

REMOVING BARRIERS

READ:
1 Corinthians 10:16-22

You are all one in Christ Jesus.
—Galatians 3:28

THE BIBLE IN ONE YEAR:
■ Habakkuk 1–3

A missionary in Calcutta said that she was profoundly influenced by a communion service she had attended during World War II. The leader of that meeting was a Swedish minister. Among those present were a Chinese pastor, a Japanese teacher, a German doctor, several English citizens, and a few Indian believers.

The missionary recalled that she felt a closeness to each person in that diverse gathering, especially when they partook of the bread and the cup. They felt a bond of Christian fellowship, even though some of them were from countries engaged in a brutal war.

The next time you celebrate the Lord's Supper, think about your oneness with all who are participating in the service with you. Resolve to look beyond all cultural distinctions and do what you can to remove the barriers between you and others.

Be merciful to those who have wronged you. Tell God you will forgive them and accept them. Determine that with His help you will show kindness to everyone, whether you feel like it or not. See the people around you as fellow members of the body of Christ.

This type of unity will enrich your life and enhance your church's influence in the world. — Herb Vander Lugt

In Christ there is no East or West,
In Him no South or North,
But one great fellowship of love
Throughout the whole wide earth. — Oxenham

WHEN CHRISTIANS DRAW CLOSE TO CHRIST,
THEY DRAW CLOSER TO ONE ANOTHER.

GOD, MY GLORY

READ:
Psalm 3

You, O LORD, are
a shield for me, my
glory and the One
who lifts up my head.
—Psalm 3:3

THE BIBLE IN ONE YEAR:
■ Zephaniah 1–3

Is God your glory? (Psalm 3:3). The word *glory* is the translation of a Hebrew word meaning "weight" or "significance."

Some people measure their worth by beauty, intelligence, money, power, or prestige. But David, who wrote Psalm 3, found his security and worth in God. He said that many stood against him. He heard their cruel voices and was tempted to believe them, to give way to discouragement and depression. Nevertheless, he comforted and strengthened his heart with these words: "You, O LORD, are a shield for me, my glory and the One who lifts up my head" (v.3).

What a change that realization made! He had God, and his enemies did not. So he could hold up his head with confidence.

Verses like Psalm 3:3 can bring peace to your heart even in the midst of a storm of trouble. God is your shield and deliverer. He will deal with your adversaries in due time.

Meanwhile, tell God all about your troubles. Let Him be your glory. You don't have to defend yourself. Ask Him to be your shield — to protect your heart with His overshadowing love and care. Then, like David, you can lie down in peace and sleep, though tens of thousands are against you (vv.5-6). — David Roper

> *Though many be against me*
> *And would attack my name,*
> *I'll glory in my Savior*
> *And trust Him just the same.* —Fitzhugh

**NO ONE IS MORE SECURE THAN
THE ONE WHO IS HELD IN GOD'S HANDS.**

SPEAK THAT WORD

READ:
Proverbs 12:17-25

**There is one who speaks like the piercings of a sword, but the tongue of the wise promotes health.
—Proverbs 12:18**

THE BIBLE IN ONE YEAR:
■ Haggai 1–2

I**n** Charles Dickens' novel *David Copperfield,* young David returns from a happy visit with friends to find his widowed mother remarried to Edward Murdstone, a harsh and domineering man. Mr. Murdstone and his permanently visiting sister Jane set out to conquer David's spirit through cruel punishment and intimidation.

Early in the process, David describes his feelings: "I might have been improved for my whole life, I might have been made another creature . . . by a kind word."

Copperfield desired so much to hear a word of encouragement, of understanding, and of reassurance that he was still welcome at home. He was sure that any act of kindness would help him respect and obey Mr. Murdstone. But to his dismay, no words of encouragement were ever given.

The tragedy of not speaking a kind word to a fearful and worried heart is as old as time. Wise King Solomon wrote: "There is one who speaks like the piercings of a sword, but the tongue of the wise promotes health" (Proverbs 12:18).

In our personal and family relationships, are we trying to force others to do what we want, or are we seeking to lead by example and encouragement? A sharp tongue leaves a scar, while a helpful word heals the heart. — David McCasland

I long to have a caring heart —
To show God's love to those in need;
So help me, Lord, to share a part
Of all I have through word and deed. —Hess

KIND WORDS CAN GIVE A LIFT TO A HEAVY HEART.

A WALL OF FIRE

READ:
Zechariah 2:1-5

"For I," says the LORD, "will be a wall of fire all around her, and I will be the glory in her midst."
—Zechariah 2:5

THE BIBLE IN ONE YEAR:
■ Zechariah 1–2

The construction of the Great Wall of China began in the third century BC. Often called the "eighth wonder of the world," it is approximately 1,500 miles (2,400 kilometers) long. The Great Wall was built to protect the people against raids by nomadic peoples and invasions by rival states.

In Zechariah 2, we read about another wall of protection. Zechariah had a vision of a man with a measuring line, who was trying to determine the length and width of Jerusalem (vv.1-2). His intention was apparently to begin rebuilding the fortified walls surrounding the city. The man was told that this would not be necessary, because the number of God's people would be so great that Jerusalem's walls would not be able to contain them (v.4). Besides, they would not need walls, for the Lord promised: "I . . . will be a wall of fire all around her, and I will be the glory in her midst" (v.5).

Physical walls can be scaled or broken through, no matter how high or strong they are. But as God's children, we have the best wall of protection anyone can have — God's personal presence. Nothing can pass through to us without first passing through Him and His will. In Him we are safe and secure. — Albert Lee

I can trust my loving Savior
When I hear this world's alarms;
There's no safer place of refuge
Than within His mighty arms. — Hess

**SAFETY IS NOT FOUND IN THE ABSENCE OF DANGER
BUT IN THE PRESENCE OF GOD.**

Tenant Of The Tunnel

READ:
Colossians 1:1-14

He has delivered us from the power of darkness and conveyed us into the kingdom of the Son.
—Colossians 1:13

THE BIBLE IN ONE YEAR:
■ Zechariah 3–6

For 16 years, John Kovacs was a "tenant of the tunnel." Along with a few others, John lived underground in an abandoned railroad tunnel in New York City. When Amtrak bought the tunnel and prepared to reopen it, John was forced to look for a place to live above ground.

According to *The New York Times*, Mr. Kovacs became the first person chosen for a new program designed to "transform the homeless into homesteaders." After spending a third of his life in a railroad tunnel, he left his underground existence to become an organic farmer in upstate New York. He was quoted as saying, "The air will be better up there. I'm not going to miss anything. I'm not coming back."

If we could see ourselves as our Lord does, we would realize that every child of God has had a similar experience. We too have been chosen to leave a dark, filthy existence for the dignity of a new life and work. If only we could see our former life as clearly as John Kovacs saw his, we too would know that there is nothing worthwhile in the dark, and no reason to go back.

Lord, help us to remember how needy we were when You found us. Forgive us for sometimes wanting to go back to the tunnel. — Mart De Haan

> *I wandered in the shades of night*
> *Till Jesus came to me*
> *And with the sunlight of His love*
> *Bid all my darkness flee.* — Van De Venter

CHILDREN OF THE LIGHT WILL NOT BE COMFORTABLE IN THE DARK.

EPITAPH

READ:
John 10:40-42

**John performed no sign, but all the things that John spoke about this Man were true.
—John 10:41**

THE BIBLE IN ONE YEAR:
■ Zechariah 7–10

John the Baptist had been dead for at least 2 years and the memory of his ministry had begun to fade. That's the way it is when a public figure leaves the scene and is eclipsed by a more illustrious successor.

As the crowds gathered around Jesus near the spot where John had taught, they remembered the baptizer's life and words, and they remarked, "John performed no sign, but all the things that John spoke about this Man were true" (John 10:41).

Like John, we don't need to perform miracles to tell people about Jesus. We can tell what we have learned about Him from the Bible, what He has done to change our hearts and lives, and what He has done for others. If we faithfully pass on the good news about Jesus, we will have served our life's purpose well.

Even long after we're dead and gone, our words may come to the minds of those to whom we've witnessed and may be the means of bringing them to faith in the Lord Jesus. Like seed buried in the ground, God's Word that we've sown can lie dormant for many years and then spring up to eternal life.

It's a great epitaph for one's life: "He did no miracles, but everything he said about Jesus was true." — David Roper

Even after we have left
This earthly scene below,
The witness of our life still speaks
Of Christ, whom all can know. — D. De Haan

**WALKING WITH JESUS LEAVES FOOTPRINTS
FOR OTHERS TO FOLLOW.**

Fishing

READ:
Matthew 4:18-22

He said to them,
"Follow Me, and I will
make you fishers of
men." —Matthew 4:19

THE BIBLE IN ONE YEAR:
■ Zechariah 11-14

A skilled fly fisherman whips his line back and forth over his head. Then he releases the line and sets the fly-like lure down on the water's surface exactly where he wants it. If he's successful, a big rainbow trout will rise, strike the lure, and the fisherman will set the hook. The battle is on!

That's one way to catch fish. Halibut fishermen use another method. They go out on the ocean and drop big baited hooks, sometimes as far down as 125 or 150 feet. When one of those big, flat fish goes for the bait and is hooked, he begins a long ride to the surface.

Jesus told Peter and Andrew to follow Him and He would make them "fishers of men" (Matthew 4:18-19). As followers of Christ today, we too are to be "fishing" for people in our world, using different methods to spread the good news. We are to be telling men and women, family and friends, young and old, about their sin, the love of God, and His offer of salvation through faith in Jesus.

Are you fishing for men? Have you tried different methods to tell others about Christ and the gospel? Have you reached out to your neighborhood and community with the good news? Keep following Jesus, and He'll teach you how to fish. — Dave Egner

THINKING IT OVER
Think of a way you can share Christ with
people in your neighborhood, workplace, or school.
Talk it over with others, then go out and try it.

**IF YOU FOLLOW THE SAVIOR,
HE'LL TEACH YOU HOW TO FISH.**

THEY'RE AFTER OUR CHILDREN

READ:
Proverbs 3:1-18

She is more precious than rubies, and all the things you may desire cannot compare with her. —Proverbs 3:15

THE BIBLE IN ONE YEAR:
■ Malachi 1 – 4

Advertisers are after our young people. They are increasingly targeting their messages to children. Because of the strong influence they have on the purchasing habits of their parents, and because they have an increasing buying power of their own, millions of dollars are being spent to get their attention. People in the advertising business are convinced that a young, satisfied consumer could become a lifelong customer — eager to buy their products far into the future.

In a similar way, we need to be influencing our young people to "buy into" the good things God has in store for them throughout all of life. According to Proverbs 3, some fantastic possibilities lie ahead for the young person who chooses God's way: long life and peace (v.2), favor in the sight of God and man (v.4), direction from God (v.6), health and strength (v.8), abundance (v.10), happiness (v.13). The person who trusts, honors, and fears the Lord finds wisdom — an incomparable prize (v.15).

The world spends millions convincing our children that they can't be happy without a certain kind of shoe. How much more we have to offer them by showing them that happiness comes by walking with God! — Dave Branon

We can help our precious children
Follow in God's way,
Living out our faith with gladness,
Praying every day. — Sper

WHAT WE LEAVE IN OUR CHILDREN IS MORE IMPORTANT THAN WHAT WE LEAVE TO THEM.

DEBTORS FOREVER

READ:
Psalm 23

Surely goodness and mercy shall follow me all the days of my life; and I will dwell in the house of the LORD forever. —Psalm 23:6

THE BIBLE IN ONE YEAR:
■ Matthew 1–4

O ccasionally it's helpful to spend a few quiet moments looking back over our lives to review how indebted we are to God for His goodness and mercy. Of course, no two personal histories are the same. But we can all echo the words of David, the poet-king, in Psalm 23:6. He wrote, "Goodness and mercy shall follow me all the days of my life." If we are trusting Jesus Christ, those few words sum up the whole of our experience in life.

God's goodness imparts what we don't deserve; His mercy withholds what we do deserve. In times of pain and sorrow, our heavenly Father faithfully meets our needs, comforts our hearts, and gives us strength to bear our burdens. Although we are believers, we still sin and fall short of the holy standard set by His Son, Jesus Christ. Yet He keeps on pouring His forgiveness into our souls as we confess our sins. We may think of ourselves as decent people, but we must still admit that "we have left undone those things which we ought to have done, and we have done those things which we ought not to have done" (*The Book of Common Prayer*).

May gratitude continually fill our hearts, because God's goodness and mercy will follow us all the way to glory. We are indebted to Him forever. — Vernon Grounds

When we stand with Christ in glory
Looking o'er life's finished story,
Then, Lord, shall I fully know —
Not till then — how much I owe. —McCheyne

**BECAUSE GOD GIVES US EVERYTHING,
WE OWE HIM ALL OUR PRAISE.**

THIS LITTLE LIGHT OF MINE

READ:
Matthew 5:11-16

Let your light so shine before men, that they may see your good works and glorify your Father in heaven.
—Matthew 5:16

THE BIBLE IN ONE YEAR:
■ Matthew 5–7

The Lake Michigan shoreline (a short drive from where I live) is dotted with lighthouses built to enable ship captains to navigate into safe harbors. The structures are varied in size, shape, and color, but each has unique charm and beauty. Pictures of the lighthouses are featured in books and calendars, and some people collect replicas and other lighthouse items.

But lighthouses were not built just to be admired; they were built to hold lights that guide sailors to safety. A lighthouse is most useful and appreciated when, in the darkness of night, only its light can be seen — not the structure itself.

When Jesus sent out His disciples, He called them "the light of the world" (Matthew 5:14). He also indicated that their task was not to draw attention to themselves, but to do good works that would cause people to recognize God's goodness and glorify Him.

Jesus said that just as a lamp's purpose is to give light, we also are to let our light shine (vv.15-16). We're most effective when we shine brightly in the darkness, guiding people who need to find safe harbor in Christ.

For a light to be effective, it has to be shining in a dark place. — Julie Link

My life was dark until the Light shone in,
That Light was Christ, who saved me from my sin;
His light that I've received I want to share
And let it shine to people everywhere. — Hess

A LITTLE LIGHT MAKES A BIG DIFFERENCE
IN THE DARKEST NIGHT.

NOT MY HAND

READ:
1 Samuel 24:1-15

I said, "I will not stretch out my hand against my lord, for he is the LORD's anointed."
—1 Samuel 24:10

THE BIBLE IN ONE YEAR:
■ Matthew 8–11

There are times when it's best to wait for God to act instead of trying to make things happen ourselves. It's a lesson we see clearly when David refused to take King Saul's life, even though the king was trying to kill him (1 Samuel 24). When Saul was alone and vulnerable in a cave, David's men told him this was a God-given opportunity to take the kingship that rightfully belonged to him (v.4). But David refused, saying, "The LORD forbid that I should do this thing to my master, the LORD's anointed, to stretch out my hand against him" (v.6).

After Saul left the cave, David called out to him, "Let the LORD judge between you and me, and let the LORD avenge me on you. But my hand shall not be against you" (v.12). David knew that God had chosen him to become king. But he also knew that killing Saul was not the right way to make it happen. He would wait for God to remove Saul from the throne.

Is there an obstacle between you and something that is rightfully yours? You believe it's God's will, but the method of obtaining it and the timing don't seem right. Think long and pray hard before taking a bad path toward a good goal.

Waiting for God to act is the best opportunity for the right things to happen His way. — David McCasland

> O God, make me one of those rarest of souls
> Who willingly wait for Thy time;
> My impatient will must be lost in Thine own,
> And Thy will forever be mine. — Bowser

**GOD'S TIMING IS ALWAYS RIGHT—
WAIT PATIENTLY FOR HIM.**

OPENING THE DOOR

READ:
1 Peter 3:1-12

Husbands, likewise, dwell with them with understanding, giving honor to the wife, as to the weaker vessel.
—1 Peter 3:7

THE BIBLE IN ONE YEAR:
■ Matthew 12–15

When my wife and I went out to lunch with some friends, I noticed that the husband went around to the passenger side of the car and opened the door for his wife. I said to him, "Some women might consider that demeaning." "That's right," he said. "One woman saw me do that and remarked, 'I'm sure she's perfectly capable of opening the door for herself!' I told her, 'I don't open the door for my wife because she's incapable. I do it to honor her.'"

Jesus treated women with the utmost respect and honor (John 4:1-38; 8:3-11; 19:25-27). Likewise, in 1 Peter 3:7, husbands are instructed to live with their wives "with understanding, giving honor to the wife, as to the weaker vessel." Men and women both have their weaknesses, but in general, women are physically weaker than men and have unique needs and sensitivities. This in no way means they are inferior. In fact, Peter said that as Christians, men and women are "heirs together of the grace of life" (v.7).

Opening a door for a woman may seem to some like an old-fashioned courtesy. But it can also be a wonderful tribute to both the man and the woman if it symbolizes the honor and respect one has for the other. — Dennis De Haan

THINKING IT OVER
Read Romans 12:10 and Philippians 2:3.
How can you apply the truths of these verses
to male and female relationships?

WE HONOR GOD WHEN WE HONOR ONE ANOTHER.

THE CHURCH INDESTRUCTIBLE

READ:
Matthew 16:13-20

> You are Peter, and on this rock I will build My church, and the gates of Hades shall not prevail against it.
> —Matthew 16:18

THE BIBLE IN ONE YEAR:
■ Matthew 16–19

The chief executive of a large and successful chain of stores made a striking statement about the future of his company. He said that a hundred years from now it would be either greatly changed or nonexistent.

The same can be said about every human organization. Leaders come and go, consumer desires change, manufacturing methods evolve. As a result, companies either change or they don't survive.

According to Jesus, this will never happen to His church. Some individual churches may go out of existence, but the "gates of Hades" will never prevail against the church that Jesus is building. When He referred to "My church" (Matthew 16:18), He had in mind all believers — past, present, and future. Paul called this vast group the "body of Christ" (1 Corinthians 12:27).

The moment we trust in Jesus, we become members of His body, the church. And when Jesus used the phrase "the gates of Hades," He was referring to death, for Hades is the abode of the dead. One by one believers die and pass through those "gates," but this neither changes nor diminishes the church. They simply join those who are already victors in the "heavenly Jerusalem" (Hebrews 12:22-24).

Praise God, the church is indestructible! — Herb Vander Lugt

Christ is made the sure foundation,
Christ the head and cornerstone;
Chosen of the Lord and precious,
Binding all the church in one. — Neale

**THE CHURCH, ROOTED BY GOD,
CAN NEVER BE UPROOTED BY MAN.**

THE JOY
OF WAITING

READ:
1 Samuel 1:19-28

**For this child I prayed, and the LORD has granted me my petition.
—1 Samuel 1:27**

THE BIBLE IN ONE YEAR:
■ Matthew 20–22

Nine months can seem like forever for a mother-to-be. In the first trimester, hormonal changes sometimes cause lingering morning sickness. Emotions rise to the surface, prolonging afternoon blues. Then a changing appetite stretches out evening hours with late-night cravings for pizza, chocolate, and dill pickles.

During the next 3 months, Mom outgrows her clothes and spends long hours looking for a new wardrobe. The last trimester turns normal activity into a chore as the final watch begins.

Then, suddenly the endless waiting is over. Nine months become like yesterday's newspaper. They are gone. They become insignificant, a faint memory — overcome by joy. Ask the new mom if she regrets enduring her pregnancy. Never!

Hannah's wait began even more slowly. For years she was unable to have a child. She felt so unfulfilled, so dishonored (1 Samuel 1). But the Lord remembered her, and she conceived. Her joy was complete.

Hannah waited patiently and saw the Lord turn her sorrow into overflowing joy. Her song (2:1-10) is a reminder that disappointment and the most bitter distress can lead to fulfillment and delight. For those who wait on the Lord, long hours of enduring will one day give way to rejoicing. — Mart De Haan

Let patience have her perfect work;
Let God refine your gold;
For in His time He'll show you why,
And blessings great unfold. —Bosch

GOD'S GIFT OF JOY IS WORTH THE WAIT.

WHAT'S A CHURCH FOR?

READ:
Ephesians 4:1-16

Where there are envy, strife, and divisions among you, are you not carnal and behaving like mere men?
—1 Corinthians 3:3

THE BIBLE IN ONE YEAR:
■ Matthew 23–25

Every time I hear about a church fight, I cringe. When my wife and I went out to eat with a pastor friend, he told us about some of the things that people in his church have squabbled about. Christians have been pitted against Christians over such issues as the color of the carpet, the thermostat setting, and whether the choir should wear robes.

Pastors have been run out of town during these kinds of arguments. Christians have cut off friendships. Churches have split because folks argued about such things.

Why does this happen? People who get caught up in petty squabbles have lost sight of what a church is for. The church is the place we go for worship, for reading the Word, for singing to God's glory, for serving others, and for helping one another to grow. It's supposed to be a place of love, forgiveness, and encouragement.

In Paul's letter to the Ephesian church, he described the unity of purpose (4:1-16) that should help us to work through disagreements without creating divisions. He knew all too well how selfish desires, personal agendas, and playing favorites could create havoc (1 Corinthians 3:1-9).

Let's make sure our churches are safe havens from squabbles by remembering what a church is for. — Dave Branon

O Lord, help us to turn aside
From words that spring from selfish pride,
For You would have Your children one
In praise and love for Your dear Son. — D. De Haan

**CHRISTIANS AT WAR WITH EACH OTHER
CANNOT BE AT PEACE WITH THEIR HEAVENLY FATHER.**

October 20

YOU ARE
NEVER ALONE

READ:
John 14:15-21

I will not leave you orphans; I will come to you.
—John 14:18

THE BIBLE IN ONE YEAR:
■ Matthew 26–28

Jesus is just as real today as He was when He walked on this earth. Even though He doesn't move among us physically, by the Holy Spirit He is here, there, everywhere — a continuous, living presence — outside of us and inside of us.

That may be a terrifying thought for some. Perhaps you don't like yourself, or you're contemplating all the bad things you've done. Insecurity and sin can create a sense of fear, awkwardness, and clumsiness in Jesus' presence. But think of what you know about Him.

Despite what you are or what you may have done, He loves you (Romans 5:8; 1 John 4:7-11). He will never leave you nor forsake you (John 14:18; Hebrews 13:5). Others may not think much of you or invite you to spend time with them, but Jesus does (Matthew 11:28). Others may not like the way you look, but He looks at your heart (1 Samuel 16:7; Luke 24:38). Others may think you're a bother because you're old and in the way, but He will love you to the end (Romans 8:35-39).

Jesus loves you in spite of all the conditions that cause others to turn away. He wants to change you to be like Him, but He loves you as you are and will never abandon you. You are family; you will never, ever be alone. — David Roper

Jesus shares your worries and cares
You'll never be left all alone,
For He stands beside you to comfort and guide you,
He always looks out for His own. — Brandt

IF YOU KNOW JESUS,
YOU'LL NEVER WALK ALONE.

FORBIDDEN FRUIT

READ:
Romans 7:7-13

The sinful passions which were aroused by the law were at work in our members to bear fruit to death.
—Romans 7:5

THE BIBLE IN ONE YEAR:
■ Mark 1–3

In Galveston, Texas, a hotel on the shore of the Gulf of Mexico put this notice in each room:

NO FISHING FROM THE BALCONY

Yet every day, hotel guests threw their lines into the waters below. Then the management decided to take down the signs — and the fishing stopped!

Augustine (354-430), a prominent theologian in the early church, reflected on his own attraction to the forbidden. In his *Confessions* he wrote, "There was a pear tree near our vineyard, laden with fruit. One stormy night we rascally youths set out to rob it . . . . We took off a huge load of pears — not to feast upon ourselves, but to throw them to the pigs, though we ate just enough to have the pleasure of the forbidden fruit. They were nice pears, but it was not the pears that my wretched soul coveted, for I had plenty better at home. I picked them simply to become a thief. . . . The desire to steal was awakened simply by the prohibition of stealing."

Romans 7:7-13 sets forth the truth illustrated by Augustine's experience: Human nature is inherently rebellious. Give us a law and we will see it as a challenge to break it. But Jesus forgives our lawbreaking and gives us the Holy Spirit. He imparts a new desire and ability so that our greatest pleasure becomes bringing pleasure to God. — Haddon Robinson

Why do we keep on trying
The fare of this world's sin
When God has set before us
The joy of Christ within? — Branon

TO MASTER TEMPTATION, LET CHRIST MASTER YOU.

October 22

EFFECTIVE PRAYING

READ:
Matthew 7:7-11

**Everyone who asks receives, and he who seeks finds.
—Matthew 7:8**

THE BIBLE IN ONE YEAR:
■ Mark 4–6

A 12-year-old Cambodian boy named Lem Cheong began to question his family's religious beliefs. He had been taught that a person seeking guidance should go to a temple and shake a container of numbered bamboo slivers until one fell out. The priest then interpreted the meaning of the number. But this practice didn't satisfy Cheong's longing for clear answers, nor did it fill the void in his heart that only God could fill.

According to Harold Sala in his book *Touching God,* Cheong asked his uncle, a priest, if he had ever had a prayer answered. The man was shocked by the brashness of his nephew's question, but he admitted that he couldn't remember a single time one of his prayers had been answered.

Later Cheong asked a Christian if God had ever answered his prayers. The man recounted several instances. Cheong was so impressed that he accepted Jesus as his Savior that day. Since then, prayer has become a vital part of his life.

Jesus said, "Ask, and it will be given to you; seek, and you will find; knock, and it will be opened to you" (Matthew 7:7). Christian prayer is effective because God is the living and true God who hears and answers according to His will. And His will is always good. — Vernon Grounds

*For answered prayer we thank You, Lord;
We know You're always there
To hear us when we call on You—
We're grateful for Your care.* —Branon

**THROUGH PRAYER, FINITE MAN DRAWS UPON
THE POWER OF THE INFINITE GOD.**

LIFE BEYOND THE GRAVE

READ:
John 11:1-44

Whoever lives and believes in Me shall never die. Do you believe this?
—John 11:26

THE BIBLE IN ONE YEAR:
■ Mark 7–10

My beloved husband Bill died of cancer at the age of 48. One tearful morning I read John 11, the story about Jesus raising Lazarus from the dead. I was reassured by two truths I found in Jesus' words to His disciples on their way to Lazarus' grave.

The first truth was revealed when Jesus said that Lazarus was asleep and that He would wake him (vv.11-14). His disciples responded, "Lord, if he sleeps he will get well." Jesus replied, "Lazarus is dead." Saying that He would waken Lazarus, I believe, was His gentle way to teach them that they didn't need to dread death any more than sleep. Because of His power, resurrecting someone from the grave was like waking someone from sleep.

I saw a second truth in Jesus' statement to Martha: "He who believes in Me, though he may die, he shall live. And whoever lives and believes in Me shall never die" (vv.25-26). Of course, believers aren't exempt from dying physically, but Jesus promised that they will live eternally. As the resurrection and the life, He will "waken" their bodies someday. His power to do this was demonstrated when He raised Lazarus (vv.43-44).

When someone we love goes to be with Jesus, these promises give us comfort and assurance. — Joanie Yoder

> *Grief will not last, joy will return,*
> *For through our tears we clearly see*
> *That while we part but for a time,*
> *With Christ we'll spend eternity.* — D. De Haan

DEATH SEPARATES US FOR A TIME;
CHRIST WILL REUNITE US FOREVER.

REMOTE CONTROL

READ:
Ephesians 5:1-17

Walk as children of light . . . , finding out what is acceptable to the Lord.
—Ephesians 5:8,10

THE BIBLE IN ONE YEAR:
■ Mark 11–13

Flick. "That's tonight at 8 on ABC." Flick. "A high pressure system is moving in." Flick. "He kicked the ball wide of the goal!" Flick. "I'll take 'World History' for $600, Alex." Flick. "In the news today . . ." Flick!

What's happening? It's a TV viewer giving the thumb a good workout with the remote control, looking for something to watch, filtering through the maze of choices.

Each time we stop on a channel, we've made a choice. We've made a decision to allow that program to influence us in some way. But have we been discerning? Are we using our time wisely and beneficially? Will what we watch build us up or tear us down? These are vital questions for the Christian, for we have been told to do all things for God's glory (1 Corinthians 10:31).

One set of guidelines is outlined in Ephesians 5. We are to steer clear of immorality, filthiness, foolish talking, coarse jesting (vv.3-4). And we are to have no "fellowship with the unfruitful works of darkness" nor "speak of those things which are done by them in secret" (vv.11-12).

We need to keep learning what is "acceptable to the Lord" (v.10). And sometimes that means taking the remote and clicking the TV off. — Dave Branon

Take heed to what you see and hear,
For it affects your soul;
Be sure it's pleasing to the Lord
And that He's in control. —Fitzhugh

THE BEST TV GUIDE IS THE BIBLE.

LOOK FOR THE GOOD

READ:
1 Thessalonians 1

**We give thanks to God always for you all, making mention of you in our prayers.
—1 Thessalonians 1:2**

THE BIBLE IN ONE YEAR:
■ Mark 14–16

I read about a young boy who had been naughty. During family devotions the father prayed for his son and mentioned a number of bad things the boy had done. Soon afterward the mother heard the 6-year-old sobbing. When she asked what was wrong, the boy cried out, "Daddy always tells God the bad things about me. He never tells Him the good things I do!"

What happened to that child underscores a shortcoming that is common to many of us. Instead of recognizing the good in people, we tend to notice their faults. We could learn from the example of the apostle Paul. In his letter to his spiritual sons and daughters in Thessalonica, he wrote, "We give thanks to God always for you all" (v.2). He remembered their "work of faith, labor of love, and patience of hope" (v.3). He told them that because they "received the word in much affliction, with joy of the Holy Spirit," they were an example to others (vv.6-7). He said that from them "the word of the Lord has sounded forth . . . in every place" (v.8). Paul's words must have encouraged them and spurred them on to even greater service for the Lord.

Let's be more ready to commend than to condemn. When we see good in others, let's tell them. It will encourage them, and that's exactly what they need. — Richard De Haan

> *Could we only see the goodness*
> *Of the ones we meet each day,*
> *We would overlook their failures*
> *As we greet them on life's way.* —Anon.

**CORRECTION DOES MUCH,
BUT ENCOURAGEMENT DOES MORE.**

A GOOD ACCOUNT

READ:
Philemon

If he has wronged you or owes anything, put that on my account.
— Philemon 18

THE BIBLE IN ONE YEAR:
■ Luke 1–3

As a young boy I watched my dad write checks and wished that I could do it. What I didn't realize was that there had to be money in an account to back them up.

The apostle Paul never wrote a check, but he did have an account good enough to pay an unusual debt if necessary. He referred to this in his letter to Philemon, a wealthy Christian whose slave Onesimus had run away and may have stolen some money from his master.

In the providence of God, Onesimus met Paul in Rome and became a follower of Christ. They agreed that it was right for him to return to his master. Paul wrote a letter to Philemon (the letter that bears his name), asking him to receive Onesimus as a brother, and assuring him that he himself would pay any debt Onesimus owed.

That's a picture of what happens in salvation. As sinners, we owed an enormous debt, but Jesus took care of it for us. Because of His sinless life, He has a limitless resource of righteousness. And by dying in our place, He paid the penalty for our sin. Now we can draw on this payment by faith. As Martin Luther said, "We are all His Onesimi." If we put our trust in Christ as our Savior, our sins are put to His account and we are free for all eternity. Praise God! — Dennis De Haan

Rejoice, rejoice, the debt is paid!
For all our sins on Christ were laid;
Estrangement once was all we knew,
But now we know a love that's true. — D. De Haan

CHRIST PAID A DEBT HE DIDN'T OWE
TO SATISFY A DEBT WE COULDN'T PAY.

"THE UNDERBIRD"

READ:
James 2:1-9

You are of more value than many sparrows.
—Luke 12:7

THE BIBLE IN ONE YEAR:
■ Luke 4–6

Charlie Brown, the comic strip character, identified with the underdog, probably because he always felt like one. In one scene he was building a birdhouse when the cynical Lucy came by. "I'm building it for sparrows," Charlie told her. Lucy said, "For sparrows? Nobody builds birdhouses for sparrows." "I do," replied Charlie Brown. "I always stick up for the underbird."

At times Christians may overlook the "sparrows," the little people in their worlds. They may ignore those they view as less valuable.

James said it's wrong for a Christian to practice partiality (James 2:1). It's a sin to show personal favoritism (v.9). The reasons may be social, economic, educational, or ethnic, but there's no excuse for disrespecting people with our attitudes and words.

Jesus didn't do this. He crossed all kinds of traditional barriers to talk with tax-collectors, sinners, non-Jews, people of mixed races, the poor, as well as the rich. He came to identify with each of us, and to pay the price on the cross for all our sins.

When a sparrow falls, the Father takes note of it. But He cares much more for people, including the "underbird." Perhaps we need a little more Charlie Brown in us. —Dave Egner

> Lord, help me to love the way that You love
> The humble, the lowly, the meek;
> And help me to care the way that You care
> For sinners, the outcasts, the weak. —Fitzhugh

NOBODY WINS WHEN WE PLAY FAVORITES.

LIKABLE CHRISTIANS

READ:
Luke 2:41-52

Jesus increased in wisdom and stature, and in favor with God and men. —Luke 2:52

THE BIBLE IN ONE YEAR:
■ Luke 7–9

The local newspaper reported the death of a semi-pro baseball pitcher I had admired during my teenage years. His name was Elmer "Lefty" Nyenhouse. He was a likable Christian. The article said that he had been active in his church and a respected member of his community until his death at 88.

On several occasions I saw "Lefty" pitch against a topnotch semi-pro team, the Chickie Giants. Knowing that Elmer was a devout Christian, some of his opponents tried to rattle him in tense situations (like when the bases were loaded with no outs). They would drop to their knees by their dugout and shout, "Better get on your knees and pray, Elmer!" "Lefty" took it in stride. Those who heckled him actually respected him.

As Jesus grew up, He "increased . . . in favor with God and men" (Luke 2:52). People were drawn to Him. Their fondness for Him, of course, alarmed the religious leaders who hated Him because of His teaching, and they "sought how they might kill Him, for they feared the people" (22:2).

Today, as always, some will hate you for being an outspoken follower of Jesus. But make sure it's not because you are unpleasant, critical, and hard to get along with. Being a likable person is to be like Jesus. — Herb Vander Lugt

Let the beauty of Jesus be seen in me —
All His wonderful passion and purity!
O Thou Spirit divine, all my nature refine,
Till the beauty of Jesus be seen in me. — Orsborn

CHRISTLIKE PEOPLE ARE LIKABLE PEOPLE
EVEN IF HATED BY SOME PEOPLE.

COME TO ME

READ:
John 10:1-18

When he brings out his own sheep, he goes before them; and the sheep follow him, for they know his voice. —John 10:4

THE BIBLE IN ONE YEAR:
■ Luke 10–13

After a hijacked plane slammed into the Pentagon on September 11, 2001, many people inside the building were trapped by a cloud of thick, blinding smoke. Police officer Isaac Hoopi ran into the blackness, searching for survivors, and heard people calling for help. He began shouting back, over and over: "Head toward my voice! Head toward my voice!"

Six people, who had lost all sense of direction in a smoke-filled hallway, heard the officer's shouts and followed. Hoopi's voice led them out of the building to safety.

"Head toward My voice!" That's also the invitation of Jesus to each of us when we are in danger or when we have lost our way. Jesus described the true spiritual shepherd of the sheep as one who "calls his own sheep by name and leads them out. And when he brings out his own sheep, he goes before them; and the sheep follow him, for they know his voice" (John 10:3-4).

Are we listening for Jesus' voice during our times of prayer and Bible reading? When we're in difficult circumstances, are we walking toward Him instead of groping in the dark?

Jesus is "the good shepherd" (v.11). Whatever our need for guidance or protection, He calls us to heed His voice and follow Him. — David McCasland

When you hear the Shepherd's voice
As He calls you, "Come to Me,"
In your life make Him your choice
And a faithful follower be. — Hess

YOU DON'T NEED TO KNOW WHERE YOU'RE GOING IF YOU'RE FOLLOWING THE SHEPHERD.

REASONS
TO REJOICE

READ:
1 Peter 1:1-9

Though now you do not see Him, . . . you rejoice with joy inexpressible and full of glory.
—1 Peter 1:8

THE BIBLE IN ONE YEAR:
■ Luke 14—17

The New Testament gives us many reasons to rejoice. For example, Jesus said, "Rejoice because your names are written in heaven" (Luke 10:20). The apostle Peter spoke of the reasons believers can "rejoice with joy inexpressible" (1 Peter 1:8). We're not asked to pretend that problems don't exist but to rejoice even in the midst of them.

The word *rejoice* reminds me of my friend Carol. She chose to rejoice throughout her long struggle with cancer. Her Christian life began within hours of surgery, when she prayed and trusted the Lord for her salvation. During her recovery she walked the hospital corridors saying to everyone, "Isn't this a beautiful day!"

Because one of her eyes had been removed, Carol had a number of decorative eye patches made to match different dresses. Every day she delighted in choosing an attractive eye patch, especially when sharing her testimony. When she became bedridden, she hung a large sign at the foot of her bed that read, "REJOICE!" On my last visit before she died, she pointed to the sign and whispered, "Rejoice!"

Carol's reason for rejoicing was her deep gratitude to Jesus for loving and saving her. Whatever you're facing today, let Carol's reason for rejoicing be yours too. — Joanie Yoder

Amid the thorny trials of life
God's buds of beauty grow;
If we'll rejoice and not complain,
His peace and love we'll know. —Sper

**IF YOU KNOW JESUS, YOU ALWAYS HAVE
REASONS TO REJOICE.**

A Walk In The Woods

READ:
Romans 6:11-14

Do not let sin reign in your mortal body, that you should obey it in its lusts.
—Romans 6:12

THE BIBLE IN ONE YEAR:
■ Luke 18–21

A friend of mine wrote to me about certain "reservations" in his life — areas of secret sin that he reserved for himself and into which he frequently withdrew.

These "reserves" are like the large tracts of wilderness in my home state of Idaho. It may sound exciting to wander around these untamed regions by oneself, but it's dangerous.

So too, each journey into sin takes its toll. We sacrifice our closeness with God, forfeiting His blessing (Psalm 24:1-5), and we lose our influence on others that comes from purity of mind and body (1 Timothy 4:12).

The wild areas in us may never be fully tamed, but we can set up perimeters that keep us from wandering into them. One perimeter is to remember that we are dead to sin's power (Romans 6:1-14). We do not have to give in to it.

The second perimeter is to resist temptation when it first attracts us. Initial temptation may not be strong, but if we entertain it, it will in time gain power and overwhelm us.

The third perimeter is accountability. Find a person who will commit to ask you each week, "Have you 'taken a hike in the wild'? Have you gone where you should not go?"

Impurity is ruinous, but if we long for holiness and ask God for help, He will give us victory. Press on! — David Roper

O Lord, help us to recognize
When we begin to compromise;
And give us strength to follow through
With what we know is right and true. — Sper

**BEWARE—THE MORE YOU LOOK AT TEMPTATION,
THE BETTER IT LOOKS!**

LEAVE THE LIGHT ON

READ:
John 1:1-14

> [John] came for
> a witness, to bear
> witness of the Light,
> that all through him
> might believe.
> —John 1:7

THE BIBLE IN ONE YEAR:
■ Luke 22–24

A motel chain once had a series of radio commercials that ended with the reassuring words, "We'll leave the light on for you." My mother used to say the same thing to me.

Sometimes I worked the late shift at the factory, or I would come home late from college. No matter what the reason or the time, the porch light was burning. Its warm beams seemed to say, "This is where you belong. Someone loves you here. You are home."

Jesus said that we who know Him as Savior and Lord are lights in this sin-darkened world (Matthew 5:14-16). We are reflections of Christ, who is "the true Light" (John 1:9).

As John the Baptist was a "witness of the Light" and pointed people to Jesus (v.7), so can we. Our faithful walk of obedience to Him is a beacon of God's love and truth. Our lives and words are beams of warm light piercing the cold darkness of this world. We are like a porch light late at night, drawing unbelievers to Jesus, assuring them that Someone loves them and waits to welcome them home.

Perhaps a member of your family is still in the darkness. Maybe you're concerned about a friend or co-worker. Don't stop praying for them. Keep finding ways to draw their attention to the Lord. Be sure to leave the light on. — Dave Egner

If we should hide our shining light
And not reflect God's Son,
Then how will people in sin's night
Be guided, helped, and won? — Branon

YOU CAN ATTRACT PEOPLE TO CHRIST
WHEN YOU HAVE HIS LIGHT IN YOUR LIFE.

LOOKING FOR LOVE

READ:
John 3:16-21

God so loved the world that He gave His only begotten Son, that whoever believes in Him should not perish but have everlasting life. —John 3:16

THE BIBLE IN ONE YEAR:
■ John 1–3

A computer virus known as "The Love Bug" spanned the globe by e-mail, infecting millions of computers in less than 24 hours. It seems that even wary people like top software engineers couldn't resist opening a message titled simply, "I Love You."

Some analysts have said that the success of the destructive computer virus reveals as much about the longings of the human heart as it does about the vulnerability of the machines in our cyber-society. Down deep, every person on planet earth is looking for love.

It's no accident that one of the best-known verses in the Bible is John 3:16. It says, "God so loved the world that He gave His only begotten Son, that whoever believes in Him should not perish but have everlasting life."

Could it be that the love we long for the most is God's love? Is Jesus Christ the special person we so eagerly seek to sweep us off our feet? If so, then accepting God's love in Christ could change our lives in remarkable ways. Hope, peace, and a zest for living — they all spring from being in love with Jesus.

When God says, "I love you," it's the message we've all been looking for. It can change our lives.

How will you respond to Him today? — David McCasland

If you're feeling alone and unworthy,
And wish for a kind, loving friend,
Remember that God longs to show you
A love that never will end. — Hess

THE DEATH OF CHRIST IS THE MEASURE OF GOD'S LOVE FOR YOU.

THE SEEKING FATHER

READ:
John 4:21-24

When You said, "Seek My face," my heart said to You, "Your face, LORD, I will seek."
—Psalm 27:8

THE BIBLE IN ONE YEAR:
■ John 4–6

When I was a young man, a friend invited me to join him in establishing a "consistent quiet time," as he put it. I knew that regular Bible reading, prayer, and worship were essential, and I wanted to spend time with God. But my friend's plan never worked for me. I would stay with his routine for a week or two, rising early each morning to work my way through a regimen of reading and praying. It was a discipline I imposed on myself—like doing 50 push-ups every day. But I couldn't sustain the effort. In time I gave up, not knowing how to satisfy my longings to spend time with God.

Then one day I stumbled across something Jesus said to the woman at the well: "The Father is seeking" those who will worship Him "in spirit and truth" (John 4:23). That's when I realized that God was taking the initiative, putting in my heart those longings for time with Him.

The psalmist said he responded to the Lord's call to "seek My face" (Psalm 27:8). It's the idea of God longing for fellowship with me that now draws me into His presence. My quiet times with God are no longer a dreary duty, but a response to my Father who yearns to spend time with me.

Do you hear your Father calling to you?   —David Roper

I sought the Lord, and afterward I knew
He moved my soul to seek Him, seeking me;
It was not I that found, O Savior true,
No, I was found of Thee. —Anon.

TALK WITH GOD—HE LONGS TO HEAR FROM YOU.

WHAT DO YOU FEAR?

READ:
John 6:16-21

[Jesus] said to them,
"It is I; do not be
afraid." —John 6:20

THE BIBLE IN ONE YEAR:
■ John 7–10

One of Grimm's fairy tales is about a rather dimwitted young man who didn't understand what it meant to shudder in fear. People attempted to shock him by putting him in all sorts of terrifying situations — but to no avail. He finally did shudder, though not out of fear. He was asleep when someone poured a bucket of cold water and wiggling fish on top of him.

Something is wrong with us if we're never afraid. Fear is the natural human reaction to any difficult or dangerous undertaking, and God doesn't condemn it. Neither does He want us to be crippled by fear. Jesus' words to His disciples on more than one occasion were, "Do not be afraid" (Luke 5:10; 12:4; John 6:20). In each case He used a verb tense that suggests continuance. In other words, He told them, "Don't keep on fearing."

We need not be overcome by our fear, nor should we ever say no to doing what we know God wants us to do merely because we are fearful. God can turn our fear into fortitude. We can trust God and "not be afraid" (Psalm 56:11).

Courage is not the absence of fear but the mastery of it. So let's resist our fear and meet it with faith in our Lord, for He has said, "I will never leave you nor forsake you" (Hebrews 13:5). —David Roper

Do not fear the darkness that is gathering all around,
For the Lord is with you, and in Him true peace is found;
When you're facing trouble, or when tragedy seems near,
Jesus is the only one to drive away your fear. —Hess

WE CAN FACE ANY FEAR
WHEN WE KNOW THE LORD IS NEAR.

DIGITAL TRANSMISSION

READ:
John 13:1-17

I have given you an example, that you should do as I have done to you.
—John 13:15

THE BIBLE IN ONE YEAR:
■ John 11–13

In 2000, a movie was digitally transmitted over the Internet from a studio in California to its world premiere in Atlanta, Georgia. It went from studio to theater screen without ever touching film. With digital distribution, electronic impulses are used instead of huge reels of celluloid.

In this age of electronics, often described as "high-tech, low-touch," it's good to remember that God is using another type of "digital transmission." In sharp contrast, though, His is a "high-touch" method to communicate His grace and love.

The English word *digital* comes from the word *digit*, which refers to a finger on our hand. As I think about the life and ministry of Jesus, I remember how He used His hands to bring hope and healing. He touched the sick, held little children, broke bread for hungry people, and allowed His hands to be nailed to the cross for our sins. In John 13 we read that Jesus, in a startling act of humility, washed the feet of His disciples and told them, "If I then, your Lord and Teacher, have washed your feet, you also ought to wash one another's feet" (v.14).

When our hearts are humble and our hands are yielded to Him, the Lord still transmits His gospel of grace to others through our human touch of love. — David McCasland

Take my life and let it be
Consecrated, Lord, to Thee;
Take my hands and let them move
At the impulse of Thy love. — Havergal

WE SHOW OUR LOVE FOR GOD
WHEN WE SHARE HIS LOVE WITH OTHERS.

First Sight

READ:
John 13:36–14:3

They shall see His face, and His name shall be on their foreheads.
—Revelation 22:4

THE BIBLE IN ONE YEAR:
■ John 14–17

When I was flying from Chicago to Tampa, I noticed a family on the plane. And from the excitement of the two children, I assumed they had never been to Florida. As we neared our destination, clouds blocked our view of the ground. Only when we began our descent did the plane finally break through the clouds.

At the first sight of the land below, the mother exclaimed to the two little ones beside her, "Look, that must be Florida!" After a few moments of silence, the young boy said, "But Mom, where are the palm trees? I can't see them!" His idea of Florida immediately brought to his mind those tropical trees, and he expected to see them first.

Christian, as you anticipate the day you will arrive in heaven, what do you want to see first? It will certainly be wonderful to greet our loved ones who have gone before. My, what a thrill to visit with the believers of the past, and how exciting to see the glorious sights of heaven! And yet, as delightful as all of this will be, our greatest joy will be to see the Lord Jesus Himself — for He is the One who made it possible for us to go there.

Yes, in the words of the old hymn, "I long to meet my Savior first of all." — Richard De Haan

I am living for the moment
When my Savior's face I see;
Oh, the thrill of that first meeting
When His glory shines on me. — Christiansen

TO SEE JESUS WILL BE HEAVEN'S GREATEST JOY.

THE CURE FOR RESENTMENT

READ:
John 21:18-25

Jesus said to him, "If I will that he remain till I come, what is that to you? You follow Me." —John 21:22

THE BIBLE IN ONE YEAR:
■ John 18–21

We may readily agree with the statement that "all men are created equal." But we don't have to live long before discovering that life treats some people better than others. This is something we must learn to accept without resentment.

Life's inequities show up on many levels. Cancer ravages the body of a child, while a hard-drinking chain-smoker lives to a ripe old age. Some people enjoy good health, others don't. Some have no physical disabilities, others have severe limitations. Some work hard and remain poor, while others are born to wealth or seem to get all the breaks.

When Jesus informed the apostle Peter that he was going to die as a martyr for his faith, Peter asked what would happen to his fellow disciple John. He seemed to think that it wouldn't be fair if John didn't die the same way. But Jesus told him that what would happen to John was not to be Peter's concern — that was God's decision. Peter's responsibility was simple: He was to follow Christ.

When looking at others makes you resent the unfairness of life, change your focus. Look to Jesus and follow Him. Life's injustices are only for a little while. Perfect fairness will be ours to enjoy forever in heaven. — Herb Vander Lugt

At times our path is rough and steep,
Our way is hard to see;
We ask God, "Why is life unfair?"
He answers, "Follow Me." — D. De Haan

**RESENTMENT COMES FROM LOOKING AT OTHERS;
CONTENTMENT COMES FROM LOOKING TO GOD.**

He Lives!

READ:
Acts 1:1-10

He also presented Himself alive after His suffering by many infallible proofs.
—Acts 1:3

THE BIBLE IN ONE YEAR:
■ Acts 1-2

When the World Trade Center towers came crashing to the ground in a deafening roar of billowing debris, citizens of New York experienced what many people in other parts of the world had already known — the fear of terrorism. Subsequent attacks in other countries have heightened the concern that mankind may be spiraling toward self-destruction.

All the unrest in the world might make us think that our future is very bleak. We might even conclude that this is not the kind of world in which to have children.

Yet one shining hope remains that can brighten our view of the future. Bill Gaither captured it in his song titled, "Because He Lives." The idea for it came to him in the late 1960s, a time of social unrest in the US and conflict in Southeast Asia. His wife Gloria was expecting a child, and they felt that it was a poor time to bring a child into the world. But when their son was born, Bill thought of the living Savior and these words came to mind: "This child can face uncertain days because He lives."

Two thousand years ago Jesus rose from the grave and gave "many infallible proofs" that He was alive (Acts 1:3). That's why we can keep going in the face of fear. Because Jesus lives, we can face tomorrow. —Dave Branon

Up from the grave He arose,
With a mighty triumph o'er His foes;
He arose a Victor from the dark domain,
And He lives forever with His saints to reign. —Lowry

CHRIST'S EMPTY TOMB FILLS US WITH HOPE.

A LIFE-AND-DEATH ISSUE

READ:
Psalm 90:1-10

The days of our lives are seventy years; ... it is soon cut off, and we fly away.
—Psalm 90:10

THE BIBLE IN ONE YEAR:
■ Acts 3–5

By altering the gene that controls aging, scientists believe they can extend the average human lifespan to 100 by the end of this century. This would be well beyond the proverbial 70 years mentioned in Psalm 90:10. But even if people do live longer, life's final chapter will still read, "It is soon cut off" (v.10).

Moses, who wrote Psalm 90, lived to be 120. He saw death as inevitable in a world cursed by the effects of sin. Yet he didn't become pessimistic. He asked God to teach him to number his days so he could gain "a heart of wisdom" (v.12). He wanted to be satisfied with God's mercy so he could rejoice and be glad (v.14). He also asked God to show His glory to the next generation (v.16). That's how Moses faced the reality of death thousands of years ago.

Like all people since Adam and Eve, we suffer the effects of sin, and death is certain (Romans 6:23). Yet we can live with hope and joy, because God sent His Son to die for our sins. Jesus conquered death when He rose from the grave. And if we receive Him as our personal Savior and Lord, we too can experience God's forgiveness and look forward to being with Him in heaven forever. Have you faced and settled this life-and-death issue? — Dennis De Haan

THINKING IT OVER
If you were to die today, would you be prepared to meet God? To be ready, embrace Jesus' promise to everyone who believes in Him (John 3:16; 11:25-26).

YOU'RE NOT READY TO LIVE UNTIL YOU'RE READY TO DIE.

COPY
THE MASTER

READ:
1 Thessalonians 1

Be imitators of God as dear children.
—Ephesians 5:1

THE BIBLE IN ONE YEAR:
■ Acts 6–9

The Louvre in Paris is perhaps the most famous art museum in the world. It displays originals by such masters as Delacroix, Michelangelo, Rubens, da Vinci, Ingres, Vermeer, and many others.

Since 1793, the Louvre has encouraged aspiring artists to come and copy the masters. Some of our most famous modern artists have done that and have become better painters by copying the best the world has ever known.

An article in *Smithsonian* magazine tells about Amal Dagher, a 63-year-old man who has been duplicating art at the Louvre for 30 years. Dagher remains in awe of the masters and continues to learn from them. He said, "If you're too satisfied with yourself, you can't improve."

Paul instructed us to be "imitators of God" (Ephesians 5:1). In his first letter to the Thessalonians, he commended the believers because they were becoming like the Lord and setting an example for others (1 Thessalonians 1:6-10).

Like the Louvre copyists, we'll never reach perfection before we get to heaven. Even so, we must resist the temptation to be satisfied with our present imitation of Jesus. We need to keep looking to Him, learning from Him, and asking for His help. Let's copy the Master. —Dave Egner

More like the Master I would live and grow,
More of His love to others I would show;
More self-denial, like His in Galilee,
More like the Master I long to ever be. —Gabriel

TO BECOME LIKE CHRIST,
WE MUST LEARN FROM THE MASTER.

THE STORM

READ:
Matthew 7:21-29

Whoever hears these sayings of Mine, and does them, I will liken him to a wise man who built his house on the rock. —Matthew 7:24

THE BIBLE IN ONE YEAR:
■ Acts 10–12

Neal Beidleman survived the ill-fated 1996 expedition in which eight climbers died on Mount Everest. Some of them had paid $65,000 for a chance to scale the world's highest peak. In assessing what went wrong, Beidleman said, "Tragedies and disasters . . . are not the result of a single decision, a single event, or a single mistake. They are the culmination of things in your life. Something happens and it becomes a catalyst for all the things you've had at risk."

On Everest, that "something" was a raging blizzard. According to journalist Todd Burgess, "If not for the storm, the climbers may have gotten away with taking so many risks. But the storm exposed their weaknesses."

The things at risk in our lives today — matters of spiritual indifference or disobedience — can overwhelm us when the storms come. Jesus told a story of the wise and foolish builders to stress the importance of obedience to His words (Matthew 7:24-27). He said, "Whoever hears these sayings of Mine, and does them, I will liken him to a wise man who built his house on the rock" (v.24).

Obedience to Christ doesn't eliminate the tempests of life, but it does determine whether we fall or stand in the storm. —David McCasland

> *Living for the Lord, fearing Him each day,*
> *Best prepares the soul for the stormy way;*
> *Then as trials come, tempting to despair,*
> *We can rest secure, safe within His care.* —D. De Haan

**THE STORMS OF LIFE REVEAL
THE STRENGTH OF OUR FAITH.**

PARENTS WHO PRAY

READ:
Matthew 19:13-15

Little children were brought to Him that He might put His hands on them and pray. —Matthew 19:13

THE BIBLE IN ONE YEAR:
■ Acts 13–14

A young mother sent these lines to a magazine: "I wish I could wrap my children in bubble wrap to protect them from the big, bad world outside."

Author Stormie Omartian understands how that mother feels. In her book *The Power Of A Praying Parent*, she writes, "One day I cried out to God, saying, 'Lord, this is too much for me. I can't keep a 24-hours-a-day, moment-by-moment watch on my son. How can I ever have peace?'"

God responded by leading Stormie and her husband to become praying parents. They began to intercede for their son daily, mentioning the details of his life in prayer.

The desire to wrap our children in bubble wrap to protect them is rooted in fear, a common tendency, especially among mothers. Wrapping them in prayer, as Jesus did (Matthew 19:13-15), is a powerful alternative. He cares more about our children than we do, so we can release them into His hands by praying for them. He doesn't promise us that nothing bad will happen to them. But as we pray, He will give us the peace we long for (Philippians 4:6-7).

This challenge is for all parents — even those whose children have grown up: Don't ever stop wrapping your children in prayer! —Joanie Yoder

If we but take the time to pray,
And seek God's guidance every day,
He'll give us strength and wisdom too,
To help our child grow strong and true. —Garka

EVERY CHILD NEEDS A PRAYING PARENT.

OUR PLACE OF REFUGE

READ:
Psalm 57

In the shadow of Your wings I will make my refuge, until these calamities have passed by.
—Psalm 57:1

THE BIBLE IN ONE YEAR:
■ Acts 15–16

It is believed that David wrote Psalm 57 while fleeing from King Saul, who had hatred in his heart for the former shepherd boy. David ducked into a cave and barely escaped his pursuer. He was safe temporarily, but the threat was still there.

We've all been there. Maybe not in a cave, but pursued by something that strikes fear into our hearts. Perhaps it is the deep sorrow that follows the death of someone we love. Maybe it's the fear of an unknown future. Or it could be an oppressive physical illness that won't go away.

In such circumstances, God does not always remove the difficulty, but He is present to help us. We wish that He would swoop in and whisk us to safety — just as David may have wished for a quick end to Saul's pursuit. We plead with God to stop the pain and make the road to tomorrow smooth and straight. We beg Him to eliminate our struggle. But the difficulty remains. It is then that we have to take refuge in God as David did. While hiding in that cave, he said, "In the shadow of Your wings I will make my refuge, until these calamities have passed by" (Psalm 57:1).

Are you in the middle of trouble? Take refuge in the Most High God. — Dave Branon

Christian, when your way seems darkest,
When your eyes with tears are dim,
Straight to God your Father hastening,
Tell your troubles all to Him. —Anon.

WE LEARN THE LESSON OF TRUST
IN THE SCHOOL OF TRIAL.

SALMON RUN

READ:
Matthew 11:25-30

**Come to Me, all you who labor and are heavy laden, and I will give you rest.
—Matthew 11:28**

THE BIBLE IN ONE YEAR:
■ Acts 17–18

S almon fascinate me. Each August I drive a few miles north of my home in Idaho and watch them make their weary way through the last stages of their spawning run to the sandbars along Lake Creek. I always think of the long journey they've taken.

Some months earlier, they leave the Pacific Ocean and begin their run up the Columbia to the Snake River, then up the main fork of the Salmon River to the East Fork, up the Secesh River to Lake Creek — more than 700 miles.

Driven by instinct, they swim against currents, up waterfalls, and around hydroelectric dams. Despite eagles, bears, and many other predators, they struggle to reach their ancestral spawning grounds to lay their eggs.

Their journey reminds me of the human journey. We too have a homing instinct. "There exists in the human mind, and indeed by natural instinct, a sense of Deity," John Calvin said. We are born and we live for the express purpose of knowing and loving God. He is the source of our life, and our hearts are restless until they come to Him.

Are you restless today, driven by discontent and a longing for that elusive "something more"? Jesus Christ is the source and satisfaction of all you seek. Come to Him today and find rest for your soul (Matthew 11:28). — David Roper

Looking to Jesus, my spirit is blest,
The world is in turmoil, in Him I have rest;
The sea of my life around me may roar,
When I look to Jesus, I hear it no more. —Anon.

**OUR HEARTS ARE RESTLESS
TILL THEY FIND THEIR REST IN CHRIST.**

FINDING OUR WAY HOME

READ:
Philippians 2:1-4,12-16

. . . you shine as
lights in the world.
—Philippians 2:15

THE BIBLE IN ONE YEAR:
■ Acts 19–21

Author Anne Lamott tells about a 7-year-old girl who got lost in a big city. The girl frantically ran up and down several streets, looking for a familiar landmark. A policeman saw the girl, realized something was wrong, and offered to help. So she got in the car and he slowly drove through nearby neighborhoods. Suddenly the girl pointed to a church and asked the policeman to let her out. She assured him, "This is my church, and I can always find my way home from here."

Many people think the church is an archaic institution, no longer relevant in our modern world. Yet I am convinced that a church that faithfully teaches the Bible and proclaims the good news of salvation through Christ provides exactly what we all need to "find our way home."

When our churches are fulfilling their God-given function, believers humbly serve and care for one another, encouraging each other to follow Christ's example (Philippians 2:1-11). Those groups of believers, by their words and lives, also point a lost world to Jesus. They serve "as lights in the world, holding fast the word of life" (vv.15-16).

A church that teaches the truth about Christ is not only relevant but desperately needed in our world. It can help people of all ages to find their way home. — Vernon Grounds

Christ builds His church and makes it strong
By using you and me;
And if we all will do our part,
The world His love will see. —Sper

**A CHURCH HELPS THE LOST TO FIND THEIR WAY HOME
WHEN ITS LIGHT SHINES BRIGHTLY.**

HANDLING CRITICISM

READ:
Amos 7:7-15

The LORD took me as I followed the flock, and the LORD said to me, "Go, prophesy to My people Israel." —Amos 7:15

THE BIBLE IN ONE YEAR:
■ Acts 22–24

As we grow older, we sometimes become set in our ways and unwilling to admit when we are wrong. Worse yet, if we don't see eye-to-eye with others, we become critical of them and try to discredit their views.

Some people, for example, when they disagree with a pastor, seem to be quick to judge motives. They may even suggest that the preacher is only looking for a paycheck.

This type of criticism happened to Amos about 750 BC. The prophet had been preaching a tough message about God's judgment of Israel. Understandably, his message was unpopular. Amaziah, the priest of Bethel, was irritated and told Amos to go back to Judah. Amaziah accused Amos of being a prophet-for-hire, preaching just to make a living (7:12). Amos responded by saying that he was prophesying only because God had told him to speak (v.15).

If we are preaching or leading, we must faithfully serve the Lord as Amos did, even if the task is unpleasant, unpopular, or rejected by our audience. And if we're in the congregation, we need to be sure that when we hear something we don't agree with, we're not actually resisting what the Lord wants us to hear and do.

That's how to handle criticism. — Albert Lee

Lord, we can't see each wrong we do,
So send us help from Christians who
Will notice faults we do not see
And tell us of them tactfully. — Branon

**NEVER FEAR CRITICISM WHEN YOU'RE RIGHT;
NEVER IGNORE IT WHEN YOU'RE WRONG.**

ROUTINELY FRESH

**That which is done is what will be done, and there is nothing new under the sun.
—Ecclesiastes 1:9**

THE BIBLE IN ONE YEAR:
■ Acts 25–26

All of us are bound to repeat our-selves as we go about our daily routine. Time after time we eat, sleep, work, and clean up. We can lose our enthusiasm for life if "there is nothing new under the sun" (Ecclesiastes 1:9).

There is another way to view life, however. The world may be likened to a stage on which the drama of eternity is being unfolded. We are the actors. The sun rises and falls like a great curtain day after day, and every time we "repeat our lines" we make a decision. We either respond to the cues of our daily circumstances just to get our part over with, or we look at our role in life as a wonderful opportunity to know and enjoy the goodness and wisdom of the great Director (5:18-20; 12:13-14).

As we gladly participate in this repetitive activity, character is formed, faith is strengthened, hope is increased, and endurance is developed. Through the normal course of events, God is saying to us that there is more to our earthly existence than the meaningless round of duties.

Part of God's plan for us is that we yield to His guidance in ordinary events that occur over and over again. Repeatedly trusting the Lord throughout this month, this week, this day, and this hour is by far the surest way to make life routinely fresh. — Mart De Haan

I wonder what I did for God today:
How many times did I once pause and pray?
But I must find and serve Him in these ways,
For life is made of ordinary days. — Macbeth

IF LIFE IS A GRIND, USE IT TO SHARPEN YOUR CHARACTER.

Let's Go Higher!

READ:
Acts 28:11-16

When Paul saw them, he thanked God and took courage.
—Acts 28:15

THE BIBLE IN ONE YEAR:
■ Acts 27–28

Author Ragnar Arlander tells about the time he and some friends scaled Mt. Rainier. When they reached a plateau, the group decided they had gone far enough.

Arlander, however, continued the climb to find a person who had traveled on ahead. Eventually he found him resting, gazing at a beautiful glacier. The man was ready to go back, but when he saw Arlander approaching, he jumped up and exclaimed, "Since you've come, let's go higher!"

This experience makes me think of the events described in Acts 28. As the apostle Paul was traveling to Rome, he met some fellow believers, and "when Paul saw them, he thanked God and took courage" (v.15).

What better compliment could be offered us than to have someone say, "Talking to you has encouraged me to continue on in my spiritual walk." The world is filled with troubled and discouraged souls who are struggling along in the Christian life. Battle weary, they are almost ready to give up. When they see you, what influence do you have on them? Do you inspire them to more noble lives of service? Or does your example tend to drag them down?

May we influence others in such a way that they will take heart and say, "I want to go higher!" — Richard De Haan

> *Oh, I would be to others*
> *A cheering ray of light,*
> *Inspiring them with courage*
> *To climb some new-found height!* — Bosch

THE HUMAN SPIRIT SOARS WITH HOPE
WHEN LIFTED BY AN ENCOURAGING WORD.

FITNESS TRAINING

READ:
Psalm 119:97-104

Oh, how I love
Your law! It is my
meditation all the day.
—Psalm 119:97

THE BIBLE IN ONE YEAR:
■ Romans 1–4

My wife is an avid exerciser. She walks, rollerblades, and bikes to keep in shape. Because of her interest in exercise, she has encouraged our children to participate in sports activities at school and to exercise along with her.

Why does she feel this is so important? It's simple: When she doesn't exercise several times a week, she doesn't feel physically fit. She feels sluggish and lethargic. She feels that her heart is not being strengthened as it should be.

But she doesn't stop with the physical part of her life. She also participates in spiritual exercise. She knows that in our walk with God we need "heart exercise" to stay fit.

The writer of Psalm 119 saw the importance of daily spiritual exercise. He loved the Word of God, meditated on it throughout the day, and obeyed it. His prayers were from his whole heart, and his hope for each new day came directly from God's Word.

How much more spiritually healthy we would be if we engaged in a godly fitness training program that matched that of the psalmist! Do you read the Bible, meditate on its truths, and pray each day? If not, begin spiritual fitness training today. —Dave Branon

Increase your knowledge of God's Word,
For in it you will find
The wisdom that you need for life,
Which comes from God's own mind. —Sper

**SPIRITUAL STRENGTH REQUIRES A TRAINING PROGRAM
OF BIBLE READING AND PRAYER.**

Take Action!

Read:
Romans 8:12-16

**If your right eye causes you to sin, pluck it out and cast it from you.
—Matthew 5:29**

The Bible In One Year:
■ Romans 5–8

S hameful behavior is being displayed in magazines, movies, and on television. Immorality is even joked about. The world is seeking to convince everyone that nothing is sinful anymore. So we must be on guard against any compromise in our hearts.

While I was in the military, I realized that I was becoming unmoved by the obscene words and conduct of some of my fellow soldiers. When I recognized what was happening, I asked the Lord to restore my sensitivity to the grievous nature of sin.

A permissive attitude toward evil will lead us to fall into sin. That's why we are to deal radically with every form of wickedness.

Jesus went so far as to say that we should pluck out our eye if it causes us to sin (Matthew 5:29). He didn't mean we should maim our bodies, but rather we are to take strong action when tempted to sin. Books, magazines, or video images that arouse wrong desires must be deliberately avoided. This is also what Paul had in mind when he said we are to "put to death the deeds of the body" (Romans 8:13). Someone who is indifferent to the sin around him or trifles with it in his own life is in grave danger.

We cannot ignore the seriousness of this issue. It's time to take action! — Herb Vander Lugt

> *Leave no unguarded place,*
> *No weakness of the soul,*
> *Take every virtue, every grace,*
> *And fortify the whole.* — *Wesley*

**TO AVOID BEING TEMPTED BY FORBIDDEN FRUIT,
STAY AWAY FROM THE DEVIL'S ORCHARD.**

GIVE YOUR HEART

READ:
Romans 9:1-5

I could wish that I myself were accursed from Christ for my brethren, my countrymen. —Romans 9:3

THE BIBLE IN ONE YEAR:
■ Romans 9–11

F̲elipe Garza was 15 when he gave away his heart. His girlfriend Donna Ashlock had become critically ill and needed a heart transplant. One day he told his mom, quite unexplainably, "I'm going to die, and I'm going to give my heart to my girlfriend." He died suddenly 3 weeks later when a blood vessel ruptured in his brain. Doctors then took Felipe's heart and gave it to Donna, saving her life.

That boy's love illustrates Paul's wish for his Jewish countrymen. He too spoke of giving his life so that others could live. Paul, though, was thinking of eternal life. He said that if it were possible (and he knew it wasn't), he would endure the loss of his eternal salvation if that would result in the salvation of the people he loved so much (Romans 9:3).

In spite of his desire to rescue the people he loved from an eternity apart from Christ, Paul couldn't endure hell for his countrymen. Yet his expression of love reminds us of what Jesus Christ did. He really did endure hell for us. He really did give His life so that we might live.

Lord, we know we can't die to gain the salvation of someone else. But by Your Spirit give us a love that cares more for the eternal well-being of others than our own temporary comfort. To You and to them, we give our heart. — Mart De Haan

> *Help me to see the tragic plight*
> *Of souls far off in sin;*
> *Help me to love, to pray, and go*
> *To bring the wandering in.* — Harrison

THOSE WHO LOVE CHRIST HAVE A HEART FOR THE LOST.

A LIFE OBSERVED

READ:
Romans 12:3-8

Having then gifts differing according to the grace that is given to us, let us use them.
— Romans 12:6

THE BIBLE IN ONE YEAR:
■ Romans 12–16

The death of C. S. Lewis on November 22, 1963, has long been overshadowed by the assassination of President John F. Kennedy on the same day. While the anniversary of Lewis' death rarely makes the headlines, the worldwide impact of this British scholar, teacher, and author continues to grow 40 years after his passing.

His books sell more than 3 million copies a year and the most famous, *Mere Christianity, The Screwtape Letters*, and *The Chronicles Of Narnia*, have been reprinted scores of times.

Converted to Christ as an adult, Lewis put his keen mind and imagination to work in the service of God. As a well-known writer and speaker, he continued a simple lifestyle. Michael Nelson has written in the *International Herald Tribune:* "Two-thirds of his book royalties were earmarked for charities. He never traveled abroad, even when fame brought invitations to lecture from around the world."

Lewis gave us the incomparable gift of a fresh, creative look at our fallen human condition and the timeless power of the gospel of Christ. He lived out the command to serve the body of believers through whatever gift God has given us by His grace (Romans 12:4-6). His example can spur us on to use our God-given gifts for His glory. —David McCasland

FOR FURTHER THOUGHT
How has God gifted you to serve?
If you don't know, prayerfully seek godly counsel
and then reach out to build others up.

GOD USES ORDINARY PEOPLE
TO CARRY OUT HIS EXTRAORDINARY PLAN.

THOUGHTFUL PRAISES

READ:
Psalm 47

**God is the King of all the earth; sing praises with understanding.
—Psalm 47:7**

THE BIBLE IN ONE YEAR:
■ 1 Corinthians 1–4

I wonder what God thinks about the way we sing at church. I'm not talking about the quality of our voices, but the honesty of our words. If we're being truthful, the following rewritten hymn titles might more accurately express what's in our hearts as we sing:

"Just As I Am" is "Just As I Pretend To Be."

"O How I Love Jesus" becomes "O How I Like Jesus."

"I Surrender All" is actually "I Surrender Some."

"He's Everything To Me" means "He's Quite A Bit To Me."

Jesus said that we are to worship Him in truth (John 4:24). Singing sincerely and with understanding is a serious challenge (Psalm 47:7).

Let's take up the challenge by seeking God's help to make the original titles of these hymns true for us. In repentance and without pretense, let's turn to Him just as we are. In His forgiving presence, let's declare total love for Jesus by surrendering all to Him. As a result, Jesus truly will become everything to us. Then we will be able to sing honestly about Jesus Christ and our love for Him.

As we make melody in our hearts to the Lord (Ephesians 5:19), let's worship in spirit and in truth. — Joanie Yoder

You are the chosen of the Lord
To sing His highest praise,
And through the melody of song
To show His wondrous ways. — Anon.

**TO SING GOD'S PRAISE,
KEEP YOUR HEART IN TUNE WITH HIM.**

PEOPLE PRESSURE

READ:
1 Kings 12:1-17

**Better to be of a humble spirit with the lowly, than to divide the spoil with the proud.
—Proverbs 16:19**

THE BIBLE IN ONE YEAR:
■ 1 Corinthians 5–8

The desire for the approval of others makes us do strange things. We wear clothing that is fashionable whether we like it or not, we accept invitations we would rather decline, and we work much harder than we want to for a level of financial success we don't need. Most regrettably, however, we sometimes choose to follow a crowd that encourages us to do what is wrong.

In 1 Kings 12, we read about King Rehoboam, who also succumbed to people pressure. He rejected the good advice of older wise men who had known his father Solomon and the mistakes he had made as king. Rehoboam listened instead to the counsel of his peers, younger advisors with whom he had grown up. They were probably motivated by pride and a desire for power, and he was obviously swayed by their influence. How dearly he paid for his mistake!

People pressure — we are all influenced by it. It bears down on us from all directions. But we can choose the path we will take. If we are swayed by the proud or by those who love money, live for pleasure, or long for power, people pressure will lead us down the path that ends in destruction. But if we heed the counsel of those who are humble, good, and godly, we will follow the way that pleases God. — Herb Vander Lugt

"Seek ye first" not earth's aspirings,
Ceaseless longings, vain desirings,
But your precious soul's requirings —
"Seek ye first!" — Anon.

**THOSE WHO FOLLOW THE CROWD
SOON BECOME PART OF THE CROWD.**

TRAVELING LIGHT

READ:
Luke 12:13-21

**Whose will those things be which you have provided?
—Luke 12:20**

THE BIBLE IN ONE YEAR:
■ 1 Corinthians 9–12

Many vacation travelers take along too much stuff. They pack more shoes, clothes, and gadgets than they will ever need. Their mindset is, "I better not forget anything because I can't go home and get it." They would be better off if they asked, "How much can I get along without?" They often end up dragging around heavier-than-necessary suitcases. Some people even purchase so many new items on vacation that they have to leave some of their other stuff behind in the hotel.

We're inclined to accumulate far too many possessions on our journey through life. We're bombarded with ads that urge us to purchase things we "just can't live without." So we buy more and more and more.

The rich man in Jesus' parable (Luke 12:13-21) may have been dreaming about all the good things he could acquire because he had a great crop. He said he would build bigger barns, and he would spend his time eating, drinking, and partying. But God told him, "Fool! This night your soul will be required of you; then whose will those things be which you have provided?" (v.20).

The principle is clear: Be "rich toward God," not rich in things (v.21). Besides, you'll have to leave it all behind when it's time to go Home. — Dave Egner

If we pursue mere earthly gain,
We choose a path that ends in pain;
But joy will stay within the soul
When we pursue a heavenly goal. — D. De Haan

LIFE IS MORE THAN THE THINGS WE STORE.

In His Presence

READ:
1 Corinthians 15:50-58

Death is swallowed up in victory.
—1 Corinthians 15:54

THE BIBLE IN ONE YEAR:
■ 1 Corinthians 13–16

As the congregation around me sang the final verse of "Amazing Grace," I couldn't sing. I found myself instead wiping tears from my eyes as I stared at John Newton's words, "When we've been there 10,000 years, . . . we've no less days to sing God's praise than when we'd first begun."

At that moment I wasn't interested in 10,000 years in heaven. All I could think of was that my 17-year-old daughter was already there. Melissa, who just a few months earlier had been looking forward to her senior year of high school, was in heaven. She was already experiencing an eternity that we can only talk and sing about.

When Melissa was killed in a car accident in the spring of 2002, heaven took on new meaning for our family. Because our bright, beautiful teen had trusted Jesus Christ as her Savior, we knew she was there. As Paul said, "Death is swallowed up in victory" (1 Corinthians 15:54). To us, heaven became even more real. We knew that as we talked with God, we were talking to Someone who had our Melissa in His presence.

The reality of heaven is one of the Bible's most glorious truths. It's a real place where our loved ones live in the presence of our great God, forever serving Him and singing His praises — all because of His amazing grace! — Dave Branon

When we've been there ten thousand years,
Bright shining as the sun,
We've no less days to sing God's praise
Than when we'd first begun. — Newton

CHRISTIANS NEVER SAY GOODBYE TO EACH OTHER
FOR THE LAST TIME.

THE MUSIC OF JOY

READ:
Nehemiah 12:27-43

God had made them rejoice with great joy . . . , so that the joy of Jerusalem was heard afar off.
—Nehemiah 12:43

THE BIBLE IN ONE YEAR:
■ 2 Corinthians 1–3

Several years ago, during a Christian men's conference in Boulder, Colorado, I stood with 50,000 men as we sang "All Hail the Power of Jesus' Name." The volume of the singing was incredible in the football stadium, and I've often wondered how it sounded outside. Could people hear it as they walked through a nearby park, sat on their patios, or drove by in cars? What impression did it leave with them?

That great sound of praise reminded me of what is described in today's Bible reading. The book of Nehemiah begins with a confession, continues with a construction project, and ends with a concert. The entire story is a study in God's faithfulness and power.

After years of hard work despite opposition, the wall of Jerusalem was rebuilt. At the dedication, two "thanksgiving choirs" stood on the wall to praise God. We are told that "the singers sang loudly . . . . God had made them rejoice with great joy . . . , so that the joy of Jerusalem was heard afar off" (Nehemiah 12:42-43).

Joy cannot be contained. It must break out in praise to God through songs of thanksgiving. Whether those who hear our outpouring of joy understand it or not, it will resound as a chorus that cannot be ignored — the music of lives lived out in praise to God. — David McCasland

Let us celebrate together,
Lift our voice in one accord,
Singing of God's grace and mercy
And the goodness of the Lord. — Sper

**EACH NEW DAY GIVES US NEW REASONS
TO SING GOD'S PRAISE.**

ORDINARY DAYS

READ:
2 Corinthians 6:1-10

In all things we commend ourselves as ministers of God: in much patience, in tribulations, in needs, in distresses.
—2 Corinthians 6:4

THE BIBLE IN ONE YEAR:
■ 2 Corinthians 4–6

Have you ever received an annual holiday letter from an acquaintance that recounts the *ordinary* events of the past year? Has anyone told you about cleaning the carpet or taking out the trash? Not likely.

An online publication called the *Journal Of Mundane Behavior* says these routine events fill most of our time. The managing editor, a sociologist, says everyday life is valuable, since we spend nearly 60 percent of our lives doing things like commuting to work and shopping for groceries.

We don't often consider the apostle Paul's ordinary days, but he wrote, "In all things we commend ourselves as ministers of God" (2 Corinthians 6:4). "All things" included not only harsh persecution but also "needs, sleeplessness, purity, kindness, love" and other everyday experiences (vv.4-10).

Oswald Chambers said that we tend to lose our enthusiasm "when there is no vision, no uplift, but just the common round, the trivial task. The thing that tells in the long run for God and for men is the steady persevering work in the unseen, and the only way to keep the life uncrushed is to live looking to God" (*My Utmost For His Highest,* March 6).

So let's live today to the fullest for the Lord, because it's such an important, ordinary day. —David McCasland

If we commit ourselves to Christ
And follow in His way,
He'll give us life that satisfies
With purpose for each day. — Sper

TO GET THE MOST OUT OF LIFE,
MAKE EVERY MOMENT COUNT FOR CHRIST.

PAIN'S PURPOSE

READ:
Hebrews 12:7-11

No chastening seems to be joyful for the present, but painful; nevertheless, afterward it yields the peaceable fruit of righteousness.
—Hebrews 12:11

THE BIBLE IN ONE YEAR:
■ 2 Corinthians 7–9

Affliction, when we accept it with patience and humility, can lead us to a deeper, fuller life. "Before I was afflicted I went astray," David wrote, "but now I keep Your Word" (Psalm 119:67). And again, "It is good for me that I have been afflicted, that I may learn Your statutes" (v.71).

Pain, far from being an obstacle to our spiritual growth, can actually be the pathway to it. If we allow pain to train us, it can lead us closer to God and into His Word. It is often the means by which our Father graciously shapes us to be like His Son, gradually giving us the courage, compassion, contentment, and tranquility we long and pray for. Without pain, God would not accomplish all that He desires to do in and through us.

Are you one whom God is instructing through suffering and pain? By His grace, you can endure His instruction patiently (2 Corinthians 12:9). He can make the trial a blessing and use it to draw you into His heart and into His Word. He can also teach you the lessons He intends for you to learn, and give you His peace in the midst of your difficulties.

The Bible tells us, "Count it all joy when you fall into various trials" (James 1:2). God is making more out of you than you ever thought possible. —David Roper

Through trials we learn to overcome,
Through Christ our victories are won;
Come lay your burdens at His feet
And find this inner peace so sweet. —Halsey

CHRIST CAN TRANSFORM PAINFUL TRIALS
INTO GLORIOUS TRIUMPHS.

UNANSWERED PRAYER

READ:
Matthew 26:36-44

O My Father, if this cup cannot pass away from Me unless I drink it, Your will be done.
—Matthew 26:42

THE BIBLE IN ONE YEAR:
■ 2 Corinthians 10–13

Have you or a friend been afflicted with an illness for which there is no medical cure? Has God denied your repeated requests for healing? Has His refusal to say yes caused you to question His purpose?

An article by Carol Bradley tells us about the wisdom of Craig Satterlee, a seminary professor in Chicago. He has been legally blind since birth, with only 20 percent of normal vision. Does he complain, saying that God has not kept His promise to answer prayer? By no means! He believes wholeheartedly that God has given him something even better.

"I am whole," he testifies, "even though I am legally blind." If introduced as a believer in the power of prayer, he graciously explains, "I don't believe in the power of prayer. I believe in the power and presence of God, so I pray." He adds, "We know that God brings light out of darkness, life out of death, hope out of despair. That's what Scripture teaches us."

Prayer isn't the way to get God to do whatever we want. It's an expression of our trust in His power, wisdom, and grace. No matter what we ask God to do for us, we are to have the attitude of Jesus, who said, "Nevertheless, not as I will, but as You will" (Matthew 26:39). — Vernon Grounds

I know not by what methods rare,
But this I know — God answers prayer;
I leave my prayers with Him alone,
Whose will is wiser than my own. — Hickok

GOD'S ANSWERS ARE WISER THAN OUR PRAYERS.

A GREAT LIGHT

READ:
Isaiah 9:1-7

The people who walked in darkness have seen a great light. —Isaiah 9:2

THE BIBLE IN ONE YEAR:
■ Galatians 1–3

I was driving through the mountains of western Maryland on a cold December night. As I topped a ridge near Rocky Gap State Park, a brilliant sea of lights caught my attention. *What in the world is that?* I wondered as the exit road flashed past. It so aroused my curiosity that 5 miles down the interstate I turned around and drove back to see what it was — a local community's celebration in lights during the Christmas season. At noon, I wouldn't have noticed anything. But at night, the dazzling display couldn't be ignored.

Strange, isn't it, that we complain about the moral and spiritual darkness of our world, yet it is the perfect setting for the radiance of the Lord Jesus Christ. At Christmas, we often read these prophetic words: "The people who walked in darkness have seen a great light; those who dwelt in the land of the shadow of death, upon them a light has shined" (Isaiah 9:2).

Jesus said of Himself: "I am the light of the world" (John 8:12), and to His disciples, "You are the light of the world. A city that is set on a hill cannot be hidden" (Matthew 5:14).

In a dark world, people don't see a great light without wondering why it's there and what it means. We get to tell them. —David McCasland

> *O Holy One of glorious birth*
> *Who lives within our heart,*
> *May we to all men everywhere*
> *Your wondrous love impart.* —Brandt

**TO LEAD OTHERS OUT OF THE DARKNESS,
LET THEM SEE YOUR LIGHT.**

THE BATTLE WITHIN

READ:
Galatians 5:13-26

**Walk in the Spirit, and you shall not fulfill the lust of the flesh.
—Galatians 5:16**

THE BIBLE IN ONE YEAR:
■ Galatians 4–6

In his letter to Christians in Galatia, Paul tried to get them to understand the inner conflict that all who belong to Christ will experience. This battle is between "the flesh" (our sinful human nature) and the Holy Spirit who lives within us (Galatians 5:17).

Because our self-centered nature wants its own way, it fights the rule of Christ within us. So we often end up doing our will rather than God's (v.17).

Once I prayed in desperation, "Lord, please show me how to overcome!" God directed me to Paul's words in Galatians 5:16 — "Walk in the Spirit." I kept reading, and came to recognize my own "works of the flesh" — my envy, anger, hatred, and selfish ambitions (vv.19-21).

I asked God for forgiveness, and I came to understand that I have been crucified with Christ (2:20). The power of my sinful flesh has been broken (5:24; Romans 6:6-7). I've gradually learned to bring this "death" into effect by allowing my flesh no more rights than a corpse! So I resolve daily to recognize and obey Christ's will alone. I sometimes fail, but repentance puts me back in step with the Holy Spirit.

We face this conflict every day, but the Spirit can overcome our sinful desires and win the battle. Which side is winning in your life? — Joanie Yoder

Lord, grant me strength from day to day —
How prone I am to go astray!
The passions of my flesh are strong;
Be Thou, my God, a shield from wrong. — D. De Haan

**GOD WILL GIVE US THE VICTORY,
BUT WE MUST BE WILLING TO FIGHT.**

A LITTLE KINDER

READ:
Ephesians 4:25-32

**The kindness and the love of God our Savior toward man appeared.
—Titus 3:4**

THE BIBLE IN ONE YEAR:
■ Ephesians 1–3

Aldous Huxley (1894–1963), one of the world's leading intellects, was visiting with Houston Smith, a well-known professor of philosophy and religion. As they were driving to an engagement, Huxley said, "You know, Houston, it's rather embarrassing to have spent one's entire lifetime pondering the human condition and . . . find that I really don't have anything more profound to pass on by way of advice than, 'Try to be a little kinder.'"

The apostle Paul saw kindness in a different light. In Ephesians 4:32, he linked being kind, tenderhearted, and forgiving with the way God has treated us. In Titus 3:4, he said that it was "the kindness and the love of God" that provided eternal salvation.

In a world where callous thoughtlessness and selfish indifference are all too common, kindness can make our lives fruitful when motivated by Christlike love. When our walk harmonizes with our words of witness, it will make a compelling impact on others by pointing them to the kind of love God has for them in Jesus Christ. If Huxley had learned what Paul had learned, he would have seen that trying to be a little kinder is one of the most profound truths of all.

What motivates us to try? There's no better reason than the love of God as shown to us by Jesus. — Vernon Grounds

He saw me ruined by the fall,
Yet loved me notwithstanding all;
He saved me from my lost estate,
His lovingkindness, oh, how great! — Medley

**KINDNESS IS TREATING OTHERS
THE WAY GOD TREATS YOU.**

TRUE LOVE

READ:
Ephesians 5:25-33

Let each one of you in particular so love his own wife as himself, and let the wife see that she respects her husband. —Ephesians 5:33

THE BIBLE IN ONE YEAR:
■ Ephesians 4–6

One day I got a call from a young man named Ewing. He and our daughter Julie had known each other for nearly a year, and they were in love. Ewing wanted to know if he could marry Julie. After asking him several questions and getting the responses I needed to hear, I gave him my approval. Then came a big surprise. I asked him when he wanted to marry Julie, and he replied, "In 2 or 3 weeks." He loved Julie so much that he wanted to be with her all the time. True love called for action.

About a month later, just 2 weeks after the wedding, my new son-in-law said to me, "I just want you to know that Julie is my best friend. We have such a great time together."

Some of us who've been married a long time may think that our experience makes us experts on matrimony. But I believe we can learn from newlyweds. First, when two people are truly in love, they will deeply care for each other and cherish their time together. Second, true love means that a couple's relationship will be characterized by the good each one does for the other. How can two people with those characteristics be anything but best friends?

Jesus is the ultimate source of love and respect (Ephesians 5:25-33). True love is Christlike love. —Dave Branon

Look upon your partner's need—
Love demands the loving deed;
Let your love be love that's true,
Prove it by the deeds you do. —Anon.

**A SUCCESSFUL MARRIAGE REQUIRES FALLING IN LOVE
MANY TIMES—WITH THE SAME PERSON.**

Is It Time To Pray?

READ:
Philippians 4:1-7

In everything by prayer and supplication, with thanksgiving, let your requests be made known to God.
—Philippians 4:6

THE BIBLE IN ONE YEAR:
■ Philippians 1–4

When people face trials, they often turn to prayer only as a last resort. I knew a man who was fighting a valiant battle with cancer. As people observed the gradual effect on his body and lifestyle, one person said, "Well, they've tried everything else. I guess it's time to begin praying."

Another man was going through an extremely difficult time at work. It was a crisis of major proportions that had ominous implications for him and for the future of his company. He just couldn't resolve it. Finally he said, "I've tried everything I know to get through this situation and nothing has worked. It's time to start praying."

In both of these instances, prayer was seen as a last-ditch effort to resolve the problem. Only after all other options were eliminated did the person decide to pray. It was a desperate "grasping at straws."

Instead of prayer being a last resort, it should be one of the first things we do. The Lord answers prayer, and He wants us to come to Him continually with all of our needs (1 Thessalonians 5:17). The Bible tells us to "be anxious for nothing, but in everything by prayer . . . let your requests be made known to God" (Philippians 4:6).

So don't wait. It's always time to pray. — Dave Egner

Any hour when helping others
Or when bearing heavy care
Is the time to call our Father —
It's the proper time for prayer. — Zimmerman

**PRAYER SHOULD BE OUR FIRST RESPONSE
RATHER THAN OUR LAST RESORT.**

IT'S ALL
FOR HIM

READ:
Colossians 1:13-20

**All things were
created through Him
and for Him.
—Colossians 1:16**

THE BIBLE IN ONE YEAR:
■ Colossians 1–4

It's a little phrase of just two words at the end of Colossians 1:16 — "for Him." Yet that little phrase gives God's own interpretation of history. In those two words He affirms that Jesus is the final and complete explanation of everything.

All that has happened and ever will happen is moving through time toward that climactic hour when every tongue will confess the lordship of Jesus Christ. Every knee, whether in grateful adoration or under compulsion, will then bow to Him (Philippians 2:10-11).

British historian H.A.L. Fisher apparently did not share that view. He sadly confessed, "Men wiser and more learned than I have discovered in history a plot, a rhythm, a predetermined pattern. These harmonies are concealed from me. I can see only one emergency following upon another as wave follows upon wave . . . nothing but the play of the contingent and the unforeseeable."

What about you? Are you overwhelmed by what seems to be the aimless sequence of events? If so, look once more at Jesus — His life, death, resurrection, and promised return. Your troubled heart will be filled with hope and confidence as you realize that there's meaning and purpose for everything in the world — when you live "for Him."   —Vernon Grounds

One life to live for Christ my Lord,
One life to do my part,
One life in which to give my all
With fervency of heart.   —Brandt

**CHRIST SHOWED HIS LOVE BY DYING FOR US;
WE SHOW OUR LOVE BY LIVING FOR HIM.**

GIVE IT AWAY

READ:
1 Thessalonians 2:1-12

We were well pleased to impart to you not only the gospel of God, but also our own lives, because you had become dear to us.
—1 Thessalonians 2:8

THE BIBLE IN ONE YEAR:
■ 1 Thessalonians 1–5

Parents, teachers, and school board members in central Texas were astounded when a retired couple offered 4-year college scholarships to all 45 children in a local school's first-grade class. The only conditions are that the child stays off drugs, graduates from the high school in that district, and attends an accredited Texas public university, junior college, or trade school. Years earlier, a company had paid half the college tuition for one of the donors, and he never forgot. "They helped me," he says, "and now it's my turn."

All of us have received a gift we can share with others. Although it may not be money, it's something that has enhanced our lives. Paul reminded the Thessalonians that "we were well pleased to impart to you not only the gospel of God, but also our own lives, because you had become dear to us" (1 Thessalonians 2:8).

What has been given to you that you need to pass along in the name of Christ? The gift of listening when someone needs to talk? Sharing in a Bible-study group where people learn to nourish themselves from the Word? Sending a thoughtful card to someone with a heavy heart?

The gospel is always most effective when it is shared by people who joyfully give themselves away. —David McCasland

The message you may give,
The words that come from you,
Most truly honor Jesus
When love is given too. —D. De Haan

GOD GIVES TO YOU SO YOU CAN GIVE TO OTHERS.

December 8

Why Am I Afraid?

READ:
2 Kings 6:8-17

Do not fear, for those who are with us are more than those who are with them.
—2 Kings 6:16

THE BIBLE IN ONE YEAR:
■ 2 Thessalonians 1–3

Columnist George Cantor told how he dealt with a childhood fear. Almost every night he would wake up in the darkness and imagine scary creatures lurking outside his room. Often he would be too scared to go back to sleep. Sometimes he would go and lie down by his parents' bedroom door, figuring that as long as he was near them, nothing would hurt him.

That child's need for some physical evidence of his parents' presence reminds me of the young servant of Elisha. He woke up early one morning and found that the Syrian army had surrounded the city. Alarmed and afraid, he cried out to Elisha, "Alas, my master! What shall we do?" (2 Kings 6:15). After Elisha prayed, the Lord opened the young servant's eyes. What he saw must have filled him with awe and wonder. The Bible says that "the mountain was full of horses and chariots of fire all around Elisha" (v.17). The Lord's army was there to protect them.

We too at times long for God to give us some kind of reassurance that He is near, and sometimes He does. But that's the exception. He wants us to learn to trust His promise that He is with us. No matter how frightening the situation, God's people always have more on their side than the enemy has on his. — Mart De Haan

At times our fears may loom so large
We long for proof that God is near;
It's then our Father says to us,
"Have faith, My child, and do not fear." — D. De Haan

**FAITH KNOWS THAT GOD IS WORKING
BEHIND THE SCENES.**

December 9

SHOWING RESPECT

READ:
1 Chronicles 13

The fear of the LORD is a fountain of life, to turn one away from the snares of death.
—Proverbs 14:27

THE BIBLE IN ONE YEAR:
■ 1 Timothy 1–3

In Myanmar (Burma), children are taught to give objects to their parents and elders with both hands. I live in nearby Singapore, and I know that in Asia it isn't polite to use only one hand to give a business card to someone. And it's extremely rude to toss it across the table to the recipient. To show respect, I should use both hands to give my business card to a person.

In 1 Chronicles 13, we see how important it is to show respect to God. David had good intentions when he decided to bring the ark back to Jerusalem. During the process, however, Uzzah touched the ark in an attempt to prevent it from falling off the cart. God struck him dead. David was stunned and upset by God's anger. Why did the Lord respond so severely?

David came to realize that what he wanted to do for God had to be done with respect for Him and His specific instructions. God had commanded that the ark be carried by the sons of Kohath on poles, not on a cart, nor was anyone to touch it (Exodus 25:14-15; Numbers 3:30-31; 4:15).

What David learned is something we too must take to heart. Showing respect for God means learning what He wants us to do and then obeying Him completely. To please the Lord, we must do His work His way. — Albert Lee

O help me, Lord, to show respect,
To always honor You;
And may I bring You highest praise
In everything I do. —Sper

WE RESPECT GOD WHEN WE OBEY GOD.

Joy To The World!

READ:
Psalm 98

The LORD has made known His salvation; His righteousness He has revealed in the sight of the nations. —Psalm 98:2

THE BIBLE IN ONE YEAR:
■ 1 Timothy 4–6

While walking home from a church service in Southampton, England, 20-year-old Isaac Watts told his father that the metrical psalms sung at their services lacked the dignity and beauty that should characterize hymns used in worship. His father encouraged him to try to create something better. So in the year 1694, Isaac Watts began writing hymns, and eventually put the book of Psalms into rhyming meter for worship.

Watts took the prophetic references to the coming Messiah in the Psalms and expressed them in their New Testament fulfillment. His hymns proclaimed that Jesus Christ is Savior and Lord. When Watts came to Psalm 98, he wrote:

Joy to the world! The Lord is come!
Let earth receive her King;
Let every heart prepare Him room,
And heaven and nature sing.
Joy to the earth! The Savior reigns!
Let men their songs employ;
While fields and floods, rocks, hills, and plains
Repeat the sounding joy.

This hymn has become a favorite of the Christmas season. It calls us to acknowledge Christ as Savior and King, and to open our hearts to His rule of love and grace.

The psalmist wrote, "Oh, sing to the LORD a new song!" (98:1). Isaac Watts did just that in his proclamation that Christ *has* come, and we can rejoice in Him. — David McCasland

---

TO FIND JOY AT CHRISTMAS, LOOK TO JESUS.

RIGHT AND WRONGS

READ:
2 Timothy 4:14-18

**At my first defense no one stood with me, but all forsook me. May it not be charged against them.
— 2 Timothy 4:16**

THE BIBLE IN ONE YEAR:
■ 2 Timothy 1–4

It's crucial to distinguish between personal wrongs, which we must be willing to forgive, and deliberate attacks on the gospel of Christ, which the Lord will judge. Paul drew that distinction in his letter to his young friend Timothy.

First, Paul wrote with respect to an opponent of the gospel: "Alexander the coppersmith did me much harm. May the Lord repay him according to his works. You also must beware of him, for he has greatly resisted our words" (2 Timothy 4:14-15).

The "harm" Alexander had done to Paul was not to him personally but to his message, and he was now engaged in stirring up opposition to Timothy's proclamation of the gospel.

Then, as if to plainly contrast and distinguish between those who oppose God's work and those who personally wrong us, Paul followed with these gracious words: "At my first defense no one stood with me, but all forsook me. May it not be charged against them" (2 Timothy 4:16).

How sad that Paul's fellow Christians would desert the apostle in his hour of deep need! What should be done to them? Surely they're deserving of his righteous anger. Not so. Paul said, "May it not be charged against them."

Lord, help us to be gracious too. — David Roper

You sacrificed Your life for us —
You shed Your blood so we could live;
So help us, Lord, to follow You,
To love each other and forgive. — Sper

**TREAT OTHERS' FAULTS AS GRACIOUSLY
AS YOU DO YOUR OWN.**

HOW GENTLE ARE YOU?

READ:
Titus 3:1-8

**Let your gentleness be known to all men. The Lord is at hand.
—Philippians 4:5**

THE BIBLE IN ONE YEAR:
■ Titus 1–3

During my years as a pastor, I encountered many Christians who were anything but gentle. They had no patience for fellow believers with character flaws or who were involved in sinful practices. They also showed little kindness toward nonbelievers. They thought that gospel messages should always include dire warnings of the torments of hell.

Recently I heard about a company that had decided to open their stores on Sunday. Because they were located in an area with many churches, the corporation received scores of condemning letters from angry Christians. Some even said they were glad there was an eternal hell for those who had made this decision. Christian and non-Christian employees were offended and embarrassed. Lack of gentleness had harmed Christ's cause.

The religious leaders of Jesus' day were quick to judge and lacked gentleness. They criticized Jesus because He ate and drank with tax collectors and sinners (Matthew 11:19). They were shocked because He showed concern for these people instead of harshly condemning them. He didn't approve of what they did, but He saw them as sinners created in God's image whom He had come to save.

Let's follow Christ's example. —Herb Vander Lugt

O to be like Him, tender and kind,
Gentle in spirit, lowly in mind;
More like to Jesus, day after day,
Filled with His Spirit, now and alway. —Ellsworth

NOTHING IS SO STRONG AS GENTLENESS, NOTHING SO GENTLE AS REAL STRENGTH. —Francis de Sales

LET GOD DO HIS WORK

READ:
1 Corinthians 3:1-11

Neither he who plants is anything, nor he who waters, but God who gives the increase.
—1 Corinthians 3:7

THE BIBLE IN ONE YEAR:
■ Philemon

In our zeal to serve the Lord, it's easy to think that it's our responsibility to produce results. This causes us to place too much faith in our ability and too little faith in God's.

Paul observed this same tendency in the Corinthian church. Certain believers extolled the seed-planting ministry of Paul, while others favored the seed-watering ministry of Apollos. In 1 Corinthians 3, Paul reminded them that it is God who brings the seed to fruition (vv.4-7). Yet Paul acknowledged that their faithful efforts were part of God's plan, "and each one will receive his own reward according to his own labor" (v.8).

Imagine a farmer sitting on his front porch. You ask him what he's doing. He answers, "Farming." You ask him what he's growing. He replies, "Wheat." "But your fields look unplowed and unplanted," you say. "That's right," he answers, "I'm farming by faith. Believing God for a harvest." "But shouldn't you be doing something?" you protest. He replies, "I am. I'm praying and believing!"

This story reminds us that God won't do our work for us, and 1 Corinthians teaches us that the results are not up to us. The best way to serve is to faithfully plant and water the seed, then trust God for the results. — Joanie Yoder

God does not expect us
To make the seed bear fruit;
Jesus said to plant it,
And pray that it will root. — Pendergraft

WE CAN PLANT THE SEED,
BUT ONLY GOD CAN GIVE THE HARVEST.

IMMANUEL

READ:
Isaiah 8:1-10

"The virgin shall be with child, and bear a Son, and they shall call His name Immanuel," which is translated, "God with us." —Matthew 1:23

THE BIBLE IN ONE YEAR:
■ Hebrews 1–4

S ince that first Christmas day 2,000 years ago, the assurance that God is with His people has taken on new meaning. Before Jesus was born, the Israelites were assured that even in judgment they could have hope because God was with them (Isaiah 8:8,10). Yet they didn't know God as fully as we can today.

We have a great advantage because through reading the New Testament we can see the glory of God "in the face of Jesus Christ" (2 Corinthians 4:6). And we can sense His presence in all situations of life because He is made real to us by the Holy Spirit (Romans 8:10-16).

When I need to be reassured that God is with me, I think about Jesus as He is revealed in the New Testament. I recall how He took little children in His arms and blessed them (Matthew 19:13-15). Then I think of His crucifixion, which reminds me of all He endured to be my Savior (27:27-54). Finally, I reflect on His promise, "I am with you always, even to the end of the age" (28:20).

The birth of Jesus gave new significance to the name Immanuel, which means "God with us" (1:23). Because He lived among us, died for us, and sent His Spirit to indwell us, we can rejoice! — Herb Vander Lugt

> *Veiled in flesh the Godhead see,*
> *Hail the incarnate Deity!*
> *Pleased as man with men to dwell,*
> *Jesus, our Immanuel.* — Wesley

**GOD CAME TO LIVE WITH US
SO WE COULD LIVE WITH HIM.**

THE GIFT OF OBEDIENCE

READ:
Zechariah 7

**Should you not have obeyed the words which the LORD proclaimed?
—Zechariah 7:7**

THE BIBLE IN ONE YEAR:
■ Hebrews 5–7

It's that time of year again when people think about God and goodwill more than they do at any other time. It seems that the nearer we get to Christmas, the more we notice that people have a willingness to express an interest in religious things. Both church attendance and church activities increase.

Does this heightened religious activity honor the Lord? We must be careful that what takes place is not what happened to the people of Zechariah's day. Although they engaged in religious activities, they were out to please only themselves. A vital element was missing — obedience to God.

Instead of their conducting empty rituals, God wanted them to show their obedience to Him by: (1) administering true justice, (2) showing mercy and compassion, (3) refusing to oppress widows, orphans, and the poor, and (4) not planning evil against others (Zechariah 7:9-10).

We can best honor God during this special season by evaluating our own devotion to Him in light of these four commands to God's people. Our Lord does not want empty, self-centered religious activities from us. He wants the gift of obedience expressed in acts of kindness and helpfulness for those less fortunate than we are. —Dave Branon

*Try to bring God's love and kindness
Into someone's life today;
Even just a gift of caring
Can the Savior's love display.* —Hess

KINDNESS IS ALWAYS IN SEASON.

December 16

WHY GO TO CHURCH?

READ:
Hebrews 10:19-25

Let us consider one another in order to stir up love and good works, not forsaking the assembling of ourselves together.
—Hebrews 10:24-25

THE BIBLE IN ONE YEAR:
■ Hebrews 8–10

In a letter to the editor of a British newspaper, a man complained that he saw no sense in going to church every Sunday. "I have been attending services quite regularly for the past 30 years," he wrote, "and during that time . . . I have listened to no less than 3,000 sermons. But, to my consternation, I discover I cannot remember a single one of them. I wonder if a minister's time might be more profitably spent on something else."

That letter sparked many responses. One, however, was the clincher: "I have been married for 30 years. During that time I have eaten 32,850 meals — mostly of my wife's cooking. Suddenly I have discovered that I cannot remember the menu of a single meal. And yet, I received nourishment from every one of them. I have the distinct impression that without them I would have starved to death long ago."

The Bible assumes the importance of going to church, and the only admonition to do so appears in the context of the danger of forsaking the practice (Hebrews 10:25). We need help to keep our faith and hope from wavering (v.23), and to love and do good works (v.24). Just as physical food keeps us alive and strong, so also the spiritual nourishment of teaching and fellowship are necessary for our survival. —Dennis De Haan

I love to worship with others,
To read the Bible and pray,
To sing the songs about Jesus,
And learn to walk in His way. —Hess

**TO KEEP GROWING IN CHRIST,
KEEP GOING TO CHURCH.**

NEVER ALONE

**I will never leave you
nor forsake you.
—Hebrews 13:5**

THE BIBLE IN ONE YEAR:
■ Hebrews 11–13

Robinson Crusoe, the chief character in a novel by Daniel Defoe, was shipwrecked and stranded on an uninhabited island. Life was hard, but he found hope and comfort when he turned to the Word of God.

Crusoe said, "One morning, being very sad, I opened the Bible upon these words, 'I will never, never leave thee, nor forsake thee.' Immediately it occurred that these words were to *me*; why else should they be directed in such a manner, just at the moment when I was mourning over my condition, as one forsaken of God and man?

"'Well then,' said I, 'if God does not forsake me, . . . what matters it, though the world should all forsake me . . . ?' From this moment I began to conclude in my mind that it was possible for me to be more happy in this forsaken, solitary condition than it was probable that I should ever have been in any other state in the world; and with this thought I was going to give thanks to God for bringing me to this place."

Have you been forsaken by a friend, a child, a spouse? God has said, "I will *never* leave you nor forsake you" (Hebrews 13:5). So you too can say with confidence, "The LORD is my helper; I will not fear. What can man do to me?" (v.6). — David Roper

*When all around me is darkness
And earthly joys have flown,
My Savior whispers His promise
Never to leave me alone.* — Anon.

**FEAR WILL LEAVE US WHEN WE REMEMBER
THAT GOD IS ALWAYS WITH US.**

THEY UNDERSTOOD

READ:
2 Corinthians 1:3-11

[God] comforts us in all our tribulations, that we may be able to comfort those who are in any trouble.
—2 Corinthians 1:4

THE BIBLE IN ONE YEAR:
■ James 1–2

A few days before Christmas, we received a beautiful floral arrangement with a card that said, "Remembering your loss and wishing you and your family a blessed Christmas and a Happy New Year. Love and prayers, Dave and Betty."

Seven months earlier, my sister Marti and her husband Jim had been killed in a traffic accident. This was our first Christmas without them, so it was a great encouragement to have friends acknowledge our loss and express their love in a tangible way.

Dave and Betty understood our need to grieve and find God's healing because two decades earlier their daughter had taken her own life. Because they had experienced the Lord's comfort over the years, they were able to come alongside us in a sensitive and caring way.

That loving act came as a striking example of Paul's words: "The Father of mercies and God of all comfort . . . comforts us in all our tribulation, that we may be able to comfort those who are in any trouble, with the comfort with which we ourselves are comforted by God" (2 Corinthians 1:3-4).

When God touches our broken hearts with His peace, we are uniquely equipped to share that with others. What a wonderful gift to give and receive at Christmas! —David McCasland

The comfort God has given us
He wants us now to share
With others who are suffering
And caught in life's despair. —Sper

GOD DOES NOT COMFORT US TO MAKE US COMFORTABLE, BUT TO MAKE US COMFORTERS.

December 19

"WHERE'S THE BABY JESUS?"

READ:
Luke 2:1-12

There is born to you this day in the city of David a Savior, who is Christ the Lord.
—Luke 2:11

THE BIBLE IN ONE YEAR:
■ James 3–5

It seems to happen earlier each year. Stores put up Christmas decorations. Newspaper ads announce "the perfect Christmas gift." Toy commercials punctuate television shows. Christmas music fills the air. Before you know it, there are banquets to attend, parties you can't miss, gifts to wrap, family gatherings to plan, baking to be done, and a host of other activities that manage to crowd out the real meaning of Christmas.

Delores Van Belkum told me a story about her young grandson that drives home the point. His mother and father had used a simple manger scene to tell Justin about Mary, Joseph, and the baby Jesus. They wanted him to know that the Child born in Bethlehem was someone very special. As the holiday approached, Justin went on a shopping trip with his mother and grandmother. One salesperson showed him a sparkling display of Santas, toys, and decorations. He was fascinated. But he spoke words that far surpassed his years when he looked up and said, "But where's the baby Jesus?"

This Christmas, let's keep foremost in our minds the reason for the celebration — the birth of God's Son. Then, as people listen to our words and observe our activities, they won't ask, "Where's the baby Jesus?"   — Dave Egner

Invite Him in this Christmas,
This Savior from above;
The gift He seeks you need not wrap —
He only wants your love.   —Berg

BEWARE OF KEEPING CHRISTMAS
BUT LOSING CHRIST.

THOUGHTFUL PRAISES

READ:
Psalm 143

**I remember the days of old; I meditate on all Your works; I muse on the work of Your hands.
—Psalm 143:5**

THE BIBLE IN ONE YEAR:
■ 1 Peter 1–2

Most of us long to praise God more joyfully than we do. One common hindrance is that no matter how hard we try, we often don't feel like praising Him.

Bible teacher Selwyn Hughes says that God has placed within us three main functions: the will, the feelings, and the thoughts. Our will, he says, has little or no power over our feelings. You can't say, "I am going to feel different," and then accomplish it by sheer willpower. What the feelings *do* respond to are the thoughts. Quoting another source, Hughes says: "Our feelings follow our thoughts like baby ducks follow their mother." So how can we make our thoughts the leader of our feelings?

David showed us the way in Psalm 143. Feeling overwhelmed and distressed (v.4), he took time to think about the Lord (v.5). He remembered God's lovingkindness, trustworthiness, and guidance (v.8); His protection and goodness (vv.9-10); His righteousness and mercy (vv.11-12). Once David got going, his feelings began to follow his thoughts.

Name your own blessings daily; contemplate them thoroughly; speak about them to God and to others. Gradually your concern about feelings will diminish and you'll be praising God with joy. —Joanie Yoder

Take control of my heart today,
Keep it filled with joy and praise
And gratitude for every good
You bestow on all my days. —Sees

JOY THRIVES IN THE SOIL OF PRAISE.

ALWAYS RIGHT

READ:
2 Peter 1:16-21

Holy men of God spoke as they were moved by the Holy Spirit. —2 Peter 1:21

THE BIBLE IN ONE YEAR:
■ 1 Peter 3–5

A weatherman boasted, "I'm 90 percent right — 10 percent of the time." That's a ridiculous statement, but some people resort to that type of doubletalk to cover up a poor record.

The Bible's prophetic record, though, truly is accurate. Let's look at a few examples.

The Lord Jesus was born in the city of Bethlehem (Micah 5:2) of a virgin (Isaiah 7:14) at the time specified (Daniel 9:25). Infants in Bethlehem were massacred as prophesied (Jeremiah 31:15). Jesus went down into Egypt and returned (Hosea 11:1). Isaiah foretold Christ's ministry in Galilee (Isaiah 9:1-2). Zechariah predicted His triumphal entry into Jerusalem on a colt (Zechariah 9:9) and His betrayal for 30 pieces of silver (11:12-13). David had never seen a Roman crucifixion, yet in Psalm 22, under divine inspiration, he penned a graphic portrayal of Jesus' death. Isaiah 53 gives a detailed picture of our Lord's rejection, mistreatment, death, and burial. These few prophecies (and there are many more) should impress us with the reliability of the Bible.

Since these predictions have all been fulfilled, let us also accept with confidence what the Bible says about the future. Remember, we have a book of prophecy that is right — all of the time! — *Richard De Haan*

> *I'll trust in God's unchanging Word*
> *Till soul and body sever;*
> *For though all things shall pass away,*
> *His Word shall stand forever!* — *Luther*

**YOU CAN TRUST THE BIBLE—
GOD ALWAYS KEEPS HIS WORD.**

GOD'S GUIDANCE

READ:
Matthew 1:18-25

**An angel of the Lord appeared to him in a dream, saying, "Joseph, son of David, do not be afraid."
—Matthew 1:20**

THE BIBLE IN ONE YEAR:
■ 2 Peter 1–3

The Christmas story contains a surprising glimpse into the way God guides those who trust in Him. When the Lord was about to turn the lives of Mary and Joseph upside down, He revealed His plans to them at different times and in different ways.

Mary received advance notice from the angel Gabriel that she would conceive the Son of God by the power of the Holy Spirit (Luke 1:30-35).

But Joseph, her fiancé, seems to have received no word from God at that time. Later, when he learned of Mary's pregnancy and pondered how to end their engagement without publicly disgracing her, "an angel of the Lord appeared to him in a dream, saying, 'Joseph, son of David, do not be afraid to take to you Mary your wife, for that which is conceived in her is of the Holy Spirit'" (Matthew 1:20).

Such is the mystery of God's guidance. Mary was told beforehand and Joseph had to struggle with what must have seemed a crushing blow. But no matter when God's word came to them, Mary and Joseph both faithfully obeyed.

We cannot predict all of what the Lord wants us to do nor how He will direct our lives, but we can be confident that He will guide us. And, like Mary and Joseph, we must be ready to follow His leading. — David McCasland

God holds the future in His hands
With grace sufficient day by day,
Through good or ill He gently leads,
If we but let Him have His way. — Rohrs

YOU DON'T NEED TO KNOW WHERE YOU'RE GOING IF YOU LET GOD DO THE LEADING.

River Of Forgiveness

READ:
1 John 1:5-9

If we confess our sins, He is faithful and just to forgive us our sins and to cleanse us from all unrighteousness.
—1 John 1:9

THE BIBLE IN ONE YEAR:
■ 1 John 1–2

According to Greek mythology, King Augeus owned a stable with 3,000 oxen. Their stalls had not been cleaned out for 30 years—hence our English word *Augean*, which refers to something exceedingly filthy from long neglect. Hercules, the mythical strong man, was commanded to clean the Augean stable in a single day.

When Hercules first saw the stable, he was dismayed by its size, filthiness, and stench. Then he noticed that it was located between two great rivers, the Alpheus and the Peneus. He put his great strength to work and diverted the rivers so they flowed through the building. Within a short time the stable was rinsed clean.

The story is a myth, of course, but myths by their very nature preserve the yearnings of the cultures that embrace and perpetuate them. The story reflects, I believe, our own longing for someone to wash from our lives the accumulated waste and filth of the years.

There is a powerful river of forgiveness that flows from the cross of Christ. No defilement, even though Augean, can withstand its cleansing flow. When we humbly confess our sins, all of our unrighteousness is washed away (1 John 1:9). We can be sure that our "sins, which are many, are forgiven" (Luke 7:47). — David Roper

Lord, give me courage to confess,
To bare my sinful heart to Thee;
Forgiving love You long to show
And from my sin to set me free. — D. De Haan

**CONFESSION TO GOD ALWAYS BRINGS
CLEANSING FROM GOD.**

December 24

A Light In The Darkness

READ:
Luke 2:25-33

I am the light of the world. He who follows Me shall not walk in darkness, but have the light of life.
—John 8:12

THE BIBLE IN ONE YEAR:
■ 1 John 3–5

An artist was painting a winter scene. Snow blanketed the ground and the pine trees. Night was falling, and the landscape was enveloped in semi-darkness. A log cabin was barely visible in the shadows. The whole scene was one of gloom.

Then the artist used some yellow tints to put the cheerful glow of a lamp in one of the cabin windows. That lone light, its golden rays reflecting on the snow, completely transformed the impression given by the painting. In contrast to the cold darkness of the surrounding forest, that light in the window created a warm feeling of love and security.

What happened on that canvas is a striking portrayal of one of the most dramatic events of all history. When Jesus was born in Bethlehem's stable, a light was placed in this sin-darkened world. The apostle John testified, "In Him was life, and the life was the light of men" (John 1:4).

During this week, as we commemorate the birth of the Lord Jesus, let's be mindful of how much brighter this world is because He came into it. Jesus declared, "I am the light of the world. He who follows Me shall not walk in darkness, but have the light of life" (John 8:12).

How has Jesus brightened your life? — Richard De Haan

The whole world was lost in the darkness of sin,
The Light of the world is Jesus;
Like sunshine at noonday His glory shone in,
The Light of the world is Jesus. — Bliss

WITHOUT THE LIGHT OF JESUS,
WE WOULD BE IN THE DARK ABOUT GOD.

CHRISTMAS CHOICE

READ:
Matthew 2:1-12

When they saw the star, they rejoiced with exceedingly great joy.
—Matthew 2:10

THE BIBLE IN ONE YEAR:
■ 2 John, 3 John, Jude

The glitter of bright decorations, the sound of joyous Christmas carols, the happy children, and the cheerful "Merry Christmas" greetings sometimes give the impression that everybody is glad that Jesus came to our planet. But that isn't true today, and it never was.

The news of Jesus' birth evoked a mixed reaction. The wise men joyfully welcomed and worshiped the Savior (Matthew 2:10-11). But King Herod was so troubled when he heard about it that he tried to find and kill the baby Jesus (vv.3-4,16). Most people, however, were unaware of the significance of what had happened.

Still today, multitudes honor Jesus and rejoice in their salvation. But many others hate Him. They grumble about the singing of Christmas carols in shopping malls and the display of nativity scenes in public places. Others are apathetic. They go along with the celebration of the season. They may join in singing Christmas carols, but they never ask themselves who Jesus is or why He came. They don't think of their need to believe on Him and receive Him as their Savior.

Are you among the indifferent? To ignore Him and His claims is to reject Him. Christmas demands a decision about Christ. The choice is yours. — Herb Vander Lugt

What will you do with Jesus?
Neutral you cannot be;
Someday your heart will be asking,
"What will He do with me?" — Simpson

**IF YOU MAKE ROOM FOR JESUS IN YOUR HEART,
HE WILL MAKE ROOM FOR YOU IN HEAVEN.**

THE COMPLETE STORY

READ:
Revelation 1:1-8

**Behold, He is coming with clouds, and every eye will see Him, even they who pierced Him.
—Revelation 1:7**

At this time of year we think about the birth of the Savior. The events of His birth are of vital importance, yet we would do well to reflect also on His earthly ministry, sacrificial death, resurrection, ascension, and promised return. Our redemption would be incomplete if any element were missing. It is fitting, therefore, to share with you a poem by L. W. Beckley titled, "The Rest of the Story."

*We are wont to sing of shepherds
And the heavenly glory bright,
Of angels and their message
On that peaceful, holy night.*

*But so oft we end the story
When 'tis only just begun,
For we fail to give the message
That this Child is God the Son.*

*Here to give Himself a ransom,
Crucified on Calvary's tree,
Through His blood providing pardon,
Perfect cleansing, full and free.*

*And the tomb, thank God, is empty;
Jesus sits at God's right hand
Now a loving, mighty Savior;
Spread the news to every land!*

The One born in Bethlehem was none other than God in human flesh. Having lived a perfect life, He died an awful death to pay the price for the sins of mankind. Now He's in heaven, and any day He could return. How wonderful to know the complete story! — Richard De Haan

---

**THE BIRTH OF CHRIST BROUGHT GOD TO MAN;
THE CROSS OF CHRIST BRINGS MAN TO GOD.**

HOLY, HOLY, HOLY

READ:
Revelation 4

**They do not rest day or night, saying: "Holy, holy, holy, Lord God Almighty, who was and is and is to come!"
—Revelation 4:8**

THE BIBLE IN ONE YEAR:
■ Revelation 4–8

"Time flies when you're having fun." This cliché has no basis in fact, but experience makes it seem true.

When life is pleasant, time passes all too quickly. Give me a task that I enjoy, or a person whose company I love, and time seems irrelevant.

My experience of this "reality" has given me a new understanding of the scene described in Revelation 4. In the past, when I considered the four living creatures seated around God's throne who keep repeating the same few words, I thought, *What a boring existence!*

I don't think that anymore. I think about the scenes they have witnessed with their many eyes (v.8). I consider the view they have from their position around God's throne (v.6). I think of how amazed they are at God's wise and loving involvement with wayward earthlings. Then I think, *What better response could there be? What else is there to say but, "Holy, holy, holy"?*

Is it boring to say the same words over and over? Not when you're in the presence of the one you love. Not when you're doing exactly what you were designed to do.

Like the four creatures, we were designed to glorify God. Our lives will never be boring if we're focusing our attention on Him and fulfilling that purpose. —Julie Ackerman Link

Holy, holy, holy, Lord God Almighty!
Early in the morning our song shall rise to Thee;
Holy, holy, holy! Merciful and mighty!
God in three Persons, blessed Trinity! —Heber

**A HEART IN TUNE WITH GOD
CAN'T HELP BUT SING HIS PRAISE.**

THE ARTIST'S DREAM

READ:
Revelation 5:1-10

**You were slain, and have redeemed us to God by Your blood out of every tribe and tongue and people and nation.
—Revelation 5:9**

THE BIBLE IN ONE YEAR:
■ Revelation 9–12

Rita Snowden wrote a book in 1937 titled *If I Open My Door*. In it she described a congregation that was planning to build a new place of worship. Central to its sanctuary would be a stained-glass window depicting children worshiping Jesus.

The congregation hired an artist to paint a picture of the proposed window. He fulfilled the assignment, and that night he dreamed he heard a noise in his studio. Going to investigate, he saw a stranger altering his picture. He cried out, "Stop! You'll ruin it." But the stranger answered, "You have already ruined it." The intruder then explained that the children's faces had all been one color, but he was using many colors. When the intruder said that he wanted children of all nations and races to come to him, the artist realized he was talking to Jesus Himself.

In a world where racial differences often lead to separation and conflict, it's imperative that Christians work for unity and peace. Jesus went to the cross to bring salvation to people of every nation (Revelation 5:9). Our witness and our fellowship must go beyond the barriers that have historically divided the human family (Romans 1:16; Galatians 3:28).

Do we reflect Jesus' love for all people? —Vernon Grounds

Jesus loves the little children,
All the children of the world;
Red and yellow, black and white,
They are precious in His sight;
Jesus loves the little children of the world. —Woolston

**JESUS LOVES ALL PEOPLE,
NOT JUST THE ONES WHO LOOK LIKE YOU.**

THE PURSUIT OF HAPPINESS

READ:
Matthew 5:1-10

**Blessed are the poor in spirit, for theirs is the kingdom of heaven.
—Matthew 5:3**

THE BIBLE IN ONE YEAR:
■ Revelation 13–15

Everyone is looking for happiness, and people follow many avenues trying to find it. They look for it in money, parties, self-improvement programs, fancy cars, luxurious homes, or promoting a cause.

That's the wrong list. The right one is found in Matthew 5. Jesus taught us that deep and lasting happiness comes from being right with God. He said we are blessed, or happy, when we are:

- Poor in spirit — recognizing our desperate need for God.
- Mourning — realizing the awfulness of sin and being genuinely sorry for it.
- Meek — demonstrating self-control, even when we are mistreated.
- Hungry and thirsty for righteousness — longing to be holy and pure.
- Merciful — showing mercy to others, just as God shows mercy to us.
- Pure in heart — being singleminded and sincere in our devotion to Christ.
- Peacemakers — sharing the peace Christ offers, and promoting peace with one another.
- Persecuted — being willing to suffer for Jesus' sake.

Looking for happiness? Follow Jesus' way. — Dave Branon

Happy are they who love the Lord,
Whose hearts have Christ confessed,
Who by His cross have found their life,
Beneath His yoke their rest. — Bridges

**HAPPINESS DEPENDS ON WHAT YOU ARE,
NOT ON WHAT YOU HAVE.**

WHAT WILL WE DO IN HEAVEN?

READ:
Revelation 22:1-5

His servants shall serve Him. They shall see His face, and His name shall be on their foreheads.
—Revelation 22:3-4

THE BIBLE IN ONE YEAR:
■ Revelation 16–18

I'm sometimes asked what we'll do in heaven. Will we sit on clouds and strum celestial harps? Will we flit about on gossamer wings? In his vision, John the apostle saw three future heavenly activities.

The first one is *serving* (Revelation 22:3). Perhaps we'll explore an unknown corner of the universe, or, as C. S. Lewis suggests, govern a distant star. Whatever that service may entail, there will be no sense of inadequacy, no weakness, no weariness. In heaven we'll have minds and bodies equal to the task to which we're assigned.

The second activity is *seeing*: We "shall see His face" (v.4). "Now we see in a mirror, dimly" (1 Corinthians 13:12), but in heaven we shall see our Savior face to face, and we "shall be like Him" (1 John 3:2). This is what Revelation 22:4 means when it says, "His name shall be on their foreheads." The name of God represents His perfect character, so to bear His name means to be like Him. In heaven we will never again struggle with sin but will reflect the beauty of His holiness forever.

Finally, there is *reigning*. We shall serve our King by ruling and reigning with Him "forever and ever" (v.5).

What will we do in heaven? We'll serve God, see our Savior, and reign with Him forever. We'll be busy! — David Roper

In heaven we'll see our Savior
And like Him we will be;
We'll praise Him and we'll serve Him
For all eternity! — *Fitzhugh*

**THOSE WHO LOVE AND SERVE GOD ON EARTH
WILL FEEL AT HOME IN HEAVEN.**

A FRESH START

READ:
Joshua 1:1-9

Do not be afraid, nor be dismayed, for the LORD your God is with you wherever you go. —Joshua 1:9

THE BIBLE IN ONE YEAR:
■ Revelation 19–22

They stand in the cold by the thousands in Times Square, New York City. What draws them to that place? There's no sporting event or rock concert. There's just a huge lighted ball that drops down a pole on top of a building. It takes only a few seconds, and it hardly seems worth fighting traffic and subway crunch to see — except that it happens on New Year's Eve.

Why have we created a holiday over such a nonevent? Other holidays celebrate famous birthdays or historical milestones or *something*. New Year's Eve just celebrates the passage of time. We make such a fuss because it signals the end of an old era and the beginning of a new one. The old year's problems and struggles become a dim memory when we think of getting a fresh start.

It must have been something like that for the Israelites who stood with Joshua and looked at the new era ahead of them (Joshua 1:1-9). Behind them were 40 years of wandering in the desert. Ahead was a land of milk and honey. And best of all, they had God's promise that He would be with them.

As we stand with our back to the past 12 months and our face toward the new year, we can have hope because we too can be sure of God's help. That makes the prospect of a new year worth celebrating! — Dave Branon

Though I know not what awaits me—
What the future has in store,
Yet I know that God is faithful,
For I've proved Him oft before. — Anon.

WE CAN TRUST OUR ALL-KNOWING GOD FOR THE UNKNOWN FUTURE.

TOPIC INDEX

Part 1

TOPIC INDEX

TOPIC INDEX

ABOUT THE PUBLISHER

RBC MINISTRIES

RBC Ministries is men and women who believe in the strategic use of media to further the mission of Christ and His church. Over 300 people serve in the home office in Grand Rapids, Michigan, USA, joined by another 300 co-workers and volunteers in about 20 offices around the globe. For 65 years, RBC has been teaching the Word of God so as to lead people of all nations to personal faith and maturity in Christ.

From a humble beginning as a Bible class aired on a small radio station in Michigan, RBC Ministries now offers 4 radio programs, *Day of Discovery* television, many devotional, instructional, evangelistic, and apologetic print resources, and a biblical correspondence ministry. In addition, the RBC Internet site (www.rbc.net) receives over 30 million "hits" a month as 500,000 people per month access the many resources found on that Web site. The signature publication, *Our Daily Bread*, is translated into more than 30 languages and used by people in almost every country in the world.

DISCOVERY HOUSE PUBLISHERS

Discovery House Publishers (DHP) was founded in 1988 as an extension of the ministry of RBC Ministries. The purpose of DHP is to be a servant to the church, the body of Christ, by publishing books, music, videos, and computer software products that teach God's Word and foster growth and godliness in the lives of His people. DHP desires to help those who, in their brokenness and sense of need, reach out for supportive materials that will assist them in knowing God through Jesus Christ and walking with Him.

RBC MINISTRIES OFFICES

AFRICA-ASIA REGIONAL OFFICE
(Africa, Middle East, South Asia)
RBC Ministries Lanka, PO Box 19, Dehiwala 10350, Sri Lanka
(PH) +94-1 2721252 • (FX) +94-1 2719766 • (E-mail) lanka@rbc.org

- **South Africa (Kenya, Nigeria, South Africa, Zimbabwe)**
  RBC Ministries South Africa, PO Box 12221, Hatfield 0028,
  South Africa • (PH) (27) 12-344-5875 • (FX) (27) 12-344-5878
  (E-mail) southafrica@rbc.org

AMERICAS REGIONAL OFFICE
(Caribbean, Mexico, South & Central America,
North America non-English)
RBC Ministries, Grand Rapids, MI 49555-0001, USA
(PH) 616-974-2210 • (FX) 616-957-5741 • (E-mail) americas@rbc.org

- **Guyana**
  RBC Ministries, PO Box 101070, Georgetown, Guyana
  (PH/FX) 592-225-1428 • (E-mail) guyana@rbc.org
- **Jamaica**
  RBC Ministries, PO Box 139, Kingston 10 • (PH/FX) 876-926-5552
  (E-mail) jamaica@rbc.org
- **Trinidad**
  RBC Ministries, #59 Southern Main Road, Curepe, Trinidad
  (PH/FX) 868-645-7402 • (E-mail) trinidad@rbc.org

ASIA-PACIFIC REGIONAL OFFICE
(East and Southeast Asia, New Zealand, Australia, South Pacific)
RBC Ministries Asia, Ltd., Geylang Post Office, PO Box 15,
Singapore 913801 • (PH) 65-67499343 • (FX) 65-67499345
(E-mail) singapore@rbc.org.

EUROPE REGIONAL OFFICE
(UK, Europe, Russia, CIS)
Radio Bible Class, PO Box 1, Carnforth, Lancs, LA5 9ES, England
(PH) In UK: 01524-733166 • Others: 44-1-524-733-166 • (FX) In UK:
01524-736194 • Others: 44-1-524-736-194 • (E-mail) england@rbc.org

RBC WEB SITE: www.rbcinternational.org

Across The Ocean

by Dave Egner

If some people were to be absolutely honest, they would have to admit that they are trying to earn their way to heaven. Their faith is in their good intentions and admirable deeds—not in the Lord Jesus Christ.

For instance, when my neighbor died, his wife said to me "Surely he is in heaven, don't you think? He was such a good man."

I agreed that he had been a fine husband and a conscientious father, but I had to add, "He'll be in heaven if he believed in Jesus Christ as his Savior."

I was thinking about our inability to save ourselves when I was fishing in my 14-foot canoe. A person would be a fool to think he could cross the ocean through gale-force winds and swelling waves in a tiny boat like that. Even the most experienced paddler with the best of equipment would not try to travel from Boston to Liverpool in a 14-foot canoe. The unstable craft just could not make it across the Atlantic Ocean.

Just as the canoe cannot carry us across the ocean, our good works and worthy intentions cannot take us to heaven. Oh, our good deeds may make the circumstances of this life more pleasant— just as sitting in a canoe on a calm lake is pleasant—but it will never meet the just demands of a righteous God. The only solution is to put our trust in Christ. The Bible tells us, "By grace you have been saved through faith, and that not of yourselves; it is the gift of God" (Ephesians 2:8).

When we accept Jesus by faith, He forgives all our sins and fully accepts us. Jesus alone can carry us "across the ocean" to heaven.

Have you put your faith in Christ?

> Not by works of righteousness which we have done, but according to His mercy He saved us. —Titus 3:5

DISCOVERY SERIES

Another benefit of receiving the quarterly devotional

When you begin to receive *Our Daily Bread* at your home every 3 months, you'll also have an opportunity to receive a helpful study booklet each time. Specially selected from the over 140 titles in our Discovery Series library, each 32-page booklet can help you grow spiritually as you consider your salvation, your relationship with Christ,

and your involvement in reaching others with the gospel. To begin receiving the quarterly *ODB*, just complete the form on the last page of this book and send it to your local RBC office.

□ YES! I'd like to receive my 3-month *Our Daily Bread* and other resources at my home every quarter!

(Please don't check this box for anyone but yourself.)

Please print

Name _____

Address _____

City _____ Country _____ Postal code _____

Complete this form and send it to your local RBC Ministries office.

Check the list of offices on page 381 to find the address of the RBC Ministries office nearest you.